Modernism ar

Series Editor: F
University, UK

MW01132300

The series Modern..... .... in a wide range of cultural, social, scientific and political phenomena to explore the relationship between a particular topic in modern history and 'modernism'. Apart from their intrinsic value as short but groundbreaking specialist monographs, the books aim through their cumulative impact to expand the application of this highly contested term beyond its conventional remit of art and aesthetics. Our definition of modernism embraces the vast profusion of creative acts, reforming initiatives and utopian projects that, since the late nineteenth century, have sought either to articulate, and so to symbolically transcend, the spiritual malaise or decadence of modernity or to find a radical solution to it through a movement of spiritual, social and political – even racial – regeneration and renewal. The ultimate aim is to foster a spirit of transdisciplinary collaboration in shifting the structural forces that define modern history beyond their conventional conceptual frameworks.

Titles include:

Roy Starrs
MODERNISM AND JAPANESE CULTURE

Marius Turda
MODERNISM AND EUGENICS

Shane Weller
MODERNISM AND NIHILISM

Ben Hutchinson
MODERNISM AND STYLE

Anna Katharina Schaffner
MODERNISM AND PERVERSION

Thomas Linehan
MODERNISM AND BRITISH SOCIALISM

David Ohana
MODERNISM AND ZIONISM

Richard Shorten
MODERNISM AND TOTALITARIANISM
Rethinking the Intellectual Sources of Nazism and Stalinism, 1945 to the Present

Agnese Horvath
MODERNISM AND CHARISMA

Erik Tonning
MODERNISM AND CHRISTIANITY

John Bramble
MODERNISM AND THE OCCULT

Modernism and...
Series Standing Order ISBN 978–0–230–20332–7 (Hardback)
978–0–230–20333–4 (Paperback)
(outside North America only)

You can receive future titles in this series as they are published by placing a standing order. Please contact your bookseller or, in case of difficulty, write to us at the address below with your name and address, the title of the series and the ISBN quoted above.

Customer Services Department, Macmillan Distribution Ltd, Houndmills, Basingstoke, Hampshire RG21 6XS, England

MODERNISM AND THE OCCULT

John Bramble
Emeritus Fellow, Corpus Christi College, Oxford

First published 2015 by
PALGRAVE MACMILLAN

Palgrave Macmillan in the UK is an imprint of Macmillan Publishers Limited, registered in England, company number 785998, of Houndmills, Basingstoke, Hampshire RG21 6XS.

Palgrave Macmillan in the US is a division of St Martin's Press LLC, 175 Fifth Avenue, New York, NY 10010.

Palgrave is the global academic imprint of the above companies and has companies and representatives throughout the world.

Palgrave® and Macmillan® are registered trademarks in the United States, the United Kingdom, Europe and other countries.

ISBN 978-1-349-49973-1   ISBN 978-1-137-46578-8 (eBook)
DOI 10.1057/9781137465788

A catalogue record for this book is available from the British Library.

Library of Congress Cataloging-in-Publication Data

Bramble, J. C.
Modernism and the Occult / John Bramble, Emeritus Fellow,
Corpus Christi College, Oxford.
pages cm.—(Modernism and—)
Summary: "Building on art-historian Bernard Smith's insights about modernism's debts to the high imperial occult and exotic, this book explores the transcultural, 'anti-modern vitalist', and magical-syncretic dimensions of the arts of the period 1880–1960. Avoiding simplistic hypotheses about 're-enchantment', it tracks the specifically modernist, not the occult revivalist or proto-New Age, manifestations of the occult-syncretic-exotic conglomerate. The focus is high empire, where the 'Buddhist' Schopenhauer cult and Theosophy, the last aided by Bergson, Nietzsche and neo-Vedanta, brought contrasting decreative-catastrophic and regenerative-utopian notes into the arts. Another instance of the Eastward turn in modernist esotericism, the Fifties 'Zen' vogue is also considered. This is the first overview of what modernists, as opposed to sectarian occultists, actually did with the occult. As such, it reframes the intellectual history of the modernist era, to present the occult/syncretic as an articulative idiom – a resource for making sense of the kaleidoscopic strangeness, fluidity and indeterminacy of modern life"—Provided by publisher.
1. Occultism.   2. Modernism (Art)—Influence.   I. Title.
BF1429.B73 2015
190—dc23   2015002150

Typeset by MPS Limited, Chennai, India.

To my Teachers

CONTENTS

SERIES EDITOR'S PREFACE

As the title 'Modernism and ...' implies, this series has been conceived in an open-ended, closure-defying spirit, more akin to the soul of jazz than to the rigour of a classical score. Each volume provides an experimental space allowing both seasoned professionals and aspiring younger academics to investigate familiar areas of modern social, scientific or political history from the defamiliarizing vantage point afforded by a term not routinely associated with it: 'modernism'. Yet this is no contrived make-over of a clichéd concept for the purposes of scholastic bravado. Nor is it a gratuitous theoretical exercise in expanding the remit of an '-ism' already notorious for its polyvalence – not to say its sheer nebulousness – in a transgressional fling of postmodern *jouissance*.

Instead, this series is based on the *empirically* orientated hope that a deliberate enlargement of the semantic field of 'modernism' to embrace a whole range of phenomena apparently unrelated to the radical innovation in the arts it normally connotes will do more than contribute to scholarly understanding of those topics. Cumulatively, the volumes in this series are meant to contribute to a perceptible paradigm shift slowly becoming evident in the way modern history is approached. It is one that, while indebted to 'the cultural turn', is if anything 'post-post-modern', for it attempts to use transdisciplinary perspectives and the conscious clustering of concepts often viewed as unconnected – or even antagonistic to each other – to consolidate and deepen the reality principle on which historiography is based. The objective here is to move closer to the experience of history and its actors, not ever further away from it. Only those with a stunted, myopic (and *unhistorical*) view of what constitutes historical 'fact' and 'causation' will be predisposed to dismiss the 'Modernism and ...' project as mere 'culturalism', a term that, owing to unexamined prejudices and sometimes sheer ignorance, has – particularly in the vocabulary of more than one eminent 'archival' historian – acquired a reductionist, pejorative meaning.

As with several volumes in this series, the juxtaposition of the term 'modernism' with the key theme, 'occultism', may be disconcerting, since one seems to belong to the history of aesthetics while the other evokes the realms of esotericism, hermetic knowledge and bizarre, even Satanic, rituals. Yet readers should be aware that the broader context for this book is a radical extension of the term modernism to embrace cultural phenomena that lie beyond the aesthetic in the narrow sense of the term. The conceptual ground for works such as *Modernism and Eugenics, Modernism and Nihilism* and *Modernism and Style* has been prepared by such seminal texts as Marshall Berman's *All That is Solid Melts into Air: The Experience of Modernity* (1982), Modris Eksteins's *Rites of Spring: The Great War and the Birth of the Modern Age* (1989), Peter Osborne's *The Politics of Time: Modernity and Avant-Garde* (1995), Emilio Gentile's *The Struggle for Modernity: Nationalism, Futurism, and Fascism* (2003) and Mark Antliff's *Avant-Garde Fascism: The Mobilization of Myth, Art, and Culture in France, 1909–1939* (2007). In each case modernism is revealed as the long-lost sibling (twin, or maybe even father) of historical phenomena rarely mentioned in the same breath.

Yet the real pioneers of such a 'maximalist' interpretation of modernism were none other than some of the major modernists themselves. For them the art and thought that subsequently earned them this title was a creative force – a passion even – of revelatory power that, in a crisis-ridden West where anomie was reaching pandemic proportions, was capable of regenerating not just 'cultural production', but 'sociopolitical production', and for some even society *tout court*. Figures such as Friedrich Nietzsche, Richard Wagner, Wassily Kandinsky, Walter Gropius, Pablo Picasso and Virginia Woolf never accepted that the art and thought of 'high culture' were to be treated as self-contained spheres of activity peripheral to – or even cut off from – the main streams of contemporary social and political events. Instead they took them to be laboratories of visionary thought vital to the spiritual salvation of a world being systematically drained of higher meaning and ultimate purpose by the dominant, 'nomocidal' forces of modernity. If we accept Max Weber's thesis of the gradual *Entzauberung*, or 'disenchantment', of the world through an instrumentalizing rationalism, such creative individuals can be seen as setting themselves the task – each in his or her own idiosyncratic way – of *re-enchanting* and resacralizing the world. Such modernists consciously sought to restore a sense of higher purpose, transcendence and *Zauber* to a spiritually starved modern humanity condemned by 'progress' to live in a permanent state of existential exile, of *liminoid transition*, now that the forces of the divine seemed to have withdrawn in what Martin Heidegger's muse, the poet Friedrich Hölderlin, called 'the withdrawal of the gods'. If the hero of modern popular nationalism is the Unknown Warrior, perhaps the patron saint of modernism itself is *deus absconditus*.

Approached from this oblique angle, modernism is a revolutionary force, but it is so in a sense only distantly related to the one made familiar by standard accounts of the (political or social) revolutions on which modern historians cut their teeth. It is a 'hidden' revolution of the sort referred to by the arch-aesthetic modernist Vincent Van Gogh in a letter to his brother Theo on 24 September 1888. In this letter, Van Gogh remarks on the impression made on him by the work of another spiritual seeker disturbed by the impact of 'modern progress', Leo Tolstoy:

> It seems that in the book, *My Religion*, Tolstoy implies that whatever happens in a violent revolution, there will also be an inner and hidden revolution in the people, out of which a new religion will be born, or rather, something completely new which will be nameless, but which will have the same effect of consoling, of making life possible, as the Christian religion used to.
>
> The book must be a very interesting one, it seems to me. In the end, we shall have had enough of cynicism, scepticism and humbug, and will want to live – more musically. How will this come about, and what will we discover? It would be nice to be able to prophesy, but it is even better to be forewarned, instead of seeing absolutely nothing in the future other than the disasters that are bound to strike the modern world and civilization like so many thunderbolts, through revolution, or war, or the bankruptcy of worm-eaten states. (Van Gogh 2003: 409)

In the 'Modernism and ...' series the key term has been experimentally expanded and 'heuristically modified' to embrace any movement for change that set out to give a name and a public identity to the 'nameless' and 'hidden' revolutionary principle that Van Gogh saw as necessary to counteract the rise of nihilism. At the same time this expansion allows modernism to be explored not primarily as the striving for innovative forms of self-expression and style, but rather as the reaction against perceived spiritual decline,

physiological and psychological degeneration, and moral decadence, which of course leads naturally to the theme of 'perversion'.
Van Gogh was attracted to Tolstoy's vision because it seemed to
offer a remedy for the impotence of Christianity and the insidious
spread of a literally soul-destroying cynicism, which if unchecked
would ultimately lead to the collapse of civilization. Modernism
thus applies in this series to all concerted attempts in any sphere of
activity to enable life to be lived more 'musically', to resurrect the
sense of transcendent communal and individual purpose that was
being palpably eroded by the chaotic unfolding of events in the
modern world even if the end result would be 'just' to make society
physically and mentally healthy.

In the context of the present volume in the series, however, it is
not Van Gogh but Wassily Kandinsky who underscores the need to
break down the mental barriers which lead experimental art and
occultism to be placed in separate cultural categories. Like several
other founding fathers of abstract modernism such as Frantisek
Kupka, Piet Mondrian, and Kazimir Malevich, Kandinsky was profoundly influenced by the notion of an occult realm promulgated
by Theosophy, after Spiritism the most popular form of occultism
of the turn of the twentieth century. The search for hidden perennial truths in art and occultism can both be seen as *modernist* experiments in the re-enchantment of the world, and reorientation of
human history away from the abyss of materialism and nihilism.
Both the gnawing malaise of anomie and angst generated by modernity, and the proliferation of countervailing visionary schemes of
cultural or political rebirth, which included occultism, are explored
at some length in my *Modernism and Fascism: The Sense of a Beginning
under Mussolini and Hitler* (2007).

The premise of this book could be taken to be Phillip E. Johnson's
assertion that 'Modernism is typically defined as the condition that
begins when people realize God is truly dead, and we are therefore
on our own.' It locates the well-springs of modernism in the primordial human need for transcendental meaning in a godless universe,
in the impulse to erect a 'sacred canopy' of culture that not only
aesthetically veils the infinity of time and space surrounding human
existence to make that existence feasible, but also provides a totali-
zing worldview within which to situate individual life narratives,
thus imparting it with the illusion of cosmic significance. By eroding
or destroying that canopy, modernity creates a protracted spiritual

crisis that provokes the proliferation of countervailing impulses to restore a 'higher meaning' to historical time, impulses collectively termed 'modernism'.

Johnson's statement makes a perceptive point by associating modernism not just with art, but with a general 'human condition' consequent on what Nietzsche, the first great modernist philosopher, called 'the death of God'. Yet in the context of this series his statement requires significant qualification. Modernism is *not* a general historical condition (any more than 'post-modernism' is), but a generalized revolt against even the *intuition* made possible by a secularizing modernization that we are spiritual orphans in a godless and ultimately meaningless universe. Its hallmark is the bid to find a new home, a new community and a new source of transcendence.

Nor is modernism itself necessarily secular. On the contrary: both the wave of occultism and the Catholic revival of the 1890s and the emergence of radicalized, Manichaean forms of Christianity, Hinduism, Islam and even Buddhism in the 1990s demonstrate that modernist impulses need not take the form of secular utopianism, but may readily assume religious (some would say 'post-secular') forms. In any case, within the cultural force-field of modernism, even the most secular entities are sacralized to acquire an aura of numinous significance. Ironically, Johnson himself offers a fascinating case study in this fundamental aspect of the modernist rebellion against the empty skies of a disenchanted, anomic world. Books such as *Darwin on Trial* (1991) and *The Wedge of Truth: Splitting the Foundations of Naturalism* (2000) made him one of the major protagonists of 'Intelligent Design', a Christian(ized) version of creationism that offers a prophylactic against the allegedly nihilistic implications of Darwinist science.

Naturally no attempt has been made to impose the 'reflexive metanarrative' developed in my *Modernism and Fascism* on the various authors of this series. Each has been encouraged to tailor the term modernism to fit his or her own epistemological cloth, as long as they broadly agree in seeing it as the expression of a reaction against modernity not restricted to art and aesthetics, and driven by the aspiration to create a spiritually or physically 'healthier' modernity through a new cultural, political and ultimately biological order, and John Bramble has enthusiastically embraced this brief. The ultimate aim of the series 'Modernism and ...' is to refashion the common-sense connotations of the term 'modernism', and hence stimulate fertile new areas of research and teaching with an approach that enables methodological empathy and causal analysis to be applied even to events and processes ignored by or resistant to the explanatory powers of conventional historiography. In an age where Hollywood has turned the praeternatural into the staple fare of millions of teenagers finding their own release from the ennui of modernity, John Bramble's *Modernism and the Occult* demonstrates how important it is to take the occult seriously as an object of historical study and as a window through which to study not the flight from modernity but modernism itself. He shows that occultism should be invited into the living room of the human sciences, rather than let it fester in a dark vault banished from the historical imagination.

ROGER GRIFFIN
Oxford
October 2014

PREFACE

Though patterns vary with changing historical circumstance and differing meta-religious geographies, the interplay of the covert and overt has long been common in the arts. The occult, on this scheme, is the covert, the sign or image the overt, and diverse forms of symbolism result from the meeting of the two. As an outcrop from late nineteenth-century Symbolism, modernism could be related to a whole family of occult symbolisms. These symbolisms began in antiquity, to be transmitted by way of the Renaissance and Romanticism to the modern age. Unlike ossified religious ortho-doxies, the occult did not stand still; nor did its outer signs and imagery. With the occultisms of earlier epochs, critics allow for clear and distinct periodization, for changing directions, functions and influences – for shape-shifting within the covert realm and varying emphases in its time- and place-bound significations and goals. They also allow for the scholarly possibility of articulating the cryptic and 'hidden', of speaking the unspeakable, without resort to nebulous cliché or jargon. But when it comes to modernism silence is the rule.

Through a series of vignettes, selected to illustrate the range and magnitude of modernism's complicity with the occult, this book joins up the dots and traces left by desultory previous scholar-ship on a normally shunned topic, to offer a historical and geogra-phical framework, and also a critical idiom, within whose terms further research might proceed. Influenced by approaches to the question of 'esotericism' in the arts (primarily of antiquity and the Renaissance) as pioneered at the Warburg Institute in London from the 1920s onwards, this is a tentative, not a definitive study, an anti-fundamentalist tale, in origin, of religio-cultural confluence and fusion under high European empires. Though it was greatly affected by an 'Eastward turn' in esotericism – a turn which loosened the hold of the older, Cabalistic-Rosicrucian-Masonic occultism of the Renaissance and Romanticism – I retain 'the occult' in my title, since that was the period term for the heterodox materials deployed by modernists in their negations, contestations and reformulations of the 'degenerate' modern condition.

Chapter 1 surveys high imperial exoticism and its most significant contribution to modernism, namely a widespread enthusiasm for the so-called 'Eastern occult'. Chapter 2 pin-points some of the more deranged excesses of the modernist 'culture of trance', a legacy from Mesmerism and Spiritualism which sought out the strange and piquant in religions, and more or less hijacked the 'metaphysical East' for its own purposes. Chapters 3 and 5 illustrate the impact of Schopenhauerian 'Buddhism', Theosophy, neo-Vedanta and Zen on a relatively continuous neo-romantic line in modernism that begins with Decadence and Symbolism and ends with American Abstract Expressionism. Less narrative in focus, Chapter 4 deals with modernist expectations of apocalypse, assumed exotic identities, the politics of a neglected interwar quarrel between 'West' and 'East', and the ingenious magical eclecticism that went into the making of Ruth St Denis's dance. The collapse and disintegration of specifically modernist forms of the occult is considered in Chapter 6, which closes with some suggestions about the workings of 'unknown forces' – interpreted as epiphenomena of the modern condition itself – within modernism's supernaturalist 'other side', imaginal realm, or 'in-between state'.

Allusive and elusive, modernist idiom is taken as 'auratic', in the occult sense of aura, precisely because of period absorption with this ghostly other side. Equally, just as the modernist occult is layered on old and new, on ancient or alien wisdom and the latest pseudo-science, so, with its mix of the shock of the old and the shock of the new, its ultra-quirky heterodoxy and refusal of mundane rules (its rejection of worldly nomos, in Roger Griffin's terminology), modernist idiom is layered as well, allusive multiplicity being its pluralistic 'anti-positivist' ideal.

Normative 'Western' categories almost necessarily pale in front of modernist complexities: a reason, perhaps, for the diversionary preoccupation with 'theoretical correctness' of modernist studies during the last thirty-odd years. Anything but tackle the problem itself: namely the kaleidoscopic interplay of overt and covert with which I began. Hence my own back-to-basics preference for a Warburgian reading of modernist imagery, iconography, myths and symbols in terms of their period occult significance. But why and to what ultimate purpose were modernist messages couched in such a recondite and 'hidden' way? To upset the materialist apple-cart is usually the answer, not out of simple cussedness, much less for free-floating 'spiritual' reasons, but rather to intimate the possibility of preferable and more diverse ways of being human (and modern) in the here and now, or near future. As I shall argue, catastrophism and utopia are the two – related – extremes of the mindset in question, as displayed in the profoundly 'reactionary revolutionary' (or new/old) modernist arts. Unregenerate modernity was unbearable: dignity, grandeur and 'magic pluralism' had to be summoned from elsewhere.

Together with the 'magical cultures' which it brought to public notice, not to mention its many parallels in the syncretism of the culturally globalizing world after Alexander the Great, the fluid and free-for-all cosmopolitanism of high empire was an ideal starting point for such a quest. This brings me to my first chapter's discussion of 'empire and occultism' as formative ingredients in the 'aristocratic' modernist quarrel with bourgeois realism and materialism, a leitmotiv of the whole book.

ACKNOWLEDGMENTS

Thanks are due to Roger Griffin for giving me the opportunity to publish this study, which is a distillation from a larger body of research into the topic. Early efforts had the blessing of senior figures like Frank Kermode, Sir Isaiah Berlin and Joe Trapp of the Warburg Institute. Their encouragement was invaluable, as was that of Roger himself, with whom I had the good fortune to work for a while. Geoffrey Samuel and Ian Harris kindly read drafts of the longer study, and Philip Hardie and Oswyn Murray commented on chapters dealing with the incorporation of Greco-Roman syncretism into the modern occult. I have profited much from discussion with Sam Richards, who helped to fill in blank spaces like esotericism in modern music and folklore studies. Tracy Thursfield kickstarted my thinking about the shape of the present study. Finding and formulating the right questions to ask of one's research materials is a lengthy business: I hope this book does justice to those who have helped me along the way with that task.

1

EMPIRE AND OCCULTISM

The Shock of the Old: Empire and Myth-making

Whatever secular rationalists say, magic and the occult, like their big-brother religion, refuse to go away. Histories of the occult, best defined as irregular/heterodox knowledge, a one-time bedfellow of religion *and* reason, fight shy of its transnational/transcultural dimensions. These were pronounced in post-classical antiquity, during the Crusades, in the Renaissance, Baroque and Romanticism, and under European high empires – where the older, Muslim-Christian-Jewish esotericism began to cede to enthusiasms for India and the Far East. 'Syncretism', the pluralistic and accommodatory opposite of fundamentalism, is the name given to the products of religio-magical confluence between different cultures. Syncretism is most observable in those laboratories of the 'religion-making imagination', borderlands, backwaters and 'contact zones'.[1] In Mikhail Bakhtin's words, 'The most intensive and productive life of culture takes place on the boundaries'.[2] Occultists and explorers like Richard Burton spent their life in such places.

This study's aim is to foreground European high empire, for the indelible transcultural mark it left on the 'Western occult'. The last pops in and out of histories, when their authors choose to see it, usually on a nation-by-nation basis. This is unsatisfactory, in that magic and occultism respect neither national boundaries nor 'orthodox' prohibitions. At journey's end, travelling magics and gods could be said to fall to three main constituencies: first, interested parties in the populace at large, second, occultist professionals

1

or magi, and third, the literary and artistic worlds of the day. The last two constituencies were important for religio-cultural mixing in the Hellenistic and Greco-Roman world and the other periods mentioned above. They are equally important for modernism, which, coinciding as it did with high empire, was open to syncretism – especially East–West syncretism.

Rivalry between Eastern and Western forms of esotericism is found in the 1890s 'occult revival'. Paying more attention to the new, interloper form of the occult, with its Hindu-Buddhist emphases, I propose to trace the history of modernist resort to East–West syncretism (the high-imperial occult) as a tool for exploring the sometimes threatening, sometimes captivating condition of modernity. Modernity's strangeness partook of the 'marvellous', an occultist staple which covered both the unnerving and seductive faces of the wondrous.[3] (Significantly, Decadent Paris had a *Librairie du Merveilleux*.) The same wonder and awe surrounded high empire, the factor which transformed Western occultism. Both faces of the marvellous, the uncanny and the alluring, at home and abroad, will figure in this study, which also develops arguments made by Roger Griffin relating to modernity's loss of transcendental coordinates.[4]

In opting for *deus absconditus* (a 'withdrawn god') as the patron saint of modernism, Griffin comes close to my concerns.[5] Like nihilism, modernist syncretism, a way of pursuing this 'occulted', hide-and-seek god, baulks at systematic definition. Born in an age of creative chaos from a union between pre-existent Western occultism, newly expanded imperial horizons, a 'second oriental renaissance' and new/old ways of construing 'religion' (those of the 'history of religions school', with it roots in the 'ancient theology' and 'perennial philosophy'), this syncretism was a sophisticated, fluctuating composite, hastily put together and rife with assumptions.[6] Like myth, the occult/syncretic was 'good to think with', and those modernists who enlisted it to rethink, dismantle or recreate modernity were usually more talented than the era's practising occultists. The role of occult sects in modernism was largely subsidiary, contributing to magical common-stock, to a mystico-occult *koine*, which eventuated, inter alia, in the modernist idea of a 'new Myth' (a 'new nomos', in Griffin's terminology).

After Baudelaire's distinction between artistic 'imaginatives' and 'realists', one of the occult conglomerate's functions in modernism was to take the imagination to new heights – and depths. Another was to explore modernity as a turbulent lived condition, sometimes rejecting it outright, sometimes (modernism's 'new Myth' enthusiasts) 'overcoming' it in utopian ways. Different sects and systems competed for attention: but in that magic and the occult served less as a form of 'belief' for modernists than as an inventive, heuristic tool, eclecticism was mostly the rule. Exceptionally, the artist Piet Mondrian remained constant to Theosophy to the end of his days.

Including its 'mystic East', modernist syncretism was an ever-accretive co-creation of many different figures. Including religio-cultural backwash from empire, the 'reconvergence', in the scholarly world, of classics, oriental studies and theology, as well as themes from what Griffin calls 'social modernism' (life-reform, naturism, the simple life), the occult-syncretic conglomerate, still visible in the countercultural sixties, stood variously for pluralism, diversity, regionalism, utopianism, the fantastic, the indeterminate, sometimes the dark and uncanny, its enemies and opportunities bureaucratic reason and 'orthodox closure'.[7]

Of this, the bid to 'put an end to religious "mutations" or ... to radically control them', Eric Mahoney writes, 'In part, syncretism is a response to ... orthodox closure; it offers a type of open-endedness in order to respond to change and crisis. As such, it has a marked flexibility that is not found in orthodox traditions'.[8] The early modernist period fits Mahoney's formula perfectly: it witnessed changes and crises for which orthodoxies, both rational and religious, had no solution. In a globalizing world in need of a spiritual lingua franca, an open-ended and flexible syncretism accordingly had its attractions: though this *could* serve as a seed-bed for new orthodoxies, even within esoteric sects. Orthodox heresy, after all, is commonplace in the New Age.

Turn-of-the-century occult revival, not synonymous with modernist syncretism but one of its tributaries – others were the just-mentioned 'second Orientalism' and *Religionsgeschichte* school, both of them related to Cambridge Ritualism (James Frazer, Jane Harrison) – was intertwined with Decadence and Symbolism, the matrix of the different modernisms. To be able to know the world differently – as a kind of Gnostic, a stance which entailed mystical nihilism as much as affirmative transcendence – was an asset for modernism's quarrel with positivism, uniformity, bourgeois master-narratives, materialist progress and the Westernization of the earth. Heretical to 'legal-rational' liberals and positivists, an anti-canonical, 'prophetic-charismatic' turn, which operated outside conventional classical and Christian boxes, lies at modernist roots.

The post-1880 influence on the arts of Arthur Schopenhauer, champion of Meister Eckhart and Buddhism, who wrote about sexuality and Mesmerism, forestalling hypotheses about an 'unconscious', explains much of the mystical nihilist component in modernist syncretism. Another influential counter-movement was Theosophy, a rambling system devised, with Henry Steel Olcott from 1875, by Helena Petrovna Blavatsky, a peripatetic spirit-medium who knew Mazzini.[9] From mesmero-spiritualist and Hermetic/neo-Egyptian origins, Theosophy, like Schopenhauer, looked to the religions of India and Tibet – less so to the Near East, which inspired an older, Gnostic-Sufistic-Cabalistic strain in Western occultism, important for Rosicrucians, Templarists, 'mystical' Freemasons and their like.[10] Under Blavatsky's successors, Charles Leadbeater and Annie Besant, Theosophy became a messianic movement, its concern the advent of a clairvoyant super-humanity.[11] To find its way into modernist manifestos, the originally Cabalistic idea of a universal restoration (tikkun olam, 'repairing the world') now took on Indianist colours. With its freewheeling eclecticism, suspicions of Christianity and liberalism, partiality to the left-overs of respectable scholarship and orthodox religion, and new avatar Krishnamurti, Theosophy was well adapted to the multi-ethnic age of high empire and the many new questions it raised.

Without necessarily joining the Theosophical Society – its 'brains' the Neoplatonists Alexander Wilder and G. R. S. Mead – modernists developed its ideas in their work in ways that upset standard Western art procedures.[12] The artistic avant-garde, which could anyway behave like an esoteric order or secret society, relied less on formal occultist organizations than hearsay, reading, travel and 'cultic milieu'. Among its aims we can count the augmentation and rearrangement of knowledge to explain the paradox of a simultaneously modern/progressive and atavistic/imperial world-dispensation, as well as the twilight, in-between states of mind and experience (the 'uncanny', the Surrealist merveilleux) generated by the clash between modernization and tradition. This clash was most pronounced in Meiji Japan, where 'professors of civilization' declared war on folk beliefs (and vice versa), but the conflict of the daimonic with 'civilization' is a Western theme too.[13] The 'ancient indecencies and monstrosities', the fantastic and grotesque, served as weapons in modernist warfare with the bourgeoisie.[14]

Modernist studies generally overlook religio-cultural backwash from the colonies, as that revolutionized Western occultism and the arts. The Romantic vision of empire was a counter-force to modernity: the genius of Theosophists – their headquarters, from 1883, in India – was to link their system to the new mysterious worlds disclosed by European imperial expansion. The natives and cultures of these last were on view at 'World's Fairs' and colonial exhibitions. Of these Paul Greenhalgh writes, 'World's Fairs were the single most important vehicle for the internationalization of visual culture between 1851 and 1940'.[15] As a vehicle of the 'colonial syncretic' – which included far more than the fringe Islam and mystical Judaism cultivated by older occultist groups – the spread of Theosophy was responsible for a similar internationalization of the occult.[16]

Where it encouraged the cult of what T. S. Eliot called 'strange gods', the Romantic vision of empire bears on Griffin's insight about the centrality of *deus absconditus* to modernism. Prevalent images of foreign deities were mystical, erotic and bursting with a 'life' now deserting the modern world. Patterned on Symbolist art, the scene of Greta Garbo dancing for Siva in the 1931 film *Mata Hari* enacts this erotic-vitalist dream. In matter-of-fact ways, ancient empires had regularly adopted the gods, learning and arts of the defeated. Modernist enthusiasms for 'strange gods' were less down-to-earth: florid, theatrical, oppositional, tending like D. H. Lawrence to emb   on their pantheons as they went along. Short of clear theological bearings, modernists, when faced by 'strange gods', fell back onto something akin to Griffin's *deus absconditus*: an intangible, withdrawn deity, apparently in hiding or 'occultation', pending the methods chosen, histrionic or quietist, to persuade him to appear. Looked at thus, occultism, twinned with vitalism, becomes the soft underbelly of modernist nihilism, the other side of *Das Nichts*.

From the modernist perspective of the Bergson-inspired French *Annales* school of history, empires had existed since time immemorial (the historical *longue durée*), modernity had not. Likewise, as ways of mapping and manipulating the world, magic and the occult had long pre-existed positivist science. It is no coincidence, then, that modernity's last turn-of-the-century discontents were drawn to magic and the occult (and in museums to the 'curious') as ways of mastering life derived from a less stifling and much older world. In the arts, the distinction between moderns and ancients – partisans of the new and upholders of the old – goes back to Greco-Roman times. So does deliberate archaism, one of the Romantic tradition's favoured tools for evoking the distant past and the geographically faraway. With its implication that the old could be new or modern under certain circumstances, this third way between hoary antiquity and the pristinely new was adopted by modernists in their attempts to contest and reframe modernity.

Taking the occult, folkloric, primitive and oriental as allies, and developing a broader, Romantic hinterland in imperial culture into a critique of bourgeois modernity, modernists, like earlier archaizers, turned the 'shock of the old' into something new. Thus, Ezra Pound's Scriabinist lady-friend, Katherine Ruth Heyman, equated the ultra-modern with the very ancient; American composer Charles Griffes declared that modern music relies increasingly on 'the archaicism of the East'; Janet Flanner spoke of Pound's 'weighty, ancient, mixed linguistics'; while Constantin Brancusi asserted that his 'new I' came 'from something very old'.[17] This sophisticated counterpart of the 'revitalization movements' studied by anthropologists – a return to the ancestral past, so as to inject new life into a failing present – was heavily reliant on what literary critics call 'myth'. The new non-classical/ non-biblical antiquities now filling Western museums were crucial to such mythopoeia, not to mention the living legatees of those antiquities, as studied by ethnographers or paraded at colonial exhibitions.

Modernism has been described as a 'continuation of Romanticism by other means'.[18] There had been various, Romanticism-related attempts to oppose or counterbalance earlier phases of modernity. For want of a developed imperial culture at home, medievalism (Pugin, Ruskin) was a favourite anti-modern ploy. But 'life', that subtle, erotic force of Bergson and Lawrence, was unlikely to benefit greatly from gazing at Gothic-revival stained-glass windows. From the 1880s, however, primitive-oriental backwash from empire, as displayed in museums or colonial exhibitions, or elaborated in imperial romances, began to take the conqueror captive, and to turn the tide against modernity more effectively than Pugin or Ruskin.[19] On show at the colonial exhibitions – and in no mood of *mission civilisatrice* – here was the *living* pre-modern. Felt affinities between the imperial primitive and oriental with Western folklore and occultism soon led to eclectic and 'polymythic', cosmopolitan art styles like Symbolism and Art Nouveau. Not simply decorative or nostalgic, these art styles, with their 'outsider' sources and layers of multi-ethnic mythic allusion, far surpassed medievalism in their celebration of 'life' by way of the shock of the old.

In its portraiture, the Enlightenment had tended to squeeze its noble savages into a Greco-Roman corset which may have enhanced their dignity, even if it strangled their 'life'. Delacroix and Baudelaire were among the first to remedy this straight-jacketing of the primitive with a wildness that was truly Romantic. But in an age of the unruly mass, high-imperial culture was less concerned with wildness than the communitarian and collective. Whether spontaneously or deliberately, this public imperial culture promoted the exotic, wondrous and vital – and Aboriginal 'good taste' in arts and crafts – as correctives for loss of social cohesion in the anomie-stricken West.[20]

It is unlikely that this culture's architects had anarcho-communitarian agendas, or that its consumers heard any Kropotkin-like message. At this public level, romantic conservatism – a vicarious, rearguard restoration of nomos – was nearer the point. But the archaic-oriental, folkloric-occult thematics of this same imperial culture are certainly reworked in *modernism* into a vision of community revivified by anarcho-communitarian return to the pre-modern animistic and organismic: not to mention the pre-modern orgasmic. Like the German Expressionist group, *die Brucke*, Lawrence was an adept of the primitive communitarianism motif, mostly done quite well. Done badly, it could be agonizing, as Wyndham Lewis demonstrates in his satire on modernist primitivism, *Paleface*.

The British may have acquired their empire in a fit of absent-mindedness, but the finished product led to two diametrically opposed schools of thought. The first, Anglicizing school believed in positivist-utilitarian-modernizing methods of rule; the second, Orientalist or Romantic conservative school believed in 'ruling the Orient by oriental methods', extending its faith in the indigenous to respect for local customs and religions elsewhere. Empire, for such Romantics, stood for all that bourgeois modernity was not. A compensation for the disappearing pre-modern at home, this was the vision of empire which, through travel or exhibitions, inspired modernists, without their necessarily being 'imperialist' in any way, let alone members of any occultist sect.

The ramifications of empire for a sea-change in Western culture have been studied to a point. It has, for instance, been established that empire led to a change from bourgeois 'obligation' and 'duty' to aristocratic 'honour code'; that it displaced the bourgeois novel with imperial romance;[21] that it won over plebeian affections through its spectacles and exhibitions; that the neo-Vedantist, Swami Vivekananda, soon to acquire celebrity followers like opera singer Emma Calve and Satanist Jules Bois, made a much-applauded debut at the 'World's Parliament of Religions', held at the 1893 Colombian exposition in Chicago.[22] But as a background to modernism, especially to the modernist liking for 'myth', empire has scarcely been studied at all. Programmatic modernist myth-making aimed to mobilize, reanimate and remagicalize. As Nietzsche proclaimed in *The Birth of Tragedy* (1872), 'Only a horizon ringed about by myths can unify a culture'.[23] Whether borrowed, as in Gilded Age America, or proprietarily owned, empire supplied that myth-ringed horizon.

The Crisis of the Modern World

In 1909 the French banker Albert Kahn, friend of Rabindranath Tagore, inaugurated *The Archives of the Planet*, a huge photographical enterprise dedicated to recording a traditional world that was being lost to modernization.[24] Kahn's images are of hallucinatory beauty, their wistful, elegiac tone close to contemporary, vitalist art and writing on the theme of the great god Pan. The enemies of what W. B. Yeats called the 'filthy modern tide', including Lawrence, another devotee of Pan, had taken against the bourgeoisie, with its banal positivism, utilitarianism and liberalism. Pining, like the Bergson-inspired Kahn, for the magic of the pre-modern, they had also taken against insensitive styles of modernization resulting from calculative-commercial applications of such derivatives from eighteenth-century Enlightenment. But just as they had not invented the oppressive, modernizing brand of imperialism – the prototype of neo-liberal globalization – 'men in periwigs' had not invented crude and tasteless modernization. There was accordingly less of a quarrel, among modernists, with the Enlightenment itself than with the self-serving mess made of it by the nineteenth-century bourgeoisie. Thus Yeats, like *Ballets Russes* impresario Sergei Diaghilev, admired the aristocratic eighteenth century, while spurning bourgeois modernity.

Many such 'men in periwigs' were Freemasons, and, as apostles of illuminated reason, forerunners of the esoteric/occultist currents of thought to which Yeats and Lawrence subscribed.[25] Enlightenment philosophers were primitivists and Orientalists, given to the idealization of Hurons, South Sea Islanders, Persians and 'wise men from the East'. Based as it largely was on travel and missionary accounts, this Enlightenment exoticism may have been superficial: but at least it provided a 'place to stand' outside the Western system, the better to critique the Enlightenment's own world, including the church's crushing power.[26]

High criticism had since undermined literal biblical truth: churched Christianity was therefore less of a problem for modernity's discontents than the part-positivist, part-religiose, mid-Victorian order of their fathers. As counter-forces to that, Symbolist-to-modernist exoticism, primitivism and Orientalism ran deeper than their Enlightenment and Romantic prototypes. For now, to return to Kahn, and as a new internationalism grew apace, fuller pictorial records of the pre-modern world were available, not to mention the high profile given to 'magical cultures' at colonial exhibitions. With improved communications, travel to mysterious, faraway places was also possible – modernism-era grand tours embraced a mystic pan-Asia, including North Africa – and even the foot-soldiers of empire could return with decidedly non-suburban, Kipling-like tales of adventure among, and often admiration for, the natives they had encountered abroad.

Not that the idea of *any* kind of modernity was rejected by the disaffected. The second industrial revolution had wrought its 'marvels', notably practical applications of electricity. At a time when electricity still equated with 'life-force', American physician George Miller Beard devised an electrical cure for neurasthenia. Electricity was also associated with Indian *prana*, so creating room for a synthesis of the scientist and the occult. Darwinism met a similar fate: no longer a threat to humankind's soul, 'evolution' was taken to a higher, spiritual level by Theosophists and the mystical German biologist Ernst Haeckel. 'Progress' was likewise retained, its focus no longer materialistic, but the omega point of the journeying soul. The invention of x-rays also proved the occultists right: solid matter was an illusion, soon to be replaced by an 'epoch of the great spiritual', in Kandinsky's expression.[27]

The reintegration, or mystico-scientistic re-synthesis, of modernity was a gradual affair. Along with a 'journey through despair', and coinciding with the perverse, world-rejecting Decadent movement, disintegration was its precondition.[28] With 'naught for thy comfort' Decadents like August Strindberg, Gustav Klimt and Alfred Kubin, the quasi-Buddhist *grand démolisseur*, Arthur Schopenhauer, was the patron saint of an illusory world without a centre, moved only by sexual desire. In France, and later in Russia, Satanism, an arm of Decadent antinomianism and catastrophism, was a way of accentuating the contradictions of both 'reason' and 'faith'. J.-K. Huysmans's novels, *A Rebour* (1884) and *La Bas* (1891), represent this trend, the first an account of a Dorian Gray-like aristocrat in flight from reality, the second a tale of Satanism and black magic. Dystopian fears of mechanization, after Mary Shelley's *Frankenstein*, appear in Villiers De L'Isle Adam's techno-occult *L'Eve Future* of 1886, its android anti-heroine, Halady, a precursor of the false Maria of Fritz Lang's 1927 film *Metropolis*.

Decadent dissipation once spent, the mystico-scientist re-synthesis of modernity, often accompanied by a new cosmogony motif (the *tikkun* idea), becomes an initially tentative, then by the twenties, more confident theme of the arts. Theosophy mirrored this trajectory. Its hashish-smoking co-founder, Madame Blavatsky (who appears in Eliot's *The Waste Land*) had not been averse to the occult's darker side. But under the Anglophone second-generation Theosophists, the movement assumed an actively millennial-restorationist cast, its point not rejection but transformation of the modern world. The breakaway Austrian Theosophist Rudolph Steiner followed suit, as did the Russian Theosophist and later Gurdjieffian Pyotr Ouspensky, whose lectures in twenties London, sponsored by Lady Rothermere, were attended by Eliot, Aldous Huxley, Gerald Heard and A. R. Orage.[29] Consolation had supervened on despair, and in no matter how strange a fashion the modern world was to be built afresh. At its best, this represented a re-magicalization of Enlightenment, a restoration of 'light' to 'reason'.

Bernard Smith's High-imperial, Occult-Exotic Theory of Modernism

In 1992, the eminent Australian art historian Bernard Smith saw the radical implications for modernism of the occult, exotic and imperial materials touched on above. Since Smith's arguments will probably be unfamiliar, I cite them at some length.[30] Of the exotic as 'the aestheticisation of the strange and the stranger', Smith writes, 'it originates out of the ... spoils of war ... After the subjugation of the defeated, what were spoils are ... transformed into trade ... what is traded ... is that which the victors covet'. Of the 'two main thrusts behind the emergence of early modernist art', the first 'comes from the so-called primitive and oriental arts' and is formal or icono-graphic. From 1900 to 1920, such borrowings from the colonies 'rap-idly subvert ... the dominance of those Graeco-Roman forms that had prevailed in European art ... since the fifteenth century'.

The 'other thrust comes from non-European religions', both Indian and tribal. Where modernist formal innovation drew on primitive/oriental models, 'it was the desire to appropriate non-European religions in the search for an exotic and syncretic world religion that determined much of the content of early modern-ist painting. The ambition was to combine ... universality of form with ... universality of spirit'. Though this, in origin largely Theosophical, universalizing ambition can be broken down into var-ious regionalist, utopian socialist or national Romantic schemes for renewal, on Smith's view a 'world art, a world religion, and a world politic' were central to modernist aims, acting as 'a critique of ... modernity'.

Taking a migrant Gauguin who wanted 'to subvert the domin-ance of Greek art' as 'the first self-conscious modernist', Smith notes how his 'desire to create an international art grounded in a mix of archaic and primitive art – Egyptian, Javanese, Polynesian – is linked with the desire for an art that expresses an international, syn-cretic spirituality grounded in the occult, and ... archaic and primi-tive cults'. Of the psychological dimension involved, he remarks: 'A primitive mind ... now lived in the basement of the rational European mind and revealed itself ... in the art of children ... the mentally ill, [and] naive, untutored painters'. As for 'the possibilities of an occult, universalising spirituality', Smith invokes Kandinsky, Kasimir Malevich, Frantisek Kupka, Robert Delauney, Franz Marc and Mondrian as exponents of this. Assured that Europe's Greco-Roman heritage was obsolete, avant-garde belief, scorning the 'dead-weight' of 'the masterpieces in their museums', was that 'primitivism and the occult would produce a new ... universal art'.

With 'the oriental, the primitive, and the occult' operating 'as a critique of Europe's parochial culture grounded in classical tradition', the new aesthetic reflected 'confidence in Europe's mastery of the world prior to World War I'. True enough of the neo-aristocratic ethic where the values of empire and modernism met – a juncture at which expanded imperial horizons elicited an expanded archaic-oriental, folkloric-occult imaginary – Smith's point about 'mastery' omits to mention the home-front crisis of modernity (the masses, urban squalor, the rising lower middle classes), and consequent upper-class anxiety and escapism. But in stressing modernism's imperial affiliations, Smith's conclusions cohere with my own:

> Modernism must be distinguished from modernity. It emerged as a critique of modernity and ended as its dominant cultural style. It may be best understood as an expression of the twentieth century European exotic. It emerges, as did other expressions of the exotic in religion, politics and language, at a time when Europe was at the height of its colonising supremacy.

Here we have the kernel of a revolutionary new assessment of at minimum *some* forms of visual modernism. But Smith's ideas apply equally well to Debussy, who frequented Edmond Bailly's occultist bookshop in Paris and enlisted new exotic sounds heard at colonial exhibitions. They also apply to Olivier Messiaen, reader of the first modern Indian guru Sri Aurobindo, who in his *Turangalila symphonie* mixed exotic sounds with occultist ideas. Equally, a combination of occult content and exotic surface distinguishes Lawrence's Mexican novel, *The Plumed Serpent* (compare E. M. Forster's *A Passage to India* to a point), while many forms of modernist poetry enlist a similar formula. As we shall see in Chapter 2, suchlike appeals to the 'redemptive' outsider meta-reality of the occult and exotic purported to solve the so-called 'language crisis', and its twin in the 'decay of cognition'.

One obvious place to pursue Smith's insights is the imperial museum, as a source for new, non-Western models for the arts. Rupert Arrowsmith has done this for the British Museum and other London venues where non-Western arts were on show, assessing their impact on Yeats, Pound, Eric Gill, T. E. Hulme, F. S. Flint and Jacob Epstein.[31] Foregrounding influential curators such as Laurence Binyon and A. K. Coomaraswamy, more in-depth studies like Arrowsmith's could considerably increase our understanding of 'back-room modernism' and 'modernism on the ground'. Travels, personal libraries, specialized exhibitions, patronage, networking and countercultural centres need attention for similar reasons: as do distinctions between alien cultures (like the Japanese and the Chinese) where there was some attempt to understand them on their own terms, as against cultures (like the ancient Egyptian, and the stranger aspects of Indian religion and art) where interpreters reached for occultism, Theosophy or Neoplatonism to explain the unfamiliar.

Nevertheless, the *exact* extent and nature of modernism's indebtedness to practising occultists and non-art-world Theosophists remains unclear. Occult content in modernist art is more easily correlated, not with current sectarian sources (compared to books of Renaissance and Baroque magic, these are visually thin), but with the cultic milieu and freewheeling, group or individual improvisation. Schopenhauer had a well-developed theory of art; the Theosophical luminaries, Steiner apart, did not. This had implications for the relatively coherent nature of the Decadent aesthetic, Schopenhauer being its main inspiration. The early, post-1910 modernist '-isms', where Theosophical allusion consorts with a larger syncretism, had a less unified aesthetic, with a fluctuating iconology and iconography. Thus, some references to sacred geometry aside, Kandinsky's *Concerning the Spiritual in Art* and the *Blaue Reiter Almanac* (both 1912) tell us more about generalized yearning for a 'new Myth' than precise occultist influences. More than sectarian affiliation, enthusiasm, improvisation, bricolage – and some vagueness about Theosophy – distinguish both texts.

Our own ideas of the occult have been affected by developments like graphic novels, Japanese manga, New Age spiritual kitsch, vampire movies and so on. Further back, there are the neo-Art Nouveau album sleeves of some sixties rock groups: 'pop Buddhism and LSD' revisited by the turn-of-the-century arabesque. Not unlike those album sleeves, glaringly occult styles, a mix of Gothic and Art Nouveau, grace the covers of *fin de siècle* esoteric periodicals: an example is the cover for a 1892 copy of the French Theosophical periodical *Le Lotus Bleu*, designed by Gauguin's pupil Emile Schuffenecker. Like Austin Osman Spare, Hugo Höppener ('Fidus'), the 'hippie' Asconan illustrator, and later Nazi, is an exponent of the same figurative-phantasmagoric manner; likewise the Dutch Symbolist, Jan Toorop, inventor of 'spook style', a variant on Art Nouveau that was adopted by Charles Rennie Mackintosh and Margaret MacDonald.[32]

There are lines of continuity to the sixties, if not the New Age, in the above: but most of it is illustration, not art, in the 'high' Kandinskyite sense of the term. And even if we add literary analogues – the bizarre/paranormal tales of French Decadents and figures like the Austrian Theosophist Gustav Meyrink – is there enough here to support Smith's notion of an 'exotic and syncretic world-religion' as an early modernist aim? Or is it the case that Smith's 'world-religion' and the narrowly occult (or seriously weird) are two different things? Where they look East, the genres and styles considered above fade into 'Oriental Gothic', with touches from what Lafcadio Hearn called 'The Shadow of the Light of Asia'. But that again, like Aleister Crowley's murals in Sicily, is more a side-show than the main event. Occult style and content are easy enough to spot in the art just cited: in the post-1910 modernisms they are not.

Unlike Schopenhauer, mainstream Theosophists, to repeat, did not have a developed theory of art. Steiner, who painted in a semi-abstract, luminous/etheric manner, came nearest to a full aesthetic theory.[33] Besant and Leadbeater produced books with illustrations of 'thought-forms' and 'occult chemistry'. Art historians have studied these for their influences on early modernism's path to abstraction. Materials concerning sacred geometry, the 'fourth dimension', occult colour theory and synaesthesia could also be found in Theosophical writings. But, for the post-1910 modernist '-isms', there is still a significant shortfall in indications by organizational occultists and Theosophists as to the proper manner of a new occultist or 'spiritual' art.

This is not to jettison Smith's 'exotic and syncretic world-religion'. Rather, to resolve this conundrum I would argue that 'occult revival', when viewed from the non-sectarian standpoint of the ubiquitously available imperial occult and exotic, was only one element in a larger syncretism; that modernists were more interested in the grand counter-cosmological idea of a 'new Myth' (or nomos/restoration) than in individual occultist systems; also, that it was the artists *themselves* who, leaving sectarian promptings behind, devised their own methods, after 1910, of producing a more than simply illustrative 'spiritual' art. With as little to inspire them visually from occultist tracts, the more inventive Symbolists and Decadents, like Jean Delville and Fernand Khnopff, had already transcended 'illustration': but once the meta-languages of 'non-objectivity' and atonality took off, the occult, in tandem, had to move on or risk irrelevance to the arts.

There were a few, specifically art-world, sectarian Theosophists, like architect Claude Bragdon and composers Cyril Scott and Alexandr Scriabin (who found a 'very strong mystic movement' in America on a 1906–07 tour); but they, too, had to go beyond the meagre hints given by mainstream Theosophical literature to find expressions and rationales for their art. Much as Zen for American Abstract Expressionists, Theosophy, for most early modernists, arguably acted as a springboard for personal creative endeavour – a raft to cross the river from figuration to abstraction, from the received to the experimental, but not to be carried around, its purpose once served. Like the exotic, too, the occult was subject to the vagaries of fashions: yesterday's 'unknown unknowns' soon became today's 'known unknowns' (or open secrets) and, as with the imperial frontier, virgin territories with a 'here be dragons' (or 'unknown unknowns') sign were sure to submit, one day, to what Rider Haggard called 'the pestilential accuracy of the geographer'.[34]

Playing mainstream Theosophy down, an interpretation like this would throw the burden of 'influence' onto the new art's syncretic conceptual hinterland, onto occultist common-stock and the broader cultic milieu, where modernists could breathe the 'spiritual' in, reshape it, then breathe it out as art. Once fully opened out – referred to empire, the second Orientalism, changes in religious-historical thinking which re-admitted Gnosticism and folk beliefs to the fold, not to mention themes from Griffin's 'social modernism' like life-reform and back to the land – the later nineteenth- and earlier twentieth-century occult and exotic, professionals of the same aside, are ample evidence for Smith's views. A narrowly localized, Yellow Nineties-style occult revival, with equally limited, in-house after-echoes (and dated attraction to Masonic 'degrees' and 'unknown superiors'), is insufficient explanation of why modernists rejected the modern world, or attempted to rebuild it along remagicalized lines.

Modernity was an unprecedented condition. Vast universal empires with sacred sites, with ancient and alien wisdom on their borders and fabled esoteric lineages running back into the mists of time, antedated modernity by hundreds, even thousands of years. Elevating archaeology (later, anthropology) to the status of imperial science, vestiges of such empires were embedded in high empire itself. Did modernists stay at home poring over Blavatsky's *Secret Doctrine* and Eliphas Levi's *Transcendental Magic*, or did they take to the open road? In a world of more numerous, remagicalizing possibilities than those of the hippie Kathmandu trail, the more enterprising did the last. At a point where cultic milieu overlaps with high-imperial globalization, worldwide esoteric circuits, dotted with sacred sites and countercultural centres like Ascona and Taos, were the result of the open-road approach.[35] These circuits and centres, with their intra-modernist syncretism, new Myths, and schemes for 'restoration' (*tikkun*, again), were more likely to have inspired the modernist 'spiritual' than any number of practising occultists. Occultism alone produced illustrative art: what modernists *did* with the occult, and *why* they did it, are more interesting questions.

'Symbols of the old noble way of life'

My aim here is to sketch a historical background to Smith's interpretation of modernism. I want to relate the post-1880 return to older, occult forms of knowledge, together with the tribal-oriental vogues, to a neo-aristocratic thirst for adventure and romance. High empire stood for antithetical, outsider values, and antithetical, outsider ways of knowing the world, to those of bourgeois domesticity. To illustrate this split, between middle-class knowledge and the imperially extended occult, and to indicate how Romantic myths of empire were processed in the period imaginary, I cite a variety of sources. Most of these bear on rearrangements of class attitudes in relation to the, after 1880, dominant Orientalist version of empire, and on the quarrel of a now resurfacing 'irregular' or heterodox knowledge with disenchanting middle-class positivism. Developing Smith, I suggest that modernism's high-imperial, occult-exotic hinterland contains pulp and elite, vulgarian and aristocratic, ingredients alike. In line with Disraeli's proposal of an alliance between upper and lower orders against their common middle-class enemy, this convergence of 'high' and 'low' gave an 'aristo-plebeian' slant to the high-imperial imaginary, a slant also found in its modernist counterpart.

Amira Bennison argues that empire in Africa and Asia was a 'Euro-Islamic condominium': European empires were tacked onto older Muslim structures, such that 'earlier universal empires continued to exercise sway'.[36] During British supremacy, the Ottoman Empire still existed, and though the Moghuls fell after the Indian mutiny, a mixed bag of emirs and other minor potentates still retained regional authority. Respect for this fact, which in turn entailed respect for local customs and religions, was axiomatic for the aristocratic, non-reformist Orientalist school of imperial thought. The middle-class Anglicist school, by contrast, rose superior to local custom – and to its different ways of knowing the world – and tried to substitute a positivist, utilitarian and reformist regime in its stead.

Just as there were two schools of imperialist thought, so there were two types of traveller: the middle-class reformist and the aristocratic traditionalist. In a study of women travellers in the Middle East, Billie Melman shows how aristocratic travellers admired what they found, wanting to change nothing, even in the case of Lady Jane Digby (a friend of Richard Burton) taking the veil on marriage to a Syrian Sheik.[37] Preceded by Wilfrid Scawen Blunt, an anti-imperial agitator-poet honoured by Yeats and Pound, 'white Arabs' like T. E. Lawrence and Wilfred Thesiger belonged to this 'aristocratic' line. So did the anti-modern Arabophile Sir Mark Sykes, of the Sykes–Picot agreement fame, not to mention John Buchan's 1916 romance of Islamic jihad, *Greenmantle*, where purification and revitalization come from the desert. Melman's middle-class travellers were, on the other hand, shocked at what they found: in the Holy Land, of all places, they discovered only dirty Arabs and ugly Jews. Cleanliness being next to godliness, reform had to follow, the more Christian the better.

The division of response was much the same, whatever the destination: some travelled with closed minds, others, including most modernists, were fascinated by ethnographic diversity and respectful of what Voltaire called 'the empire of custom' (provided it was free from modern taints). In trying culturally to reproduce or imitate this age-old empire of custom, however, it was usually the case with modernists, of 'first world plus third world equals the fourth world remake', as one critic of musical exoticism puts it.[38] As familiar Western knowns, the categories of the exotic, the occult and the Gothic, as applied to non-Western unknowns, could set up expectations and alter the finished product ('oriental mysticism', 'tribal cults') in ways that were foreign to earlier, genuinely 'gone native', religio-cultural crossovers.

Expectations could also result in disappointments, like Antonin Artaud's, when his preconceived 'ancestral' Mexico (shades of Carlos Castaneda) turned out on a visit to be too modern. Gauguin, who had a Theosophist neighbour in his island retreat, devised an alternative: he gave his bedraggled South Sea Islanders the myths they *ought* to have had. In India, quondam 'gone civilized' indigenous elites began to 'appear native', aped by sympathizing Theosophists.

As Edwin Luytens remarked of dress code as a sign of anti-colonial nationalism under the Raj, 'India expects every man to do his dhoti'. Doing one's *dhoti* (reinventing nomos) also included mystical revival, now just as much a hybrid, in India, as the 'magical eclecticism' found in Germany by Hugo Ball.

The reverse side of imperial expansion was Europe's disorientation at finding itself part of a much larger, more heterogeneous and mysterious world than ever expected (note Gauguin's question, in the title to one of his Tahitian paintings, 'where do we come from, where are we going?'). Hence, along the lines of Kahn's 'archive of the planet', needs for a new, worldwide imaginary; for new and more varied, indigenist pasts; and including the now imperially extended occult, needs for new knowledges and representational idioms, can all be discerned. Greece, Rome and the Bible, traditional cornerstones of older Western knowledge, availed little in front of high-imperial globalization. Romanticism, true, is as much a distorting lens as positivism: but positivism alone was hardly able to supply the new high-imperial desiderata. Nothing short of an epistemological and representational sea-change could save Europe and America from the religio-cultural blowback, and shocks to inherited worldviews, created by turn-of-the-century globalization. Embracing the transnational groundswell, this was Theosophy's opportunity to proselytize its 'universal restoration' as a global brand.

Perceptions needed to be adjusted, paradigms changed: duly expanded like the occult, and aided by empathetic-analogical thinking – the ability to see the other as an ally not an enemy – a remodelled Romanticism was the best available tool for these tasks. Long before they coalesced into a new, earlier twentieth-century cultural establishment, this impulse to rearrange knowledge and representation was most pronounced among the potential losers and threatened species of bourgeois modernity: dreamers, utopians, poets, aristocrats, cosmopolitans, anarchists, all of whom, as 'heathenish' outsiders, were more attracted to the occult and distant 'myth-ringed' horizons than (Cook's Tours excepted) the stay-at-home middle class. In repentant 'irrationalist' guise, some bourgeois switched sides, to throw in their lot with the colonial syncretic and revenant pre-modern: whence moneyed, not landed, members of the early counterculture like Mabel Dodge Luhan, married to an American Indian and hostess of Lawrence at Taos. Dennis Hopper later bought her house.[39]

But how did this story of a heterodox and cosmopolitan, transnational class politics of the exotic, the primitive and the occult begin? How did aristocrats, and later plebeians, come to espouse the primitive and pre-modern, even if, as the imperial theme shaded into Barnum and Bailey, that was in a 'fourth world remake', faux tribe sense? Early Enlightenment primitivists, mostly aristocrats, had neither known the Terror nor strayed too far from Europe. The Terror's aristocratic survivors knew it only too well, many of them, with other beleaguered aristocrats, taking to distant travels, most likely in the knowledge that, absent anti-democratic reaction, their writing was on the wall.

Harry Liebersohn, historian of 'aristocratic encounters' with American Indians, answers some of these questions: 'the "savage"', with his vital role in the 'modernist dream of merging with the primitive', was 'an alternative to bourgeois Europe and an ally of the aristocrat in a democratic age'.[40] Contact with savages 'opened up a moment of peculiar affinity between the destiny of warrior elites from two worlds'. In Europe, a post-Napoleonic alliance between 'successful survivors of the old order's collapse' and 'wealthy and educated members of the upper middle class' formed a new elite. 'This new aristocracy was adept at taking up *symbols of the old noble way of life* and streamlining them into an acceptable culture for an increasingly industrial, commercial, and emancipated society' (my italics). Balancing this, 'Indian societies seemed to their admirers more aristocratic than Europeans themselves in their cultivation of warrior values'. Liebersohn's aristocrats came 'just in time to observe [President Andrew] Jackson's policy of forced removal of native peoples to territories beyond the Mississippi. The exterminating logic of democracy as they knew it … from the Terror once again displaced classes and peoples as part of the cost of progress'.[41]

For Georges Sand and Delacroix, American Indians 'were to be honored as fellow aristocrats'; equally, Baudelaire was 'the first of a succession of artists who turned to native peoples for a heroism, vitality, and expressiveness that were being eradicated from the modern world'.[42] Such admiration for 'natives' had repercussions, not just for the later nineteenth-century return of pluralist and multi-ethnic aristocratic ideals, but also for the Orientalist/collaborative way empire was ruled. Not to mention Rice Burroughs's Tarzan, himself of aristocratic descent, Buchan's *Prester John* and *Greenmantle*, with their accounts of revitalization movements in

South Africa and the Muslim world, are later expressions of the same longing for an anti-modern nomos: a mood picked up, in the Taos and Ascona countercultures, by modernists like Lawrence, Dodge, Hesse and Rudolph Laban, guru of modernist dance. Here, then, strangely enough – since transposed from empire, aristocracy, imperial romance and high Bohemia to a levelling, life-style key – is an ancestry for hippie tepees and the Amerindian shamanism professed by the New Age.

Of the revival of 'Eastern spirituality', Stephen Hay makes similar points to Liebersohn's. Their aim 'the revitalization of ancient or medieval ideals', the Asian revivalists 'work[ed] together, in Tokyo ... Boston ... Peking, or Paris, but most often in Calcutta and London ... form[ing] an international community, a largely English-speaking confederation of rebels against the Westernization of the globe'. Assisted by 'such Western allies as ... Fenollosa, Nivedita, Besant, ... Rolland [and] Keyserling' (more on these figures later), these 'Asian intellectuals were much encouraged by the Orientophilia of Western intellectuals ... disillusioned with their own Judaeo-Christian or Greco-Roman cultural heritages'.[43] East–West art-world interchange flourished on comparably equal terms: as potter Bernard Leach writes of his inspirational friendship (after 1909) with Yanagi Soetsu: 'I gave him Blake and Whitman; seeds which fell on fertile ground, for he wrote ... about both poets. In turn he made me aware of mystics ... East and West, such as St John of the Cross, Meister Eckhart ... Lao Tze, Confucius, and Chuang Tse ... We dealt authors and artists like playing cards'.[44] This (1880–1920) was the age of the 'second oriental renaissance', the first having petered out with Romanticism. Paradoxically, this new Orientalism was most 'furious' under the German *Kaiserreich*. France, Russia, Britain and Holland had their Eastern possessions: the reality as well as the dream. Minor annexations apart, Germany only had the dream, from the Romantics to the Third Reich.[45]

Modernist roots run deep in the would-be reanimating, countermodern strains of empire-related culture touched above. Savages, Orientals, peasants – with the Jazz Age, American negroes too – were the antithesis of the moneyed bourgeois. As Hermann Bahr put it in 1914,

> The way ... Expressionism proceeded in an uncontrolled ... fashion is
> excused by ... circumstances ... We live almost in the state of a primitive

tribe ... Bourgeois rule has made wild men of us ... to save ... mankind
from the bourgeoisie, we must all become barbarians ... We flee from a
civilization that devours the soul of man.

To be developed by figures like Lawrence, Stravinsky, the Russian
Futurists and Georges Bataille, Nietzsche felt the same: 'the domes-
tication (the culture) of man does not go deep – where it does it at
once becomes degeneration ... The savage (or in moral terms the
evil man) is a return to nature – and in a ... sense his recovery, his
cure from culture'.[46] Finding a 'cure' for civilization was also a concern of occultist Simple Lifer Edward Carpenter, a notion repeated
by a 'jungle' strain in modernism, fashionable in the twenties.

Imperial Gothic

Following J. A. Hobson, who influenced Lenin, literary historian
Patrick Brantlinger notices the period 'desire to revitalize not only
heroism but aristocracy', commenting that 'imperialism offers a
swashbuckling politics and a world in which neither epic heroism
nor chivalry is dead'. He interprets imperialism as a diversionary
'political and cultural regression', a rearguard bulwark 'against the
corrosive effects of popular reform and democratization', productive of 'fantasies of aristocratic authority at home and abroad'.[47]
For all his left-liberal bias, Brantlinger has a nose for links between
empire and occultism, including what he calls 'imperial Gothic'. Of
the revivification of imagination and fantasy, he writes, 'India is a
realm of imaginative license ... *a place where the fantastic becomes possible in ways that are ... circumscribed at home*'.[48] As within modernism
itself, the laws of 'civilization', of Newton, Descartes, Euclid and
Aristotle, were suspended in the colonial world. With consequences
for styles of representation – flight from domestic realism into
oneiric-visionary or magic realist modes – the 'unknown forces' or
Sakti of the tropics came into this break with 'civilized' laws.

Thus in *The Hidden Force*, a novel by the Dutch Decadent Louis
Couperus, written during a 1900 stay in the East Indies, the
European characters 'are defeated by the hidden forces of the land
they rule'. Apropos these forces, Ian Buruma quotes Couperus on
the supernatural: 'I believe that benevolent and hostile forces float
around us, right through our ordinary, everyday existence; I believe

the Oriental … can command more power over these forces than the Westerner who is absorbed by his sobriety, business and making money.'[49] Often letting two worldviews collide, the magical and the materialist, but scarcely resolving the resultant liminoidality (an ever-present 'in-between state'), this was precisely the belief of Smith's modernists when they rejected the 'civilized' West in favour of the exotic and occult.

Quoting the novelist William Hale White's 1885 assertion that 'our civilization is nothing but a thin film or crust lying over a volcanic pit', a comment that could apply to Stravinsky's *Rite of Spring*, Brantlinger writes that imperial Gothic's 'three principal themes' are 'individual regression or going native; an invasion of civilization by the forces of barbarism or demonism; and the diminution of opportunities for adventure and heroism in the modern world'. Comparing the Theosophical and occultist vogues, he continues: 'In the romances of Stevenson, Haggard, Kipling, Doyle, Bram Stoker, and … Buchan the supernatural or paranormal, usually symptomatic of individual regression, often manifests in imperial settings'. Noting Anglo-Indian fiction's Hammer House of Horror-like obsession with 'inexplicable curses, demonic possession, and ghostly visitations', Kipling's 'Phantom Rickshaw' is cited as typical of the genre.

Of occultism's link with imperialism, Brantlinger notes parallels between defences of spiritualism and Theosophy and Haggard's and Conrad's complaints about contracting geographical frontiers. 'Not only were occultists seeking proofs of immortality and of a spiritual realm … they were also seeking adventure. The fantasy element in such adventure seeking is its most obvious feature, as … also in the literary turn away from realism to romanticism.'[50] The 'anti-modern vitalism' diagnosed in Gilded Age America by T. J. Jackson Lears was another such backlash against contracted horizons: with the closing of the American frontier, a cult of 'strenuosity', intended to remedy 'nerves' – subscribed to by Teddy Roosevelt and later Ernest Hemingway – was another way of finding adventure in an overly civilized world.[51]

For some adventure seekers, the dangers proved seductive. Alluding to Conrad's Asia as 'the lands of the brown nations, where a stealthy Nemesis lies in wait, pursues, overtakes, so many of the conquering race', in his 1924 autobiography, the 'teacher and journalist, globe-trotter and man of action, travel-writer and novelist' Edmund Candler wrote that 'it was just that Nemesis which attracted me. I believed that the contacts and collisions of East and West still provided adventures akin to the medieval ... Chivalry could not attain full stature in a milieu of pavements and chimney pots'.[52] Kipling's tale 'The Man Who Would Be King' is a fictional prototype of Candler's heroic atavism: feeling short on places to 'Sar-a-*whack*' (a reference to the White Rajahs of Sarawak), the British protagonists go off to found their own kingdom in Kafiristan.

With its mix of animism, occultism, swashbuckling politics and new frontiers, Lears's 'anti-modern vitalism' was commonplace by the turn of the century – a triumph, in its way, for Liebersohn's displaced gentleman travellers, and a pivot for warring, liberal and neo-Romantic worldviews. Indian religion, its atavism a theme of Forster's *Passage to India*, was especially unnerving for the bourgeoisie. According to a 1902 review of Anglo-Indian novels, 'It is in the religious atmosphere above all of India that the Englishman feels himself to be moving in a mysterious ... world'. Suggesting he 'surround [himself] with English atmosphere, and defend [himself] from the magic of the land by sport, games, clubs ... the chatter of fresh-imported girls, and ... fairly regular attendance at Church', the reviewer warns that the newcomer 'does well to resist the seduction which this atmosphere exercises upon those too curious about it'.[53] In which connection, the Calcutta art historian E. A. Havell, said to believe 'any sadhu he meets', allegedly went mad through dabbling in Tantra.[54]

In an account of colonial novelists with mystical-Nietzschean leanings, Hugh Ridley notes how they rejoiced at missionary failure and were keener to dilate on civilization's shortcomings than to extol any *mission civilisatrice*. M. A. Leblond saw an anti-degenerate, post-liberal 'new man' in the settler; the Taoist initiate and associate of Rene Guénon, Albert de Pouvoirville, believed that 'only by outdoing the old [Indochinese] order in heroic and uncivilized ruthlessness could France lay claim to imperial expansion'; Frieda von Bulow 'often compared ... [her] characters with Nietzschean figures', including the '*Willenmensch*'. In *The Explorer* (1908), Somerset Maugham depicted 'the ruthless colonial pioneer with his contempt for the weak and their morality, and his readiness to sacrifice lesser mortals to the accomplishment of his will'.[55] While in Edgar Wallace's 1909 *Sanders of the River*, a commissioner in Africa 'outsavages the savages, partly through police brutality ... partly ... through knowledge of witchcraft'.[56] Alternatively, as an 'affirmative' counterpart to Conrad's 'Mistah Kurtz', there is Perken, the self-appointed guardian of the tribal Stieng in Andre Malraux's 1930 Indo-Chinese novel *La Voie Royale*, a freedom-fighting member of the anti-modern ethnic protectorate who, like Tolstoy and Che Guevara, has rejected the civilized world.

From 1880s origins, a new myth-making politico-cultural style had emerged by around 1900. This political 'expression of the exotic' (Smith) sought to inject vital energy into the new post-bourgeois, or post-European, order which the era's counter-modern revolutionaries envisaged as supervening on liberalism. With Bergson and Nietzsche presiding over the synthesis of the materials involved – their ideas acted as a solvent for the Eastern lore and Western occultism that went into the mix – the reach of the new style was international, extending to anti-colonial nationalism in India. The Bombay revolutionary B. G. Tilak acknowledged his sources: 'It was the articles of Europeans who studied our ancient books which made them attractive to our … people … we began to recognize the importance of the contents of our home only after the foreigners showed us [them].'[57] With its implications for a complicity of outlook between imperialism's romantic advocates and equally romantic foes, the reactionary revolutionary revival of the 'rejected knowledge' theme is visible here.

For the Cambridge-educated Aurobindo, bicultural terrorist then guru, India was 'a mighty Shakti, composed of the Shaktis of all the millions of units that make up the nation'. But she was 'inactive, imprisoned in the magic circle of tamas, the self-indulgent inertia and ignorance of her sons. To get rid of tamas we have but to wake the Brahma within.'[58] Aurobindo's fantasy is the same as turn-of-the-century Europe's: if decadence is the necessary outcome of civilization, then the only hope for regeneration is a return to the vital and sacred. Though its immediate basis was later nineteenth-century neo-Romanticism, the new counter-modern, revivificatory style can ultimately be traced to the 'symbols of the old noble way of life' synthesized by Liebersohn's aristocrats, as they fled the 'exterminating logic of democracy' and the urban-industrial ravages of the modern world.

The connection of such holistic-organismic vitalism with the Romantic vision of empire is clear. Of this and its liberal contender, David Cannadine writes,

> there were … two discrepant views of the societies and polities thus acquired. The first was that the native regimes and hierarchies were

backward, inefficient, despotic and corrupt, and had to be overthrown and reconstructed according to the more advanced model of western society and politics. The second view was that they were traditional and organic, an authentic world of ordered, harmonious, time-hallowed social relations [such as] the Industrial Revolution was threatening ... in Britain, and that ... had to be ... preserved and nurtured overseas as a more wholesome version of society than could now be found in the metropolis.[59]

Dubbed 'Toryentalist' by Niall Fergusson, and opposed to what he calls the 'Anglobalizing' strain in British imperialism, it was the second vision which Romantic imperialists lent to native cultural nationalists, Theosophists and modernists.

To flatter high society, Diaghilev's *Ballets Russes*, with its Slav primitivism and Indian opulence, staged latter-day rearrangements of Liebersohn's 'symbols of the old noble way of life', as codified now within an imagined archaic-oriental primordium. Bursting with 'life' and occult marvels, this primordium was central to the new, post-realist imaginary within whose counter-modern terms the new illuminated politics and artistic culture came to the fore. And just as the faraway, with its sacred geographies, could be politicized to make it usable by anti-liberal renegades, so within such neo-aristocratic rearrangements of Liebersohn's 'symbols of the old noble way of life', the distant past, with its sacred histories, could be politicized as well.

The Russian Symbolist Andrei Bely put it thus:

The really new in Symbolism is the attempt to illumine the deepest contradictions of contemporary culture seen through the prism of various cultures: we are now experiencing, as it were, the whole of the past: India, Persia, Egypt, Greece ... pass before us ... just as a man on the point of death may see the whole of his life in an instant ... An important hour has struck for humanity. We are indeed attempting something new but the old has to be taken into account; there is a novelty in the plenitude of the past.[60]

As if in some Art Nouveau 'total artwork', humanity's ancestral inheritance, the shock of the old, is as important as any shock of the new; and like a dying man, an otherwise, under liberalism, terminally sick Europe can benefit from a review of antiquities which *exclude* the Roman and Hebraic. Diaghilev made similar omissions: the centre of world history had moved elsewhere, away from Rome and (Salome excepted) away from the Bible.

To switch from the *Ballets Russes* and Bely, from polite affectations of the archaic and the exotic in Symbolist culture to their less patrician counterparts. In his 1892 *Degeneration*, Max Nordau noted that 'Ghost stories are very popular, but … in scientific guise, as hypnotism, telepathy, somnambulism … So are esoteric novels, in which the author hints that he could say a great deal about magic, kabbala, fakirism, astrology and other white and black arts if he … chose.'[61] On a similar tack, Conan Doyle wrote of the popularity of occult romances of 'the animal-magnetico-electrico-hysterical-biological-mysterious sort'.[62] Taken with imperial Gothic, whose readership was doubtless legion, Doyle and Nordau imply that, far from being elitist, an elevated aesthetico-spiritual movement apart, modernism, at a 'semi-animistic, mystical-unconscious' level (Wyndham Lewis's characterization of Schopenhauer's legacy to the modernist twenties), chimed with more popular fashions.

These fashions included not just the occult and the Orient, but also what anthropologist E. B. Tylor called 'savage philosophy'. Analogies with popular Western trends came readily: as Doyle's Professor Challenger noted, 'the "soul talk" of … spiritualists is the "Animism of savages"'.[63] Likewise, for Tylor, modern occultism was 'a direct revival from … savage philosophy and peasant folk-lore', while contemporary poetry evoked 'the mental condition of the lower races'. For Tylor's follower, Andrew Lang, modern romances were 'savage survivals', and modern men and women (unlike Japan's 'professors of civilization') longed to feel 'the stirring of ancient dread in their veins'. The reason for this (anti-positivism again) was that 'as the visible world is measured, mapped, tested, weighed, we seem to hope more and more that a world of invisible romance may not be far from us'. Lang continues: 'The ordinary shilling tales of "hypnotism" and mesmerism are vulgar trash enough, and yet I can believe that an impossible romance, if the right man wrote it … might still win us from the newspapers, and the stories of shabby love, and cheap remorses, and commonplace failures.'[64]

Modernism is arguably just such an 'impossible romance', a last stand for the imagination (or 'mythopoetic function': a term of F. W. Myers, founder of The Society for Psychical Research), a meeting of old and new, rearguard and futural, a reanimating venture which spurns the decay of domestic culture. Making elitist hypotheses about modernism unlikely, the evidence suggests that the savage was an ally not only of aristocrats, but also of plebeians: unless, with high-minded progressives, we find merely cynical diversionary tactics behind the popularity of colonial exhibitions, of penny romances of empire, of the Buffalo Bill shows (as attractive to the barbarophile Queen Victoria as to her less-tutored subjects), of a 'Coney Island Orientalism' which entranced the masses, among them the vulgarian Ruth St Denis, future star of modern dance. Developing Smith – and without necessary intervention by professional occultists – the imperial occult and exotic were unmissable in elite and plebeian culture alike.

2

MODERNIST INTERWORLDS

Codes of the Soul and the Culture of Trance

As symptoms of the nervous, hunter-gatherer nature of modernism's foraging on the 'other side' – its attraction to a frantic, speedily thrown together syncretism where the absolute and wondrous fused – I now probe the curious autism (and automatism) of modernist communication, selfhood and consciousness. Magic, Mesmerism and Spiritualism had pointed the way. Communication at the here-requisite subtle, pre-vociferous level being covert and 'vibrational', not overt, the mediumistic/hypnotic 'second state' of recent occultism duly served as a basis for magnetic rapport between the modernist artist and his 'suggestible' audience. Modernist metalanguage included 'metaphysical codes' or 'soul codes', their aim to supersede mass idiom, renovate cognition, and promulgate new, perception-changing optics, acoustics and literary forms.[1] As proposed in 1917 by Russian Formalist Victor Shklovsky, 'making it strange' in the arts was an antidote to 'decay': but the occult-hypnotic nature of this strangeness, a relative of the 'marvellous', is seldom spelt out. 'Occult-hypnotic' implies imagination: a faculty with access to other realms, especially 'intermediate states', complete with their 'treasure house of images', available for use in entranced and entrancing art.[2]

In this originally Symbolist schema, much depended on the state of health of the imagination, and of the magical images it claimed to translate from 'astral/etheric' into aesthetic terms. *Flectere si nequeo superos, Acheronta movebo*, wrote Freud at the beginning of his *Interpretation of Dreams*: 'if I cannot bend the upper powers, I will

28

stir up the powers of hell'. But who was able to distinguish clearly between the divine and the demonic? Suggesting its cures were worse than the *mal de siecle* it tried to shake off, Symbolism has been described as a history of 'ruined lives'.[3] Descent into hell was all too easy – *facilis descensus Averno* – as shown by a catalogue of madness, addiction and suicide in Decadent/Symbolist and modernist quarters.[4] As in the myths of Sisyphus and Prometheus, hybristic presumptions on the divine rebounded on modernist millenarians and redeemers, concluding in torment.

With the 'mythic forties' and 'mystic sixties' in mind, Hugo Ball will guide us through the 'lawless', hypnotico-magical interworld of the Expressionist Teens. Samples of modernist meta-language will follow. Because of the eclecticism involved – a mix of magic, multiple personality, hypnagogic imagery, hallucinosis, mesmerism and reverie – this is an elusive subject. But through a series of snapshots of the different myth-makers, Gothic psychologists, occultists and mediumistic 'imaginatives' who contributed to this deeply arcane side of modernism, I hope to show how the modernist 'second self', the unconscious and imagination, all interworld denizens, came to operate as sources for phantasmagoric 'second state' art.

Psyche, Cosmos, Mythos: The Modernist Canon

The sourcing and processing of the colonial syncretic, as food for the imagination, is my initial theme. For its contributions to modernist myths about Psyche and Cosmos, a resume of current sources of 'Eastern spirituality', a relatively new player which overtook Cabala, the earlier source for such myths, might be a helpful place to start. The first of these sources was textual; others were more informal, part of the cultic milieu. Besides colonial exhibitions, non-textual sources included mystical tourism, countercultural roving and contacts with gurus and esoteric networks. The textual basis was roughly fourfold. First, traditional, though not necessarily in origin canonical, texts like *The Upanishads, Bhagavad-Gita, Tao Te Ching, Lotus Sutra, The Life of Milarepa* and *The Tibetan Book of Dead*, all coalesced into a Western canon, available in various translations.[5] Next, there was a scholarly secondary literature, like the works of Eugene Burnouf, Paul Deussen, Max Muller and Henry Clarke Warren, as read by such figures as Wagner, Strindberg and Eliot.[6]

Third, a mixed bag, and varying in their closeness to Asian sources, we have the American Transcendentalists, the 'cosmically conscious' Whitman–Bucke–Carpenter trio, and the German counter-philosophers, Schopenhauer, Nietzsche and Heidegger. Other middle-men include the Theosophists, East Asianists like Arthur Waley and Laurence Binyon, and Traditionalists like Guénon, Coomaraswamy and Julius Evola. Here, too, we find savants such as Heinrich Zimmer, Henry Corbin and Mircea Eliade, members of the Jungian Eranos circuit, interested in symbolism and the 'theophanic' imaginal realm. Important for the higher vulgarization, many such middle-men withdrew increasingly from the academy: though the Traditionalist and Eranos-conference pundits, even if sectarians, were undeniably scholars. Finally, we encounter the non-traditional – modernizing, revivalist or independent – teachings of Asians like Vivekananda, Tagore, Aurobindo, Krishnamurti and D. T. Suzuki.

In developing the new gnosis, 'modern mystics' like Huxley ranged freely within all categories, adding Western esoterica. In his 1944 *The Perennial Philosophy*, Huxley drew on Oriental translations, scholarly commentary, Krishnamurti, Swami Prabhavananda and Western mystics. In subsequent works like *The Doors of Perception*, *Heaven and Hell, Island* and *The Devils of Loudun*, interests in trance-mediumship, possession and psychotropic drugs further diversified his counter-cosmology. Common in modernist circles, Huxley's part-occultist, part-Gothic psychological, part-Orientalist world-view is that of the *bricoleur*.

The type provided answers to the 'big' questions about cosmos and consciousness that accompanied the quest for new transcendental coordinates. Thus in Robert Musil's 1906 novel, *Young Torless*, the Symbolist dilemma of 'whence, why and whither' elicits resort to India's Sacred Books:

> in the ... act of opening a book he sought to enter ... *exquisite knowledge as if through a secret gate*. They had to be books whose ... possession was like *the sign of a secret order* and ... *the guarantee of superterrestrial revelations* ... [H]e found that ... only in books of Indian philosophy, which he did not consider mere books, but *revelations, reality-key works* like medieval books of alchemy and magic.[7]

With titles like *La Mort et l'au delà – L'homme et ses corps – Les sept principes de l'homme – Karma – La clef de la Theosophie – A B C de la Theosophie – La doctrine secrete* – *Le Plan Astral*, the library in Pirandello's 1904 novel, *Il fu Mattia Pascal*, provides its owner with similar 'exquisite knowledge' of the invisible world.[8]

Proof of the older Nordic-Asian mythology's pre-eminence – Raymond Schwab, historian of the Oriental Renaissance, opposes the West's 'Latin–Christian' and 'Nordic–Asian' axes of thought – Musil's Theosophist seeks illumination from Indian, not East Asian texts.[9] He also yearns for cosmosophical System, of a kind that, on his deathbed, Ouspensky feared might not exist. In the Eastern religions themselves, this kind of System (which in context, of course, is neither Oriental nor exotic) is not so much primary/spelt out, as secondary/implicit, the focus being less on cosmo-conception than liberation from mental and worldly snares. As for the 'occult phenomena' implied by the titles in Pirandello's library, for austere Self-realized figures like Ramana Maharshi and Nisargadatta Maharaj, such 'next world' signs and wonders were just another trap.

Musil's 'reality key' approach to Eastern texts predominates in the dynamic, 'post-Euclidean' counter-cosmologies of modernism's neo-Romantic schools – Symbolism, German Expressionism, American Abstract Expressionism – where the vital, fluid and mysterious carry great weight. In such cases, there are echoes of the sympathetic-magical universe which accompanied what Catherine Albanese calls 'kinetic spirituality' – post-Romantic spirituality being drawn to 'spirit on the move'. Albanese notes that, as enlisted by American Transcendentalists, the Swedenborgian doctrine of correspondences, which assumes a fluid, multi-dimensional, interdependent cosmos of 'signatures' unlike the modern West's, is paralleled by archaic-Oriental notions of magical sympathies and synchronicities.[10]

A sympathetic-magical worldview of this type (common in folk religion, including Mormonism) was a godsend for modernity's higher intuitive discontents.[11] But where their teachers strayed, from Emerson, through the Theosophists, to Huxley and maybe Suzuki, was in assuming that cosmosophical know-how, not liberation, was the point of the magical and, in the sense of a re-ensouled nature, *Naturphilosophie*-like Systems they sought to expound. As opposed to pursuing methods for loosening its hold, establishing the mere existence of such a magico-sympathetic universe was the goal of devotees of the 'reality key' (or the later and related 'Tao of Physics') approach. More than by China (or Japan: a source for 'little epiphanies' prior to the Zen vogue), anti-classical modernist myth-makers were inspired by India, as regarded, not from a static Vedantic, but from a dynamic, yogic-Tantric perspective (Chapter 4). Virtuosos like Eliade and Evola acted as spokesmen for this vital-istic, psycho-cosmic India, their aim the extrapolation of System and 'grades of being' from what they saw as a life force-rich, hence potentially reanimating, subtle energy universe, not unlike that of the *Natur-* and *Lebensphilosophie* complex of ideas.

Links exist between the different countercultural networks where Psyche, Cosmos and Mythos assumed their modernist, then 'mystic sixties' and New Age forms. By way of the writings and career of Joseph Campbell, one such set of links involves the turn-of-the-century German occultism behind Jungian thought, and that now international 'Californian cosmology', to whose development the Esalen Institute's neo-Theosophical mythopoeia contributed so much.[12] Signalling the demise or marginalization of the esoteric currents (Cabala, Hermetism, alchemy) once carried by 'irregular' Freemasonry, Esalen, founded in 1962, hosted Huxley, Campbell, Timothy Leary and Alan Watts among others. Because of his connections with the Jungian Eranos circuit and Bollingen Foundation on the one side and Esalen on the other (where he lectured for 19 years from 1968), the most important figure here is Campbell. Reared on a modernist diet of Joyce, Mann, Spengler and Jung, Campbell knew or met several Orientalist figures: Karlfried Graf von Durckheim, Zimmer, Krishnamurti, Swami Nikhilananda, Suzuki.[13] His best-known book, *The Hero with a Thousand Faces* (1949), influenced the Abstract Expressionists and George Lucas, director of *Star Wars.*

Returning to my proposed links between turn-of-the-century Germanic occultism and the New Age, the still semi-Theosophical Eranos Conferences, convened by Olga Froebe-Kapteyn, Theoso-phist friend of 'Aquarian' Alice Bailey, were held in the German counterculture's heartland at Ascona. Granted that the next port of call after Ascona and Eranos was the Mellon-financed Bollingen Foundation and then the Esalen Institute – and given Campbell's intermediary position between the Eranos and Esalen milieux – a bridge now seems to have materialized over which the German occultism on which Jung was reared could travel to America and find a new home. In short, further to their post-Second World War influences on counter-cosmology and late modernism in the

USA – via the Bollingen Foundation's connections to the arts, and the Abstract Expressionist cult of *The Hero* – shades of pre-First World War Germanic occultism live on in the Jung- and Campbell-influenced magic worldview of America's New Age. (Mary Mellon, Jungian wife of millionaire Paul Mellon, was the force behind the Bollingen foundation.[14])

Even if the cosmosophical and interworld emphases of the modernist Mythos (including Jungianism) pose problems, the cultural consequences of adopting a new imaginary derived from it were rich. Many typically Symbolist or early modernist themes and procedures draw on archaic-Oriental influences from within that imaginary. There is, for instance, the period topos of lost wisdom and unmediated vision – the 'childhood of the race' or 'self-ancestral' motif – as assumed from primal, pre-Christian histories, whether indigenous (see later) or like those mentioned by Bely (Chapter 1). There is a further modernist tendency to multilayered, transcultural reflections on a modern reality, which Bely describes elsewhere as being 'like a diamond, a prism, the play of light, simultaneity'. With its subtle energetic and mesocosmic preferences in 'higher worlds', the new Mythos also encouraged Symbolist techniques like synaesthesia: engagement of all the senses at once with a sympathetic-magical universe which transcended classical norms. Another by-product of this 'prismatic' Symbolism was the high modernist profile of paranormal consciousness, as witness Mikhail Matiushin's all-round 'see-know' vision, an 'expanded viewing' approach to art based on yoga.[15] Radiance, aura and freshness – the preternatural colours of intermediate reality – were crucial for making it new in the arts.

Not that interworld pyrotechnics, astral excursions and occultist phantasmagoria were the whole story. Some of the figures involved, like Victor Segalen, Gustav Holst, Eliot, Christian Dotrement, Ad Reinhardt and Gary Snyder, took university-level courses in Oriental studies, thereby (sometimes) curbing occultist excess. Not noticeably chastening their approach, others, such as Strindberg, Alma Mahler (a Theosophist since 1914), Rene Daumal and Yves Klein taught themselves Oriental languages like Japanese, Sanskrit or Mandarin. (Hebrew and Arabic were their precursors in the older occultism.) Except among conservatives like Eliot's teacher Irving Babbitt, interest in Pali was less pronounced: nor did 'rational' Pali Text Society Buddhism, like its living relative, the 'Protestant

Buddhism' of Ceylon, appeal to neo-Romantic sensibilities absorbed by the otherworld.

With Andre Malraux, Rudolph Otto, Eliade, Jung, Bruno Taut, Frank Lloyd Wright, Tobey, Leach, Henri Michaux, Sam Francis and Yves Klein, travel to or extensive stays in Japan, Indo-China or India, even time spent in ashrams and Zen monasteries, added to their knowledge of the aesthetic and metaphysical East (Chapter 5). Finally, a system of countercultural 'little Orients' – based on Ascona, Green Acre Maine, Taos in New Mexico, the Cornish School in Seattle, Dartington in Devon, Black Mountain College in South Carolina, Theosophical Adyar and Tagore's Santiniketan – fed visitors the latest fashions, as well as fostering networks of patronage and influence. Dedicated initially to something like Coomaraswamy's 'postindustrial' Arts and Crafts vision, these 'little Orients' attracted such already-mentioned figures as Hesse, Ball, Jung, Laban, Lawrence, Dodge, Tobey and Leach, as well as Marsden Hartley and Walter Gropius, not to mention Merce Cunningham, Robert Rauschenberg and Cage.[16]

Professional occultists are absent from the above list. Survivals from the pre-materialist West's 'magic worldview', both learned and folkloric, are doubtless involved in modernist receptivity to Eastern cosmologies. But where mediation is involved, there is no need, Theosophy aside, to emphasize 'occult revival'. Not unlike nineteenth-century America's utopian commune-dwellers (who drew on the Western world-picture's pre-modern magical substrate, and sometimes the Orient), modernists had their own authorities and resources for remagicalizing the dispirited, bourgeois worldview that had flattened Eden.

The Modernist Unconscious

Thomas Mann remarked that the earlier twentieth century 'surrendered to admiration of the unconscious, to a glorification of instinct, which it thinks is overdue to life'.[17] Mann's 'instinct' is easily referred to Nietzsche and Bergson. But what of his 'unconscious'? By the 'mythic forties', my choice would certainly be Jung, whose mistress, Toni Wolff, was a Theosophist; less so Freud, who reasonably feared 'a black occultist tide'. But as a vehicle, like instinct, for the reception of the colonial syncretic, what William James called 'Gothic psychology' – the study of hysteria, spirit mediums, and paranormal mental states – was more important than either. Jung, especially, drew on this older psychology, whose 'unconscious' was more magico-occult, interwoven with mesmero-spiritualism (then, with high empire, entangled with the tribal/Oriental), than 'psychological' in today's sense of the term. For Blavatsky, 'psychologized' and 'mesmerized' were at any rate synonymous, suggesting that a still actively magical psyche is most relevant to modernism's formative phase. The Gothic unconscious, as old in the arts as Fuseli, E. T. A. Hoffmann and Poe, was intimately connected with imagination: the very image-making faculty which took hypnotic command of the arts after 1880.

Alan Gauld's history of hypnotism shows how a pan-mesmeric model of religious experience became the mid-nineteenth-century free-thinking norm.[18] Anticipating the 'spectrum of consciousness' theories of the 1970s, this, the first 'transpersonal psychology', assumed that Mesmer's animal magnetism was the common denominator of the most diverse, meditative, ecstatic and enthusiastic, religio-mystical states.[19] J. C. Colquhoun's 1851 *History of Magic* illustrates the gist: 'Somnambulistic or ecstatic visions, accompanied … with cataleptic insensibility, and … the faculty of *clairvoyance* appear to have occurred among the religious mystics and fanatics of all ages … the Eastern Brahmins and Bonzes, the Hebrew Prophets, the early Christian Saints … Mahometan devotees, and … Protestant sectaries.' With its ascription of ecstatic self-vacation to 'Eastern Brahmins and Bonzes', Colquhoun's wild comparativism fails to distinguish between meditation and trance.

Gauld also cites Otto Stoll's 1894 work on hypnotic suggestion, which, casting its net yet wider, lumps together

> shamanism, possession by Oriental fox-spirits, the powers of yogis and fakirs, possession in the New Testament, analgesia during torture, temple sleep, epidemic suggestive ecstasy, epidemic possession, the crusades and other religious wars, the flagellants, convulsive and dancing epidemics, tarantism, the witch-craze in … Europe, the tremblers of the Cevennes, revolutionary movements … stock market crazes, and the vagaries of fashion.

Stoll's assumptions are not so different from those of the second transpersonal psychology: one pan-mesmeric – from the 1970s neo-Jungian/pan-shamanic – model fits all.

Paralleling James on the interworld's 'snakes and seraphs', Myers characterized the intermediate realm as a 'rubbish-heap as well as a treasure-house'.[20] Beset with new mysteries from the colonies, the era saw a proliferation of neo-mesmeric terminology, in relation to a faculty which stood part-way between the old Neoplatonic, Hermetic and Paracelsan *vis phantasticus* or *imaginatio*, and the Jungian then transpersonal unconscious.[21] Its quasi-shamanic 'energy and imagery' sphere serving as the creative field of the 'mythopoetic function', *imagination creatrice* and *fonction fabulatrice* theorized by Myers, Theodore Flournoy and Pierre Janet, the neo-Romantic occult self or magnetic double was variously figured in this not-yet-settled terminology. Options included Myers's 'secondary', 'inner', 'unconscious' or 'subliminal' self (from 1885), Alfred Binet's 'double consciousness' (1890), James's 'hidden self' (from 1890), Max Dessoir's 'underconsciousness' (1889), and Boris Sidis's 'subwaking self' (1911).[22]

Gothic psychology permeates imperial Gothic, drawing on occultist obsession (Levi, Blavatsky, the Golden Dawn) with 'magnetic fluid' – 'ethereal substance', as Levi's friend Balzac called it.[23] The 'subtle' sub-self idea recurs in this occultism. Thus in Meyrinck's 1915 *Der Golem* we read,

> The circle of people emitting blue-tinted rays who were standing around you constituted the chain of inherited *Ichs* which every man … drags around with him. The soul is nothing 'unique' – it will become unique later and that is called 'immortality'; your soul is still composed of many *Ichs* – as an ant colony is composed of many ants.[24]

Gurdjieff, too, saw man as a plural being: 'When we speak of ourselves ordinarily, we speak of "I".' But 'There is no such "I", or rather there are hundreds, thousands of little "I's" in every one of us. We are divided in ourselves but … cannot recognize the plurality of our being except by observation and study.'

The prospect of an extra sub-self or two proved popular with modernists. Familiar from Yeats and Eliot, the tactic of faking a double is a favourite of the Portuguese poet Fernando Pessoa, correspondent of Aleister Crowley and self-styled 'nomadic wanderer through consciousness' like the Whitman he discovered in 1914.[25] In Hesse's *Steppenwolf* (1927), the sub-self idea allows the novel's protagonist, Harry Haller, a double identity as alienated bourgeois and primitivist wolf from the steppe; it also underlies the novel's 'magic theatre' episode where Haller experiences his own fantasies in an 'etheric', proto-psychedelic fashion. In his 1923 essay on Poe, Lawrence plays on the metamorphic nature of selfhood and consciousness in a comparably Gothic and primitivizing way:

> Poe has no truck with Indians or Nature … He is absolutely concerned with the disintegration processes of his own psyche … the rhythm of American art activity is dual. 1. A disintegrating and sloughing of the old consciousness. 2. The forming of a new consciousness underneath. Fennimore Cooper has the two vibrations going on together. Poe has … only the disintegrative vibration … the old white psyche has to be … broken down before anything else can come to pass.[26]

Gothic psychology had a negativist complement in Ernst Mach's 'impressionist' quasi-Buddhist philosophy. As a mere waiting room for sensations, the ego was 'untenable' (*unrettbar*) on Mach's view. More usually, ostensible identity's loss was the second self's gain, as in the fluidic dilemma of Henry James's 1881 *The Portrait of a Lady*: 'What shall we call our "self"? Where does it begin? Where does it end? It overflows into everything that belongs to us – and then it flows back again.' Noting recent hypnotic experiments, an article in the *North American Review* (1908) similarly argued, 'the human self is a … more complex and unstable affair than has … been supposed … the self of which … man is normally conscious is but a self within a larger self, of which he becomes aware only in moments of inspiration, exaltation, and crisis'.[27] The second self was benignly regarded, mostly, in North America, as witnessed in the 'cosmic-utopian' selves of Whitman and Bucke at one end of our period, and Abram Maslow and the Esalen Institute psychologists at the other. In Europe, where the sinister tales of Maupassant and Meyrinck, like Strindberg's *A Dream Play*, evince a less sanguine mood, it was more often a cause for frisson or horror.

The Self-Ancestral

Gothic psychology could be adapted, hybridized and even politicized to deal with themes and worlds outside the province of the home-grown hypnotic subject and spirit medium. William Sturgis Bigelow's identification of Japanese Buddhism's 'void' (*ku*) with 'what is called subliminal consciousness or subconsciousness by modern psychologists' is an early example of fusion between neo-mesmeric psychology and Eastern thought. A later example is Suzuki's identification of Zen's 'no-mind' with 'the unconscious', a questionable move perhaps occasioned by his co-option onto the Jungian Eranos circuit. Bigelow, who spent seven years in Japan from 1882, saw Buddhism as 'a sort of Spiritual Pantheism … Emerson, almost exactly', remarking that 'separate personal consciousness … is … the only obstacle to complete freedom of the will … [T]he self is coextensive with the universe. The difference between … beings is … how much of themselves they realize.'[28] With their Transcendentalist and Gothic psychological base, Bigelow's beliefs anticipate a Promethean strain in modernism, which equates redemption with cosmic merger, after the fashion of Whitman, Lawrence and Malevich (Chapter 3).

An example of the coincidence of an imperfectly understood Orientalist lexicon with neo-mesmeric deep grammar is found in some comments on Buddhism and psychology by one Reverend Arthur Lee, member of Orage's Leeds circle. Here we find an equation between the world of ancestral spirits ('the massed efforts of countless inherited ghostly wills latent in all of us'), Myers's 'composite self' or 'multiple soul', and Edwin Arnold's version of *nirvana*, whereby 'the real "I" would be to the personal "I" what the ocean is to the dewdrop'. From an orthodox Buddhist perspective, this flight into muddled Oneness – known in Zen as 'bad sameness' (*aku-byodo*) – *could* describe the total mental and cosmic continuum within which Enlightenment finally takes place. As it stands, Lee's transpersonal soup merely applies to the greater *samsara*. On a Buddhist view, this would be full, not of the 'sacred', but of the intermediate world's trials and terrors as described in *The Tibetan Book of the Dead*.

Lee's spectral development of what Bucke called 'cosmic consciousness', Jung 'the collective unconscious' and Huxley 'mind at large', shows how easily 'advanced' thought could flounder. Part of a quasi-Indian 'One Mind', Lee's 'personal "I"' surrenders its conventional integrity, becoming instead an appendage to Myers's 'multiple soul' and a window for apparitions of the dead. In a 1904 lecture, again to Orage's circle, Carpenter expressed a similar view. Entitled 'Deities and Devils in the Light of Race Memory', the talk gave 'a resume of the evolutionary steps in the production of those … figures [imaginal fauna, like Lee's] which dwell not in …

ordinary consciousness but in the deeper or racial consciousness'. Arguing that 'the remote past of the world' is 'stored in the profound depths of the race (of which each individual is but a momentary point)', and that 'through our eyes look the eyes of dead ancestors', Carpenter equated the continued, modern presence of 'deities and devils' with the fact that these ancestors create a 'halo or glamour' around objects of perception.[29]

Yeats's 'great memory', stored in the *Brahman*-like world-soul, and the 'self-ancestral' of AE (the pen name of Yeats's friend George Russell) further illustrate this same florid and polymorphous Art Nouveau-like unconscious. Adjusting the Upanishadic *Atman* to Celtic revivalist concerns, Yeats also spoke of an 'Ancient Self'.[30] Jung's variant on this ancestral unconscious, recurrent in the pandaemonic imaginings of transpersonal psychologists like Stanislav Grof, has been referred to Haeckel's 'monistic' Darwinism, with its theories about ontogeny repeating phylogeny.[31] On a Haeckelian view, the result of visionary evocation of atavistic gods and demons like Carpenter's would be an intrapsychic recapitulation of our race's early history – an 'ontogenetic' (and regenerative) repetition of the originary, pre-Judaeo-Christian scenario of our phylum or tribe.

Though anathema to its 'professors of civilization', who pathologized the occult, similar chimaeras were found in late Meiji Japan. For the folklorist Yanagita Kunio, reader of Yeats's *The Celtic Twilight*, if they were to 'reconstr[uct] the everyday life of the folk', his countrymen 'had to plumb the depths of the folk consciousness for archaic religious beliefs that had been forgotten and bring them to the surface of life in the present'. Equally, 'People had to work for … reunion with their true self, even though it appeared uncanny, other and strange',[32] In Lears's summary, an editorial in *Scribner's* for 1909 privileged the artist's role:

> archaic man was 'a mere bundle of susceptibilities' dominated by 'fear, passion, and … [a] sense of mystery'; his worldview, preserved in folklore … composed of 'stammerings … in the face of cosmic events'. Only a few gifted artists could consciously recapture those stammerings; but ordinary people could recover them in their dreams.[33]

Well suited to 'Holy' Symbolist theatre or ceremonial magical staging by the era's many occultist leagues – like Yeats's 'Castle of the Heroes' project – such archaic-indigenist thinking, still common in the mythic forties, had strong 'poetic political' potential too.

Favouring anti-Decadent life-reform causes, like sun worship, body culture and naturism, there was a physical as well as a psychic dimension to the way the racial unconscious was viewed. For Carpenter, the 'gods', like 'race', were situated in the 'ganglia' or *chakras*. This gave a quasi-anatomical location to the redeeming quintessence ('life' or 'blood') as idolatrized by Lawrence in his American fiction. The ganglia also provided the – yogic or quasi-Tantric – location of Haeckel's 'life force', which, in addition to its embodied functions, could double as a proto-Jungian unconscious.[34] Darwinian biology thus found its mysteriosophic apocrypha, tricked out in a syncretic biosophical discourse which assigned *elan vital* and life force to the same family as *Kundalini, Sakti, Prana,* and yogically enhanced power.

The regenerative progress-through-primitivism rationale behind attempted retrievals of the racial past appears in a 1909 comment of the mystical anarchist/dramatist Vyacheslav Ivanov:

> symbols ... are the experience of *a lost and forgotten heritage* of the people ... They have been deposited since time immemorial by the people in the souls of its bards *as basic forms and categories in which alone any new vision can be framed* ... the poet ... is the organ of *collective awareness and collective recollection.* Through him *the people recalls its ancient soul.*[35]

The folk-soul's 'basic forms and categories' (myths and symbols) promise unity and community, the goal of Dionysian Symbolist theatre; while the poet's ability to re-enter the primeval racial scenario acts as a guarantee of a future folk-utopia.[36] Such *volkisch*-occultist beliefs, whereby a regenerative 'lost wisdom' was recovered through psycho-archaeological and mediumistic means, comprised the transnational lingua franca of neo-Romantics set on rebirth. Their formula for salvation from 'civilization' being one of neo-pagan soul-retrieval in a recreated magical culture, such advocates of the 'aristocratic-folk ideology' developed a 'magic socialist' style in politics, heavily indebted to occultism and obsessed with cultural renewal.[37] Initially left-wing, the style – 'rainbow fascism', as Sam Richards (private communication) calls this politico-cultural exoticism – migrated to the far right, then with American Abstract Expressionism, back to the anarchist left.

Modernist myth-makers saw the 'ancestral' conglomerate as a means of reintegrating fallen urban-industrial man into the (would-be nomic) unity and community of the 'sacred' first age. Besides the figures cited so far – Ivanov, Yeats, AE, Lawrence, Carpenter, Yanagita, Haeckel, Jung – Blavatsky, Steiner, Bely and Bergson have their variants on the racial memory and folk-soul motifs: Bergson's 'biological unconscious', for instance, contains race-memories, while Blavatsky's folk-soul leaves its imprints on the 'akasic records'.[38] Clairvoyantly divined, the ether/akasa/astral light became a source for alternative gospels, pre-histories and cosmic-cycle lore. Liebersohn's Native America (Chapter 1) now belonged to the same psycho-physical 'ancient wisdom' circuit. The American Theosophist James Pryse, who inspired Lawrence's yogic doctrine of the embodied unconscious, lived among Red Indians (as did Aby Warburg); while the Dodge-circle *litterateur* Witter Bynner, interested in Orage, tried to reconcile Amerindian and Taoist ideas.[39]

At political levels, such animistic or panpsychic beliefs subordinated the personal to the collective, magical retrieval of aboriginal energies by initiates hopefully leading to group transformation and rebirth. The folk-soul, early man and a versatile racial unconscious having upstaged Decadent perversity as a focus of interest, such palingenetic archaism was widespread: another instance is Pound's enthusiasm for the 'djinns, tribal gods, fetishes, and spirits of our ancestors' who inhabit the intermediate world.[40] Conceived during Pound's Yeats-inspired readings in the elemental magic of the seventeenth-century *Comte de Gabalis*, these variants on Carpenter's 'deities and devils' foreshadow Surrealist primitivism and the occult/Jungian fauna of forties myth-makers like Pollock.

To say that the modernist subject was 'decentred' is an enormous understatement: but fully to understand this loss of centre – this reckless abandonment of the Cartesian cogito and the bounded individual ego – we must enter the spectral world of Gothic psychology and the turn-of-the-century culture of trance. The liminoid interworld (or limbo) of the 'sub-waking self' was also the operative sphere of the modernist imagination, as that incorporated the colonial syncretic and exotic into its kingdom of dreams. Modernists and their forbears having discovered not Enlightenment, but the ungoverned imagination's greater *samsara*, the procedures and assumptions outlined above were metaphysically suspect and dangerous, as the Asian visitors I discuss next could have pointed out. The syncretism of the *longue durée* was time-tested and workable: the undigested materials just surveyed were not.

'Alternate' Consciousness: Critique from the East

Along with growing speculation about an unconscious, hypnagogic and oneiric-visionary states are central to Symbolism and
modernism. Yeats's 'daimonic images' were drawn from such states,
likewise the Baudelairean 'forest of symbols' approach to modernist art-making. Rimbaud's claim to be a 'master of phantasmagoria',
subsequent to deliberate derangement of the senses, should also be
referred to the point where neo-Romantic occultism and Gothic
psychology met. So should the 'artificial paradises' of the drug-
taker, declined by Anaïs Nin as 'tourism in the house of images',
when offered LSD by Huxley. Spirit mediums were virtuosos of the
in-between, but their quasi-shamanic forms of imagery cultivation
were matched in ingenuity by Symbolist/modernist expertise in
phantasmagoria – a favourite term of Walter Benjamin in contexts
involving the magical and uncanny in modern life. Pending occultist or psychological emphases, imaginal fugues could be exter-
nalized as astral excursions, or interiorized as journeys into the
unconscious.

Twinned with the reform or demise of those religions which
once sanctioned a modicum of the pagan/occult, the decline of traditional symbologies paved the way for the chaotic yet artistically
fruitful situation after 1880. The Sufi mystic al Hallaj said there are
two steps towards God: a step out of this world, followed by a step
out of the next. Prone as they were to explain all mystico-religious
phenomena in mesmeric terms, psychical researchers, occultists and
most Symbolists/modernists ignored (or did not know) al Hallaj's
second step. Lacking traditional restraints, the 'next world' accordingly became open to unruly embroidery and individual whim.
Eliot had this in mind when he attacked Yeats's 'lower mythology' and 'wrong supernatural world': on the 'lower' view, an ever-
shifting mass of etheric/astral pre-particulate matter (the 'daimonic')
becomes the upper-storey of a once three-tiered, but now only two-
tiered, universe. The 'mystic' West's befuddlement by wonders and
marvels – by a borderline, 'no exit' sub-spirituality which effectively
reduplicated the lawless and nomocidal, impassably liminoid nature
of modernity itself – was noticed by early emissaries of the 'rational'
East like Vivekananda and Zen Master Soyen Saku, both present
at the 1893 World's Parliament of Religions, and exponents of an
'ordinary' non-thaumaturgical view of Enlightenment.

The rationality and simplicity of the 'ordinary' view, with its suspicion of the unreconstructed visionary experience in which the West's Romantic tradition abounds, were paramount considerations for Vivekananda. His aim was to simplify and to 'make out of the philosophy and … intricate Mythology and queer starting Psychology [of Hinduism] a religion which shall be easy, simple, popular … meet[ing] with the requirements of the highest minds'. It followed that 'abstract Advaita must become living – poetic –; out of … hopelessly intricate Mythology must come concrete moral forms; and out of bewildering Yogism must come … scientific and practical Psychology'.

The bewildering and paranormal proved more to Western tastes than Vivekananda's rationalism. To quote his pupil, Kripananda (Leon Landsberg),

> This hotbed of pseudo-religious monstrosities, devoured by a morbid thirst for the abnormal … the occult … the exceptional – whence … credulity leads to the dissemination of hundreds of societies: goblins, ghosts, mahatmas, false prophets – this refuge for aliens of all colours was an abominable place to Vivekananda. He felt himself obliged to cleanse this Augean stable at the outset.

Vivekananda himself was more poised: 'I am perfectly aware that although some truth underlies the mass of mystical thought which has burst upon the Western world of late, it is for the most part full of motives, unworthy or insane.'[41] Such objections availed little in a climate where, as spiritualist Elizabeth Phelps wrote in 1886, 'Silken society seeks … the esoteric … It is *au fait* to be a Buddhist … A live Theosophist is a godsend in a dead drawing room.'[42]

Though Vivekananda's vision precluded magical hocus-pocus, his followers and admirers, including Jules Bois, Emma Calve, Sarah Bernhard, Carpenter and Malevich, ignored him. The elaborate counter-cosmologies of neo-Vedantists Gerald Heard, Christopher Isherwood and Huxley were equally at odds with the simplicity of Vivekananda's spiritual style. Thus, where Heard cheerfully combined Ufology with lessons from Swami Prabhavananda, rather like Yeats – who, side by side with his ghostland beliefs, translated the *Upanishads* with Sri Purohit Swami – Huxley and Isherwood wrote Vedantic tracts, while courting Eileen Garrett, the famous spirit medium who knew Carpenter, Mead, Lawrence and Joyce.[43]

Another sign of continued influence from the culture of trance, Huxley followed Yeats in likening *samahdi* to self-hypnosis. This contradicted Vivekananda on Realization as 'de-hypnosis' from the habitual mind, and the explanation of Huxley's own teacher Prabhavananda, that where the results of auto-suggestion and hypnosis are subjective and different in every case, those of meditation are always the same.

Similar reservations were voiced by Soyen Saku, who, during a two-year stay in America from 1905, taught *zazen* and *koan* practice to a Mrs Alexander Russell of San Francisco.[44] This itself was exceptional, in that Gilded Age American tastes in Japanese Buddhism, like those of Fenollosa, Beatrice Lane Suzuki and Bigelow (who thought 'leaving the body' was the point of meditation), ran to Shingon, its more ornate Tantric form. Against such visionary emphases, Saku stated the 'ordinary' view in a 1906 sermon, published by Suzuki's patron Paul Carus:

> Those who have had no spiritual experience ... frequently speak of enlightenment as an *abnormal psychical condition*, and try to explain it under the same category as *hallucination, somnambulism, self-suggestion* ... But ... enlightenment is not *a special psychic state* which excludes or suppresses the ordinary exercise of other mental faculties. Enlightenment goes ... along with all psychological phenomena. If enlightenment is to be gained through the *suspension of mentation*, religion is false ... Enlightenment ... does *not stand separate from other states of consciousness*, sending its commands from a ... vantage ground ... Enlightenment is *constant and not sporadic* ... It is not something *extraordinary* that takes place by fits and starts.[45]

Saku's allusions to Gothic psychology ('abnormal psychical condition'), the pan-mesmeric hypothesis about religious experience ('hallucination, somnambulism, self-suggestion') and the culture of trance ('suspension of mentation', 'separate from other states of consciousness') all display acute awareness of Western misconceptions, reinforcing neo-Vedantic scepticism on the same score. Thanks to its absorption in a seductive, but spurious and hastily built, occultist interworld, the 'mystical West' was unprepared for 'Eastern rationalism' when its merely incarnate apostles appeared. One hundred and ten years later, the situation has not greatly improved.

The German Expressionist Cultic Milieu

Hugo Ball's account of what he calls the 'aesthetic gnosis' of the Teens combines acuity with ambivalence. Of Expressionist trance-states, he remarked in 1917 that 'everyone has become mediumistic', referring this to the antinomian or crisis-cult factors of 'fear … terror … agony, or because there are no rules any more'. In a comment that could apply to Yeats's spirit-dictated *A Vision* and Jung's channelled *Seven Sermons to the Dead*, he adds, 'Perhaps it is only that our conscience is so frightened, burdened, and tortured that it reacts with the most stupendous lies and pretences (fictions and images) at the least provocation.'[46]

As for the 'house of images', quoting Johannes Baader on Paracelsus and Boehme, Ball aligns 'metaphor' (the image) with 'magic, imagination and magnetism' as keys to these two Hermetic thinkers:

> Baader says … 'Our philosophers and theologians have long kept a safe … distance from the words imagination and magic … Whereas the German natural philosophers, Paracelsus and Jacob Bohme, found the key to all spiritual and natural creation in the concepts of magic, imagination, and magnetism.' … The spiritus phantasticus, the spirit of images, thus belongs to natural philosophy. *Metaphor, imagination, and magic, when they are not based on revelation and tradition, shorten and guarantee only the paths to nothingness; they are delusive and diabolical.* Perhaps all associative art, which we think we capture time with, is only … self-delusion.[47]

Ball doubts Expressionist attempts to create a non-contingent heterocosm ('which we think to capture time with') out of images taken, not from genuine spiritual tradition, but from amateur otherworld excursions.

This later student of exorcism knew his heresiology: 'modern artists are gnostics and practice things that … priests think are long forgotten; perhaps even commit sins that are no longer thought possible'. Asking, 'What is a visionary?', he answers, a 'reading master in the supernatural picture-book' – a virtuoso of the house of images – and yet 'To be a visionary, you would have to know the laws of magic. Who knows them? We are playing with a fire that we cannot control.'[48] Apropos current syncretism, he asks, 'Do we not steal the elements from all magical religions?', adding the pointed query, 'Are we not magical eclectics?'[49]

Ball's quartet of metaphor, imagination, magnetism and magic was central to early modernist schemes for world-renewal. Contrary to believers like Yeats and Jung, Ball, though himself a modernist, detected something illicit, the occult as the pornography of genuine spiritual tradition maybe, in the motives and methods involved. Outside degenerationists like Nordau, scourge of the new mysticism in 1892, the infallibility of the imagination's visions from a 'next world' that had become art's definitive sphere was taken for granted by most of Ball's peers. This makes his scepticism the more remarkable: comparable, perhaps, to Kenneth Rexroth's reservations about the Beats.

Not that Ball is entirely consistent:

> Yesterday I gave my lecture on Kandinsky … Total art: pictures, music, dances, poems – now we have that … The painter as administrator of the vita contemplativa … As herald of the supernatural sign language … Is sign language the real language of paradise? Personal paradises – maybe they are errors, but they will give new color to the idea of paradise, the archetype.[50]

A moment ago, the post-traditional imagination's designs for an alternative order were cast as diabolic. Here, the same utopian stirrings are ascribed, not to ungoverned fancy, but to contemplation. Returning to 'Eastern critique', except in Tantra and magical Taoism, where the imagery is precise and consensual, Eastern meditation ('contemplation') has no 'supernatural sign language' of the type envisaged by Ball. The hypnagogic reverie of free-form trancers like Blake, of 'anarchists of perception' like Rimbaud and Daumal, is more relevant to Ball's 'total art' than the vita contemplativa he invokes.

Doubts, however, remained: 'The nervous systems have become extremely sensitive. Absolute dance, absolute poetry, absolute art – what is meant is that a minimum of impressions is enough to evoke unusual images.'[51] From a perspective like this, while Manuel Cordova-Rios, 'The Wizard of the Upper Amazon', was being taught by his tribal captors to hallucinate in a sober, orderly manner, Ball's Expressionists were proving the truth of Nordau's charge that modern 'mysticism' was a compound of 'degeneracy' and 'hysteria', with aesthetic pretensions thrown in.[52] As Ball hesitates between mysticism and pathology as explanatory categories, what Viennese critics called Nervenkunst springs to mind.

A short digression could make Ball's predicament clearer. In 1919 Mead translated the Neoplatonist Synesius' *On Visions*. Warning against self-deception, Synesius wrote 'Let no one whose imaginative spirit [*phantastikon pneuma*] is diseased, expect clear and unconfused visions.'[53] The crux is critical discernment, given the provenance of vision and dream from an unstable middle-world sphere. Anticipating the 'transmarginal/subliminal' talk of James and Myers, Synesius depicts the imagination's cosmological *mise en scène* in 'in-between' terms: 'this [imaginative] spirit is precisely the border-land between unreason and reason, between body and the bodiless. It is the common frontier of both, and by its means things divine are joined with lowest things'. On a tacitly tripartite view of the religious cosmos like this, vision is not automatically divine, but, as the Neoplatonic/Hermetic tradition teaches elsewhere, arises from the intermediary realm of the subtle body or 'lesser soul'. This was the province of modern spiritualism and occultism, both of which ignored Synesius' principle that 'psychical purification' is a prerequisite of visionary clarity and truth. Where modernity enjoys enormous and sometimes anti-social visionary latitude, tradition, with its concerns for society's needs, does not. Indeed, the further we stray on the modernist side of Romanticism – where, after Paracelsus' opposition between *fantasia* and *vis imaginativa*, for Coleridge 'fancy' and 'imagination' were still two different things – the laxer the situation becomes.[54]

Ambivalence also marks Ball's assessment of madness. Contrary to Synesius' warnings about hallucinosis, but true to modernist habits of exoticizing the naïve and mad, Ball wrote in 1916,

I got Lombroso's *Genie und Irrsinn* [*Genius and Madness*] from the library. My opinions of the inmates of lunatic asylums are now different … The childlike quality … borders on the infantile, on dementia and paranoia. It comes from the belief in a *primeval memory*, in a *world that has been supplanted and buried beyond recognition*, a world … liberated in art by *unrestrained enthusiasm*, but in the lunatic asylum … freed by disease … The *primeval strata*, untouched and unreached by logic … emerge in the … infantile and … madness, *when the barriers are down*; that is *a world with its own laws and its own form*; it poses new problems and tasks … like a *newly discovered continent*.[55]

Reminiscent of Symbolists on the folk-soul (and R. D. Laing), this is the reasoning that led Russian Futurists to co-author books with

children.⁵⁶ The further the modernist departs from the Cartesian cogito, the better for the unmediated 'primary process' aspects of his art.

Elsewhere, Ball sounds more like Synesius:

> So it depends on the inner constitution whether someone with artistic
> talent conveys only *meaningless visual and auditory hallucinations, as a mad-*
> *man does* … *Wild ideas and romanticism may result,* but also classical works
> and new limbs on a mystical body. *The receptive soul can be pure or impure,*
> *confused or clear, wicked or holy.*⁵⁷

Clearly, there are important, unexplored affinities between mysticism, the unconscious, madness and late Romantic/modernist
aesthetics.

For all his Dadaist 'Negro-poetry', Ball was not convinced by ethnological primitivism either:

> Why do we have to go so far back to find reassurance? Why do we dig
> up thousand-year-old fetishes? … From the Negroes … we take only the
> magical-liturgical bits … We drape ourselves like medicine men in their
> insignia … but we want to ignore the path on which they reached these
> bits of cult and parade.

Equally, 'Rimbaud's discovery' of 'the European as the "false Negro"'
led nowhere:

> When he arrived at Harar and Kaffa, he could not help but realize that
> even … genuine Negroes did not correspond to his ideal. He was looking
> for a world full of wonders: ruby rain, amethyst trees, ape kings, gods in
> human form, and fantastic religions in which belief becomes fetishistic
> service to the idea and to mankind.⁵⁸

The occult as the marvellous, again, as brittle as the drug-taker's
high.

Foreshadowing Lears on the counterculture's futile quest for
alternative identities, Ball senses self-deception in the strip-mining
of alien cultures for masks to trickout a jaded post-bourgeois self.
'Their effort to create a coherent sense of selfhood', writes Lears,
'seems fated to frustration. Every failure inaugurates a new psychic
quest, until the seeker is embroiled in an interminable series of self-
explorations. This continually frustrated search is the logical outcome of antimodernism in America.'⁵⁹ Internationally speaking,

the logical outcome, too, of an occultism- and colonial backwash-indebted *embarras de richesses* for the recreation of self and conscious-ness, for the fabrication of exotic masks and arcane syncretic beliefs. The psychological exotic, like Kafka's obsession with dreams, and Ball's testimonia, needs adding to Smith's list of modernism-defining factors.[60]

Modernist Meta-languages

The modernist 'aesthetic gnosis' involves solipsism and self-deception. Of his painting *Departure* Max Beckmann wrote in 1938, 'The picture speaks to me of truths impossible … to put in words and of which I did not … know before. I can only speak to people who … already carry within them a similar metaphysical code.'[61] This statement, which excludes most of humankind – a high price for transcending consensual idiom – raises the question of mod-ernist assumptions about an 'anterior' code of the soul, as known among occultists, Jungians and spirit mediums, but not to the degenerate 'mass'. Mediumistic trance was never distant from soul codes like Beckmann's: nor indeed from current perceptions of new styles in art. Detecting 'phantasmagoric' circumventions or 'vegetative-technological' reconstructions of modernity in *Jugendstil*, Benjamin likened its interiors to the shifting astral expanses of Steiner's otherworld; while Breton compared Art Nouveau's ecto-plasmic arabesques to spirit-medium drawings.[62] The exquisite hab-itations of turn-of-the-century men and women already had a foot in the 'next world'.

Among spiritualist automatists, in 1903 Myers found a 'remark-able correspondence of literary style', reminiscent of translation, or 'the compositions of a person writing in a language he is not accustomed to talk'. This was the case, whether the automatic script was 'incoherent' or not, and just as pronounced 'when … the automatic script surpasse[d] in intelligence, and … eloquence, the products of the waking mind'. Of 'those strange … arabesques which have been baptized … "spirit-drawings"', he stresses their 'rudimentary symbolism; as though the subliminal intelligence were striving to express itself through a vehicle … more congenial to its habits than articulate language'.[63] Related to Arthur Machen's inclination 'to think that … art is distilled from the subconscious

... not ... the conscious self', such Gothic psychological accounts of the channelling-zone bear on Pollock's claims to paint 'straight from the unconscious'.[64] Prone to a similar sameness as that of some modernist house- and signature-styles, the key to spiritualist art and writing – its psychographic 'rudimentary symbolism' in many ways comparable to Surrealism and Abstract Expressionism – is an automatism of the second self.[65]

Theosophy gave such 'rudimentary symbolism' a more recondite cast: for Blavatsky, the secret doctrine of 'the great Asiatic and early European religions' was 'hidden under glyph and symbol'.[66] In proto-'mythic forties' vein, Lawrence's 1923 *Fantasia of the Unconscious* embellishes Blavatsky:

> in the [previous] world a great science and cosmology were taught esoterically in all countries ... In that world men ... were in one complete correspondence over all the earth ... knowledge, science was universal ... cosmopolitan as ... today ... Then came the ... world flood ... some retained their ... innate ... life-perfection, as the South Sea Islanders ... some, like Druids ... Etruscans ... Chaldeans ... Amerindians or Chinese refused to forget, but taught the old wisdom ... in ... half-forgotten, symbolic forms ... And so, the intense potency of symbols is part at least of memory ... [T]hese myths now ... hypnotize us again, our own ... scientific way of understanding being almost spent ... [B]esides myths, we find the same mathematic figures, cosmic graphs ... among the aboriginal peoples ... mystic figures and signs whose true cosmic or scientific significance is lost, yet which continue in use for ... conjuring or divining.[67]

In the 'primal markings' of his mid-forties *Guardians of the Secret* and *Pasiphae* phase, Pollock, too, embraced the psycho-archaeological cause of Blavatsky's 'glyphs' and Lawrence's 'mystic figures and signs'.

Thanks to their nose for 'the intense potency of symbols', modernists like Gauguin, Brancusi and Pollock were expert readers in Ball's 'supernatural picture-book'. Behind this expertise stood a consciousness revolution alert for new expressive modes. As Dodge asserted, 'Many roads are being broken today and along these ... consciousness is pursuing truth to eternity ... Gertrude Stein ... is impelling language to induce new states of consciousness ... A further consciousness than is already ours will need many new forms of expression.'[68]

Occultism and spiritualism had anticipated Dodge's call. One spirit medium, Hélène Smith, became a turn-of-the-century cause célèbre, then a Surrealist heroine, through her channelling of 'Martian'. Her case was studied in a 1900 book, *From India to Planet Mars*, by Theodore Flournoy, and her meta-languages – Martian ('astane esenale puze mene simand ini mira'), ultra-Martian ('bak sanak top anok sik'), Uranian ('pa lalato lito namito bo te zozoti zolota matito yoto') and Nazar ('spik antik flok skak mak tabu mila-hatt') – were investigated by Ferdinand de Saussure, founder of modern linguistics.[69] Occultists also knew strange languages: Blavatsky purported to understand the astral language 'Senzar'; while Saint Yves d'Alveydre, author of books on the world's secret history, allegedly learned Sanskrit and 'Vattan' from a Hindu in Le Havre.

Among modernists, such love affairs with the borderline and incomprehensible were driven by a quest for 'primary process' means of soul-to-soul communication. Artaud's 1931 comment that Balinese theatre 'finds its expression and even its origin in a secret psychic impulse which is Speech anterior to words' implies an undifferentiated level of will-to-expression, prior to its assuming familiar outlets.[70] This kind of 'anterior speech' (the art of children, mediums, magicians, the mad, the untutored) was the language of modernism's interworld. In 1916, Ball claimed an inspiration akin to Artaud's:

> two-thirds of the wonderfully plaintive words that no human mind can resist come from ancient magical texts. The use of 'grammologues', of magical floating words and resonant sounds characterizes the way we [Ball and Huelsenbeck] … write. Such word images, when … successful, are irresistibly and hypnotically engraved on the memory.[71]

With their coloured paper, 'single incoherent words', syllables, numbers, letters and sometimes blank pages (Chapter 3), Nordau's 'fatal' Decadent books belong to the same magical, anti-mass idiom lineage as do Russian Futurism's deliberately slipshod and tribal/infantile books.

Alexei Kruchenykh, 'transrational' *zaum* poet and associate of Malevich and Matiushin, programmatically invoked Ouspensky's 'art goes in the vanguard of … psychic evolution'. As with Velimir Khlebnikov's theurgical 'world-creation' – Khlebnikov styled himself 'a dervish, a Yogi, a Martian'[72] – this was to validate his view that 'for the depiction of the new and the future completely new words and a new combination of them are necessary'. With this same millennial future in mind, like Dodge on Stein's 'superconscious' poetry, Kruchenykh asserted that 'a new content is only revealed when new devices of expression, a new form, is attained'.[73]

Like Dadaist phonic poetry, Surrealist automatism and the primal markings of forties art, as trance-forms that bypassed the cogito to reveal the second self's 'anterior speech', *zaum* was inspired by current syncretism:

> Kruchenykh and the Cubo-Futurists turned to the ecstatic speech of … Russian religious sects … [M. V.] Lodyzhenskii [author of *Superconsciousness and Ways to Achieve It*, 1911] cited the ecstatic 'speaking in tongues' of … Russian sectarian[s] … and referred to D. G. Konovalov's … *Religious ecstasy in Russian mystical sectarianism* (1908). Lodyzhenskii claimed that … when the sectarians emit an automatic stream of senseless words, they are 'in a state close to samahdi'.[74]

As a third-hand beneficiary of Vivekananda, newly translated into Russian and available to Lodyzhenskii, his source, Kruchenykh typically confuses trance with meditation, offering the sound-world (or *barbara onomata*) of the in-between state as a route to 'the new and the future'. It needed a modernist, not an occultist, to dream that up.

Would-be 'transcendental' sound effects figure in Steiner's art theory too. Referring to Josef Beuys's repetitious chant 'uh uh uh uh … ' during his 1963 performance *The Chief*, John Moffitt remarks on Steiner's 'precocious (after 1912) advocacy of the artistic means of nearly pure sound effects'. With Hugo von Hofmannsthal, Shklovsky, Khlebnikov, Kruchenykh and Artaud, Steiner's enemy was everyday language:

> the poet has to fight against the conventionality of speech in order to be able to draw from speech that element which could make of it a way leading to super-sensible worlds … the chief concern of the poet is the embodiment of his poetic inspirations in [nonrepresentational] *sounds* which are imaginative, plastic, and musical.

This way lies 'the possibility of perceiving the archetype, of which speech is but the shadow'.[75]

Despite his wooden prose, Steiner inspired Bely, not just in Bely's thought-form-infested *Petersburg* (Chapter 3), but also his *Glossolalia*, a work on sonic symbolism. In H. E. Salisbury's words,

> Biely never created a symphonic polyphony of the order of *Finnegan's Wake*, but from … *Glossolalia*, 'a poem on sound' (1917), we gather that he had reached the stage of thinking in terms of a new universal language in the … Joycean sense: 'Hail to the brotherhood of peoples: the language of languages … will break up the languages.' In *Glossolalia*, he attempted … to arrive at a unifying symbolical, phonetic principle behind words in many different languages: *ero, ira, ire, terra, earth, airtha, Erde*.[76]

Kandinsky, too, recommended a phonic (or mantric) transcendentalism: 'repetition of [a] word, twice, three times or even more frequently … will … tend to intensify the inner harmony [and] bring to light unsuspected spiritual properties of the word itself … frequent repetition of a word … deprives [it] of its original external meaning'.[77]

The fruits of this sonic occultism are, however, scarcely more alluring than Esperanto, or the grass-roots spiritualist and Pentecostal glossolalia and xenoglossia which accompanied the trans-rational tradition's rise. In Kandinsky's *Yellow Sound*, voices-off shout 'spiritual' nonsense words like 'Kalasimunafakola'.[78] Nordau's lonely 'syllables' and 'incoherent words' recur in Kruchenykh's 1913 'dyr bul shchyl / ubeshshchur / skum / vy so bu / r l ez', and Ball's 1916 'gadji beri bimba / glandridi lauli lonni cadori … / hollaka hollala / anlogo bung … bosso fataka / u uu u'.[79] In 1931, we encounter the phonemic 'shamanism' (or neo-gnostic mantras) of the Chilean poet, Vicente Huidobro: 'Ai aia aia / ia ia aia ui / … Isonauta / Olandera uruaro / Ia ia companuso campasedo / … Lalali / Io ia / iiio / Ai a i ai a iiii o ia'. Then, with the insane late-forties Artaud, we read 'o dedi / o dada orzoura / o dou zoura / a dada skizi / o kaya / o kaya pontoura'.[80]

In her 1930 *Three Chants for Womens' Chorus* the American composer Ruth Crawford devised 'a language of my own – consonants and vowels in a … chant that sounds quite Eastern'. CHYAH CHYAH AH NAH NYE … SRAH KYO SRAH NYE TE … NGE NAH ZO A NGYA SO: Crawford's invented liturgy looks as much a period piece as the trans-rational soul codes studied so far.[81] Based on a text from the *Popul Vuh*, Varese's *Ecuatorial*, as 'drama and incantation', was intended to convey the 'elemental, rude intensity' of pre-Columbian sculpture, and 'a little of that rough-hewn and elemental intensity that characterized their savage and primitive works'.[82] At Artaud's suggestion, Dada-like meta-language was employed in *Ecuatorial* and again in Varese's 1961 *Nocturnal*, a composition based on a text by Anaïs Nin. 'Hengh bengh whoo … ho o ha', in *Ecuatorial*, or in *Nocturnal*, 'whah / ya whoo whoo / sh / gara ya ga ra': 'Varese's love of primitive rites and incantations' (so his one-time Dadaist wife, Louise Norton) ends up in dated embarrassment, compared to its visual counterparts in Gauguin's faux Polynesian mythology.[83]

Helene Smith's imaginary languages, de Saussure's interest in them, Blavatsky's Senzar, Saint Yves's Vattan, Dada non-sense, Cubo-Futurist *zaum*, and Crawford's and Varese's meta-liturgies corroborate Smith on 'expressions of the exotic in language' as a distinguishing mark of modernism (Chapter 1). Unlike its visual equivalents, however, 'literary non-objectivity' was an idea without a future, based on the illusion of a parity between the arts that could somehow magically cancel the inherently (or conventionally) representational nature of words. The meta-linguistic soul codes of the modernist 'second state' take Shklovsy's calls for 'making it strange' to incomprehensible extremes. But with their vernacular base in spiritualism, and regardless of distinctions between the absolute and the fanciful, extra-ordinary cognition and cosmology, extra-ordinary authorial postures and soul-to-soul idioms were now in charge of the arts. The ordinary, 'epiphanic' *Japoniste* strain in modernism ran counter to this, as did the twenties' 'call to order', but belief in a potentially world-changing (if lawless) 'reality behind reality' that required a special, trans-rational idiom was not easily dislodged.

3

DESTRUCTION–CREATION: FROM DECADENCE TO DADA

Destruction–Creation: A Bipolar Rhythm

As tradition's magic worldview waned and religion became more exclusionary, the Pandora's Box of the supernatural and daimonic fell to new management: occultists, Gothic psychologists, neo-Romantics, folklorists.[1] From 1880 to 1920, the made-over supernatural joined with the colonial syncretic in creating modernist 'myth': an almanac-like tool, not just for revitalization, but also for mapping and articulating geopolitics, history, cosmic cycles, and the fluctuations of modern experience. Occult revival sects part-adopted the wandering daimonic: but large tracts of the mysterious still lay open, as common, useable property for spiritual orphans, aspiring artists and ruthless Svengali-like figures. Particularly in America, Russia and Germany, intra-modernist supernaturalism was larger than occult revival: more flexible, more easily adapted to aesthetico-metapolitical and historico-cosmosophical agendas. One of these was 'destruction–creation': the decomposition and reconstitution of the modern world, a reworking of the dual, catastrophic/utopian nature of millenarian thought.[2]

The Golden Dawn and the 'little religions' of turn-of-the-century Paris had surprisingly little impact on modernism, the older Cabalistic Freemasonry, not the 'further Orient', being the focus in both cases. This lack of correlation between experimental/advanced aesthetics and formal sect membership probably implies two different constituencies. Creatively speaking, subscription to a modernist '-ism' had advantages over occultist sectarianism, being less bound by rules. An impression of independent modernist syncretism is certainly given by the period 1880–1920, an age which lurched from Decadent decomposition to qualified early modernist optimism around 1910. Thanks to shared intellectual roots (Nietzschean, Bergsonian, Theosophical), the immediate pre-war modernist '-isms', if formally different, were relatively consistent in outlook, except where divided by the extent of urban-industrial development in their countries of origin.[3] Outside Russia itself, the Great War and Russian revolution gave the more stridently utopian, intoxicated modernisms of the earlier Teens pause for thought, leading to introspection and reduction, and the birth of Dada in 1917.

The origins of modernist destruction–creation derive from complementary, 'yeah-saying'/utopian and 'nay-saying'/catastrophist strains in Decadence and Symbolism. When Lawrence wrote in 1916, 'If we have our fill of destruction, then we shall turn again to creation', he drew on these two apocalyptic-related leitmotivs.[4] Where did people stand within the current cosmic cycle? At its end or a new beginning? Was more demolition necessary, or could building afresh commence? The nay-saying trend permeated the part-Schopenhaucrian, part-Satanic Decadence, a pan-European, not simply French, revolt against realism and modernity. Its yeah-saying complement belongs to the more optimistic forms of Symbolism/ early modernism, where Whitman, Bucke, neo-Vedanta, Nietzsche, second-generation Theosophy and Bergson promised a new dawn. The German *Blaue Reiter* group, Orage's New Age circle in London, Russian 'mystical anarchism' (Chulkov, Ivanov) and Malevich's Suprematism exemplify this trend. But given the era's instability, fear of an approaching Armageddon could accompany hopes for rebirth, giving destruction–creation a cyclothymic cast.

The war- and revolution-torn Teens saw the consolidation of the 'pattern of expectation' – the death of the bourgeois subject, 'voices prophesying war', degenerationist anxieties – of the 30 years before 1914.[5] As some epochal upheaval, some 'battle of the nations' maybe (Serusier, Chapter 4), catastrophe was expected, affording a glimpse, at best, into the first pangs of rebirth. Anticipating the 'cosmic' Teens, the 'coming war' and death/rebirth themes had been popular with Celtic revivalists. Its hoped-for sequel a 'multitudinous influx' from Joachim of Fiore's Holy Spirit, Yeats and MacGregor

Mathers awaited 'a magical Armageddon' from 1893; in 1896, Yeats wrote his apocalyptic 'The Valley of the Black Pig'; in 1895, following Blavatsky's prophecy of an upturn for 1897, AE declared 'the morning cycle is in the air'; in 1896 Symbolist Stuart Merrill praised Yeats's 'lofty level' on 'social questions' like the coming war and revolution.[6] Influencing Lawrence, who foresaw a 'vast death-happening' as a form of millennial hygiene, Carpenter predicted in 1912 that the 'negative Christian dispensation' was ending, as did Yeats's 1920 'The Second Coming'.

Pre-war intimations of apocalypse like the sinking of the Titanic and the appearance of Halle's comet spread panic. In this inflammatory climate of expectation, could minds remain married to an art complicit with the four-square world of the age of 'Christianity and commerce' – with a set of representational canons which, far from envisaging its decomposition and reconstitution, insisted on the preordained integrity of the manifest world? Explaining the strangeness of Decadent/Symbolist idiom (Nordau, below), and heralding 'non-objectivity', mimetic realism met its nemesis amid questions like these. The world and self were not as solid as once thought: both could be decomposed or disassembled, then working from their underlying occult energies, reconstituted by the artist-initiate in a 'new creation', a new nomos, in Griffin's terms.

Decadence: Decomposition in a Foundationless World

Robert Pynsent remarks that 'The Decadents produced a literature of disaster – that had not yet taken place.'[7] The Schopenhauer vogue can assist our understanding of this catastrophism, and its relationship to end-of-cycle despair. 'Destruction' and 'creation' being two faces of the same coin, modernist utopias had to contend with a catastrophic shadow-side rooted in Schopenhauerian Decadence. A reworking of traditional millenarianism, agonistic struggle between the two extremes, interspersed with prophetic and apocalyptic allusions, became a modernist trademark. The 'Buddhist' *néantisme* and mystical nihilism bred by the Schopenhauer fashion – Franz Marc alludes to 'Schopenhauer's wish to pass away into nothingness' – represented the anomistic deliquescence which, 'under Nietzsche's banners' (Marc again), 'creative', new nomos-seeking modernists tried to overcome.[8]

Schopenhauer, dead by 1860, entered Decadence through Wagnerism.[9] Following Hans von Bulow's tone-poem *Nirvana*, Wagner employed chromaticism to capture the self-annulling quality of Schopenhauerian ascesis. Burnouf's *Introduction a l'histoire du buddhisme indien*, mentioned in 1856, and Schopenhauer's *The World as Will and Representation*, read in 1854, were the sources of Wagner's Buddhism. As shown by his comment, 'for me Nirvana … becomes very quickly, *Tristan*', this was compatible with Celtic mythology and the *Liebestod*, as a 'gateway to union'. Wagner's *nirvana* coincided with what he called the 'violet' or 'deep lilac' hues of *Tristan*. Mann, who projected a novel entitled *Maja*, caught the mood when he spoke of German bourgeois descent, 'from revolution to disillusionment, to pessimism and … resigned, impregnable inwardness'.[10] In 1856, Wagner sketched a Buddhist music-drama, *The Victors*, left unfinished at his death, though fragments are scattered around his *oeuvre*, especially in *Parsifal*.

Read as a 'modern Buddhist' – at which point he enters occult revival, broadly understood – Schopenhauer, in Theodule Ribot's 1874 summary was important for French Decadence. Subscribers to *Schopenhauerisme*, or *Bouddhisme moderne*, included Elemir Bourges, Paul Bourget, Jules Laforgue, Guy de Maupassant, Remy de Gourmont, Villiers de l'Isle Adam and Henri Cazalis.[11] Alias the *Indianiste* poet 'Jean Lahor', Cazalis was a friend of Mallarme, who famously claimed an 'impersonal' mystical experience. Denying prior knowledge of Buddhism (unlikely, given friendship with Cazalis), Mallarme here became 'an aptitude for the spiritual universe for seeing and developing itself through what used to be me'.[12]

Anatole Baju's 1886 Decadent manifesto linked *Schopenhauerisme* and 'morphinomania', showing how, like some 1960s guru, Schopenhauer was prized for his vision of reality as illusion or *maya*.[13] Nordau dismissed the fashion: 'The degenerate who … is without will-power … calls himself … a Buddhist, and praises Nirvana, as the highest … ideal … [T]he degenerate and insane are the predestined disciples of Schopenhauer and Hartmann.'[14] His own Orientophilia notwithstanding, Debussy was also unimpressed:

Nothing is more exciting than playing the little Buddha, living on an egg and two glasses of water a day and giving the rest to the poor; ruminating on interminable … reveries of the nature of nature, and of luxurious confusions of ego and non-ego reabsorbing themselves into the cult of

the universal soul … It's pretty, and makes nice conversation, unfortu-
nately it's not worth two cents in practice and can even be dangerous.[15]

Creating representational difficulties from the start, Decadents,
after Schopenhauer, saw reality as a libido-spun web of illusion suspended in nothingness: perverse and troubling oneiric-visionary
modes, or Mallarmean white voids (Le Vide), followed from that
anti-ontological stance. Negative 'Buddhist' epiphanies are recorded
by several Decadents: on reading Schopenhauer, the Belgian Max
Elskamp experienced an 'anxiety attack', his compatriot Maurice
Maeterlinck had 'typhoid visions', while the Austrian artist Alfred
Kubin underwent a 'Buddhist crisis' in 1911[16]

In Belgium, home of many proto-modernist initiatives, Schopenhauer also attracted poet Georges Rodenbach and painter
Fernand Khnopff; and in Scandinavia, Strindberg and Munch,
painter of psychic limbos and life's weary biological cycle.[17] Other
Schopenhauerian artists include Max Klinger, Klimt and de Chirico:
Decadents, all, if a phantasmagoric mystical nihilism is a qualify-
ing criterion.[18] Like Elskamp, Laforgue, Strindberg, and later Blaise
Cendrars, Kubin, the odd man out in the 'yeah-saying' Blaue Reiter,
overtly professed Buddhist beliefs. In Austria, Ernst Mach's 'psycho-
physical' writings did similar work to Schopenhauer's, in eroding
beliefs in a stable subject and world. Among novelists, Schopenhauer
influenced Tolstoy, Turgenev, Melville (who was also drawn to
alchemy and Cabala), Edouard Dujardin, Mann, Hardy, Conrad,
Proust, Ferdinand Celine and Samuel Beckett.[19] Wittgenstein was a
Schopenhauerian, as was Jorge Luis Borges.

Entailing fascination with evanescent images, Decadent 'destruction' evokes a 'death of the real': substance is replaced by simulacra,
and an older cognitive certainty about the world's spatio-temporal
coordinates, by aporia as to the ontological status of modern
chaos and flux. Encoding Schopenhauer's view of reality as a 'cerebral phantasmagoria' in images that suggest co-identity between
the imaginal and phenomenal spheres, art based on these quasi-
Buddhist 'Mind Only' assumptions exudes dream-like unreality,
from Khnopff's elusive half-worlds, to de Chirico's pittura metafisica.
Shaped by an 'anti-epiphany', de Chirico's enigmatic canvasses, their
chaosmos a mind-arisen phantom, influenced magic realism, Surrealism and German New Objectivity.

In this deadpan, anomie-ridden art, where appearances melt into hallucinatory images, the manifest surface of things is no longer self-explanatory: more, we find incongruous juxtapositions, indicating a hidden, but ultimately non-signifiable mystery. Worldly manifestations, for Decadents, are illusory provisional signatures, or tantalizing 'correspondences', for Schopenhauer's inscrutable first principle, the representation-creating will. Being undifferentiated, all-pervasive and imponderable, the world of will ('primal procreative energy' or *Sakti*) has neither an agreed iconography nor a distinct symbolism for the web with which it beguiles us: for manifest parts, that is to say, which have no separate existence aside from the unspeakable non-manifest whole. Thus, in the very different manners of Khnopff and de Chirico, will's presence is conveyed through the entire pictorial surface, not through individual symbols, a surface that evokes the free-floating fictions and signs from which, like a dream-machine, the will-possessed mind manufactures a world.

Contrary to Theosophical beliefs, the consequent desolidification of actuality discloses no cosmic 'plan' or 'hierarchy', no benign upward-evolutionary dynamism, on will's part. Schopenhauer's overtly anti-Hegelian and anti-historicist doctrine was totally incompatible with utopian metapolitics: a source for repugnance or horror, the chaotic and unstable modern condition – its enigmatic liquefaction being a correlative of their art's Protean volatility – lay unredeemed and unredeemable among Decadents. Within will's unpredictable universe, there is no consolatory mysticism, no world-affirming 'cosmic consciousness', only the metaphysical uncanny or absurd. Unlike the reconstructive impulse in German Expressionism and Russian Cubo-Futurism, and quite different from the China/Japan-based modernist strain which offers little, immanentist epiphanies, Decadence is an art of deliquescence and futility, not self-expansion and renewal.

Nor is its aesthetic truly 'correspondential', in the sense of its images equating with agreed otherworldly energies and forces. Thus in Strindberg's 1907 *The Ghost Sonata*, subtitled 'Kamaloka, a Buddhist Play', Schopenhauerian man inhabits a metamorphic, hellish and draining world of obscure events and signs, indecipherable except in terms of a circular, vampiristic craving for life. A sign that the occult was changing, Strindberg experimented with alchemy and abstract painting, learned Chinese in 1874 and Japanese in 1880, claiming Schopenhauer, Edward von Hartmann, and Nietzsche as his 'Buddhist masters'. This romantic German Buddhism recurs in Eliot's attack on Hardy in *After Strange Gods*, though Melville, Conrad and Mann could have qualified as targets too.

A 1901 diary entry reveals Strindberg's drift after writing *A Dream Play*:

> Am reading about the teachings of Indian religion – The whole world purely an illusion … The divine archpower … let itself be seduced by Maja or the urge of procreation. The divine archmatter thereby committed a sin against itself … The world thus exists purely because of a sin, if indeed it does exist – for it is merely a vision seen in a dream (thus my *Dream Play*, a vision of life), a phantom whose destruction is the task of asceticism … now the 'Indian religion' has given me the meaning of my dream play … The Secret of the Door = Nothingness. All day I read about Buddhism.[20]

For Schopenhauer, the only escape from will's snares was its suspension through ascesis or music. Already tacit in Wagner's *nirvana*, this aesthetico-mystical belief, in a more robust, ontologically supported version, migrated via the Kandinskyite 'spiritual' to the Theosophical religion of modern art. Unsuspended, however, will's empire ran to the hallucinatory visions of 'unreal' or 'dead' cities found in Belgian Symbolism and the pre-conversion 'Buddhist' Eliot, to de Chirico's paradoxical anti-epiphanies, or the unrelenting nightmares of suffering depicted by Strindberg and Munch. In Europe, the Schopenhauer cult shook inherited assumptions about substantiality, selfhood and perception in a conventional Euclidean world. Was the world actually there, as common sense taught, or was it just a transient mental figment? Did the self correspond to anything more than a subconscious set of blind impulses? If we cancelled both cosmos and self, what was the nature of the nirvanic cessation or ascetic nothingness beyond? These were some of the questions that Schopenhauer's quasi-Buddhist philosophy posed.

In optimistic America, reared on Transcendentalist pantheism and Whitman's world-affirming ecstasies, Buddhist *néantisme* had less appeal. A healthy-minded, melioristic mysticism here sought self-expanding raptures, not teachings on *samsara* or its cessation, from its 'mystical East'. In a land where 'Wagner was cleansed' and 'Schopenhauer purged',[21] the world-hating Melville aside,

I have found only one Schopenhauerian, Edgar Saltus, author of *The Philosophy of Disenchantment* (1885) and *The Anatomy of Negation* (1887).[22] For Saltus, 'According to Schopenhauer, art should be strictly impersonal, and contemplation as calm as a foretaste of Nirvana, in which the individual is effaced and only the pure knowing subject remains': advance notice, perhaps, of 'anonymous' and objectivist modernists like Eliot and Wallace Stevens.[23] More self-effacing than Emerson, this Buddhist stance of no-self/*anatta* has been seen in Mallarme's loss of individuality in the macrocosm: a loss resulting in an impersonal objectivity later affected by Americans particularly, from Imagism to Cage. The hallucinatory work of Edward Hopper and David Lynch (the last a TM meditator) is perhaps the nearest we get to Schopenhauer in twentieth-century America.

Angst about a disappearing subject and object – Schopenhauer speaking to the blur of the modern – overlapped with other period insecurities. These included entropy, degeneration and the perceptual impact of the era's new material culture. Further to the expansion of the railways, itself a cause for 'nerves', the second industrial revolution's innovations, if less unsettling for Americans and Theosophists, placed the stable, classical universe yet further beyond humanity's grasp. For all its 'exquisite' phantasmagoric solipsism and enigmatic imagery, European Decadence brims with anxiety about an *actually* no longer reliable outer reality; characterized as 'the decomposition of ideas' in Huysmans's *La Bas*, these anxieties stemmed from the cognitive uncertainty at the modern experience's core. Like other crisis-cults, Pynsent's 'disaster' originated in perceived reality *and* the catastrophic side of millennial time.

Through transvaluation of its aesthetic, the yeah-saying, pre-First World War avant-gardes aspired to conquer Decadence's legacy of doubt, acting as if decomposition had disclosed the primal ground of 'life', where Schopenhauer's 'void' becomes an unbounded, horizon-less universe, accessible to superconscious states of mind. As the unsure Decadent account of cognition and existence met its Nietzschean/Theosophical come-uppance, decreation began to cede to reconstitution and, as in millenarian movements generally, catastrophe to utopia. But Schopenhauer had set the pace: the *serious* – non-precious, non-sensationalist – modernist occult is largely a set of responses to the difficult but necessary questions he raised.

'Occult Revival'

The outlook on modernity of French *fin de siècle* occultism and the Golden Dawn was hesitant, dismissive or escapist. Ignoring the imperial milieu, and caught between Baudelaire and Catholicism – blasphemy or 'throne and altar' – the Parisian sects were notorious for their in-fighting, as was the Dawn. The official French Empire was anyway assimilationist, its natives taught to speak of 'our ancestors, the Gauls'. To that extent, Gauguin, if father of the Theosophically inclined *Nabis*, was a one-off, a lone adventurer into a faraway magical culture, free to invent a private mythology. France did, in fact, have an imperial culture: Pierre Loti's exotic romances, the usual colonial exhibitions, and museums of Oriental and primitive art (the Guimet and Trocadero). Hindu troupes visited Paris, and Debussy met the Sufi musician Inayat Khan, as did Scriabin. Paul Sedir wrote on yoga and fakirism, while Edouard Schure's semi-Theosophical *The Great Initiates* (1889) influenced several Symbolists (Schure later co-authored mystery dramas with Steiner). But like the Golden Dawn, French occultists generally preferred Western esotericism – the 'restorationist' tradition of irregular, Cabalistic Freemasonry – making less of the Blavatskyite 'Eastern occult' than their Anglophone, Germanic and Russian coevals.

Josephin Peladan, with his strange 'Assyrian' pose, was another, temporarily important – conservative, non-Theosophical – figure for Symbolism. With Stanislas de Guaita and Gerard Encausse (Guénon's Martinist mentor, 'Papus'), Peladan revived a flagging Rosicrucian Society. After quarrelling, Peladan created his own neo-Catholic Mystic Order of the Rose + Croix in 1890, then a Salon de la Rose + Croix, which promoted Symbolist work in six salons, from 1892 to 1897. Erik Satie's music, and the paintings of Felicien Rops, Arnold Böcklin, Khnopf, Redon, Jan Toorop, Ferdinand Hodler, Delville, Gustave Moreau, Puvis de Chavannes, Carlos Schwabe and Charles Filiger, were all showcased at these salons.[24] This was the first attempt at a (semi-)internationalist 'religion of modern art', grouping artists whose spiritual sources were as legion as their styles, but with Symbolism's sudden eclipse by the cult of 'life' and fresh air, it became a dead end.[25]

Yeats, briefly a Theosophist, and an editor of Blake, was the only Golden Dawn member to achieve fame as a modernist, unless we add Surrealist Ithell Colquhoun, member of the *Ordo Templi*

Orientis and biographer of MacGregor Mathers. The hair-raisers of Arthur Machen and Algernon Blackwood are relatives of imperial Gothic; the occultist novel, with Tarot symbolism, was a speciality of Charles Williams, who belonged to the Oxford Inklings. Edith Nesbit wrote fantasies, mainly for children, while the Scottish writer William Sharp ('Fiona Macleod') is best assigned to a Gaelic branch of Celtic revival. Constance Wilde was a Dawn member for a time. More attractive is the Tarot designer (with A. E. Waite) and book illustrator Pamela Colman Smith. Jamaican folklore was an interest: she also illustrated Yeats's nineties poems, Bram Stoker's *The Lair of the White Worm* (its author perhaps a Dawn member) and Ellen Terry's book on the *Ballets Russes*. Except where affiliated with activist causes like Celtic revival, most of the Dawn's legacy to the arts falls outside standard definitions of modernism, if not of its tributaries.[26] This is surely a sign that modernists were less attracted to Western esotericism than to the Theosophical 'Eastern occult'. Subordinate, for present purposes, to intra-modernist occultism and syncretism, 1890-ish 'occult revival' turns out, aesthetically speaking, to be a damp squib.

The shift from figuration to abstraction in visual art deserves comment. Announcing departure from known realities, deformation and abstraction in modernist art, like chromaticism and atonality in music, are signs of the occult and exotic. Classical art procedures are suspended in grotesque and occult-exotic contexts, such that even customary figurative styles assume a visionary-phantasmagoric cast. Long before 'non-objectivity', Nordau was worried by Decadent/Symbolist supersession of 'art's known and standard forms' (below). The dilemma facing Decadents and Symbolists was one of how far to go: deformation after Gauguin or Munch, a distressing and splintering of surfaces with Russian Symbolist Mikhail Vrubel, or outright abstraction. No one achieved full abstraction until the Teens: but three not so well-known artists predated Kandinsky, Mondrian and Malevich in deriving a form of abstraction from Decadent/Symbolist practices. The halfway house abstraction of these artists – the Theosophical *Nabi*, Paul Serusier, Lithuanian painter and composer M. K. Ciurlionis, and Czech Theosophist and spirit-medium Frantisek Kupka – illustrates an important moment of transition from Decadence/Symbolism to abstraction.[27] Even if en masse 'Great Awakening' had to await the American countercultural sixties, Sphinxes, devouring women, human embryos and sado-Christianity fell out of favour as Kandinsky's age of the 'Great Spiritual' loomed.

Blind alleys included, the variety of Decadent/Symbolist modalities is instructive, as might be expected of a major new aesthetic's incubation phase. Until Theosophy achieved arts-primacy around 1910, this age's occultism was equally variegated, thanks to divisions between 'Western' and 'Eastern' schools and the proliferation of different sects. As expressions of the liminoid, J.-K. Huysmans's novels, Baudelaire's poetry, Redon's *noirs* and Flaubert's *Temptations of St Antony*, all of them adrift in a hot-house intermediate world, are black romantic founding monuments for French Decadence. Most early modernists had a Symbolist or Decadent phase: good reason for considering the cultic milieu of their formative years.[28] To do the last full justice is impossible here: because of the importance of its 'disintegrative vibration' for modernist destruction–creation, I therefore expand on Decadence. Largely Schopenhauer's child, this was also awash with the occult.

The 'Disintegrative Vibration': Nordau and Bely

Nordau's 1892 *Degeneration* rails against modern poetry's cryptic and nomocidal nature:

> Printing is now only on black, blue, or golden paper; on another colour are single incoherent words, often nothing but syllables … even letters or numbers only … which have a symbolical significance … to be guessed at by the colour and print of the paper and form of the book, the size and nature of the characters … Some poets who publish … isolated letters of the alphabet, or whose works are pages on which is absolutely nothing, elicit the greatest admiration … New forms! Are not ancient forms flexible … enough to lend expression to every sentiment and thought? Has a true poet ever found difficulty in pouring into known and standard forms that which surged within him?[29]

Nordau could be writing about magical spells or diagrams – Blavatsky's 'glyphs', Lawrence 'mystic figures and signs', the idiolects of the 'second state'.

In that pre-material proto-plasma could only be represented by magical signs, Decadents and Symbolists set the fashion for meta-art pitched in the interworld of the 'lesser soul'.[30] Traditionalist 'triple world' theory, which apportioned the arts to distinct physical, subtle and spiritual dimensions, was known to but a few, like the Russian critic Nicholai Berdyaev, who assigned an 'astral' music, novel and painting to Scriabin, Bely and Kandinsky. It was also known to Mondrian's associate, Theo van Doesberg, who postulated three (sensory, psychic and spiritual) forms of knowledge; and through Coomaraswamy, to the Seattle painter Morris Graves. Since the 'wrong supernatural world' with which he berated Yeats was synonymous with the intermediate realm, the 'triple world' was probably known to Eliot too.[31] Slighted for its 'lower psychism' by Guénon, the proto-plasmic interworld, which had no obvious exit except a crash to earth, was the modernist occult's default position.

Matching the colonial exotic with its disregard for 'Euclidean' laws, the interworld's main characteristic, like modernity's, was extreme instability. For Steiner, everything in this realm's limbo, a cousin of the *Bardo* in *The Tibetan Book of the Dead*, was in a state of constant transformation and motion. While for Strindberg the idea that 'anything may happen' governed the weird astral workings of his 1902 *A Dream Play*. Another example of this alogical 'next world' fluidity is Bely's 1916 novel, *Petersburg*. Though he claims it for Cubo-Futurism, Berdyaev's review of *Petersburg* stresses its quintessentially Decadent, catastrophic/decompositional thrust. Apropos Bely's 'artistic technique of the cosmic division, scattering, and decrystallization of all things … the destruction and disappearance of all firmly fixed boundaries', he notes how 'the solid borders which separate one person from another, and from … the surrounding world, are lost'.[32] Remarking how 'one person turns into another, one object becomes another, the physical shifts to the astral, the cerebral is transformed into the existential', Berdyaev compares E. T. A. Hoffmann's magnetic tales, where 'all boundaries and planes blend, everything splits and turns into something else'.

As expounded in the preface to Strindberg's *A Dream Play* ('the characters split, double, multiply, vanish, solidify, blur, clarify'), this torturing of contours evokes Lawrence (Chapter 2) on the 'disintegrative vibration' in Poe. Decadent *néantisme* is also suggested by the fact that Nicholai Apollonovich, the novel's mystical revolutionary, is a 'Mongolian-Turanian' Kantian in thrall to *Nirvana* and Buddha. Encapsulating the essence of destruction–creation, such Schopenhauerian 'Buddhism' is the obverse of the life-affirming 'Hinduism' of Whitman, with his futurological dedication, in Symbolist Konstantin Bal'mont's words, to 'world-making' and 'building … new forms of life'. Perched on the 'modern Buddhist' abyss, *Petersburg* harbours no hopes for a millenarian new dawn. Adding a Satanic twist, Bely's equivalent of Strindberg's splitting and multiplication draws on Steiner, whom he met in 1912, to spend 1914–16 at Anthroposophical Dornach in Switzerland.

Berdyaev's 'Everything becomes everything else, everything intermingles and crumbles' evokes Steiner on the astral world: 'in it there exist everywhere constant motion and transformation, nowhere are there points of rest'. Besant's astral world is likewise 'full of continually changing shapes … vast masses of elemental essence from which continually shapes emerge and into which they … disappear'.[33] Paralleling Blok's refusal to 'differentiate life from dreaming [and] … death, [and] this world from the other world' (compare Valerii Bryusov's 'there is no border between reality and reverie, between life and death'), for Steiner, 'birth and death are ideas that lose their significance' in a realm where 'a continual transformation of one thing into another' is the norm.[34] Other 'astral', Russian-sphere modernists like Ciurlionis, Kandinsky and Scriabin draw on similar ideas. But where they share Theosophy's evolutionary optimism, Bely's 'idle cerebral play' with the idea of 'self-thinking thoughts' (alias Besant and Leadbeater's 'thought-forms') serves merely to exacerbate the already ambiguous world of a Russia torn between East and West.[35]

Petersburg's philosophical syncretism is complex: a mix of Schopenhauer, Vladimir Solov'ev and Steiner. But how far its techniques of imaginal–phenomenal merger surpass those of Hoffmann, Poe and Meyrinck, and Decadent artists like Toorop and Kubin, is doubtful. In Hoffmann's day, the 'magnetic spiritist' J. H. Jung-Stilling 'believed that, through magnetizing, the human soul can be separated from the body … and that – once "ecstatic" – it experiences everything differently'.[36] Nonetheless, such second-state 'difference' can eventually pall, particularly given that the psychic-clairvoyant borderlands reduplicate life on earth. As Besant explained, 'Astral world-scenery much resembles that of the earth in consequence of its being largely made up of the astral duplicates of physical objects.'[37] Conventionally Toorop's creation, 'spook style' rose no higher than dreamlike astral confusion, itself a jumbled reduplication of the already known.

Just as Decadent attraction to Schopenhauer's 'cerebral phantasmagoria' trope led to morbid self-enclosure, so Bely's 'idle cerebral play' diminishes humanity, not expanding it like Whitman. Apertures for astral influx in the shape of 'self-thinking thoughts' or 'thought-forms', his characters are puppets of a tyrannical and sense-less Beyond. Contrary to the open cosmicism of the extended, Whitmanesque view of the self, Bely's worldview is claustrophobic and sinister: a side-light on Decadence's *homo clausus*, as a figure *au courant* with the 'next world', but otherwise turned in on himself. A feature of Charles Williams's novels and Castaneda's 'separate reality', the liminoid pseudo-ecstasies of Bely's interworld offer no exit into a truly spiritual world.

Contrary to the 'life-creating' strain in Russian Symbolism that led via the pre-war avant-garde's 'people of the future' to the 'life-building' Constructivist twenties, Bely's shifting borderlands suggest Decadent liquefaction and anomie, states of half-being provoked by modernity's disorientating strangeness and flux. *Petersburg*'s upshot is decreative, not cosmogonic: like Strindberg's, its god-forsaken, limbo-universe is one where 'anything may happen': an adage as true of modernity as of the new, destructive-creative consciousness and culture it produced. Threatening as elsewhere in Decadence, the soul's meta-world in Bely is not the graduated evolutionary sphere of the Theosophists, much less the distant spiritual Olympus of Eliot and the Traditionalists. Sub-spiritual 'no exit' equivalents of modernity's ever-changing but 'iron cage'-like nature – a Decadent speciality – were the Proteus with which modernism's 'creative' strain had to wrestle.

'Creation' in Whitman, Expressionism and Cubo-Futurism

In 1913 Mabel Dodge wrote of the mind-expanding impact of the New York Armory Show: 'Men began to talk and write about the fourth dimension, interchangeability of the senses, telepathy, and many other occult phenomena.'[38] Theosophical millenarian-ism is one background factor here. Another is Nordau's bugbear, Whitman (a 'teacher of energy' for Maurice Barres) whose influence as a prophet of redeemed and expanded cognition was crucial for 'overcoming' Decadence. To repeat Bal'mont, Whitman 'takes us to the morning of world-making' and 'sings of his young country chaotically moving towards … building … new forms of life'.[39]

A cosmogonic thinker, the American seer's self-designation as 'Walt Whitman, a Kosmos, of Manhattan the son' implies an *Atman– Brahman* unity, such as, heralding cognitive renewal, became popular after 1910. In contrast to Europe's disillusioned, post-1880 retreat into impersonal self-denial, Whitman fuses absolute with relative to celebrate cosmic merger and extended subjectivity.

Whitman's *Bhagavad Gita*- and *New York Herald*-based brand of cognitive renewal was accompanied by 'self-teaching exercises'. Recalling his profession to 'contain multitudes', these look like Hermetic mind-expansion techniques:

> Abstract yourself from this book; realize where you are … located, the point you stand that is now … the centre of all. Look up overhead, think of space stretching out, think of all the unnumbered orbs wheeling safely there … of the sun around which the earth revolves; the moon revolving round the earth … the different planets belonging to our system … Then … realize yourself upon earth … Which way stretches the north, and what country, seas … ? Which way the south? Which way the east? Which way the west? Seize these … with your mind, pass freely over immense distances.[40]

Apropos the Indian ingredients in Whitman's 'cosmic consciousness', V. K. Chari indicates 'a metaphysical self borrowed from Sankhya, Vedanta, and Yoga'. Noticed by Vivekananda, Aurobindo and Coomaraswamy, this 'dynamic cosmic I' is complemented by 'an assumed role as an American bard, and Whitman's own private self'. Capturing the pragmatism of American meta-religion, which, contrary to Europe's, at least until the sixties, contains little weird or bizarre (Poe and H. P. Lovecraft apart), this self's absolute and relative dimensions are well summed up by Lawrence: 'When he is infinite he is still himself. He still has a nose to wipe. The state of infinity is only a state, even if it is the supreme one.' For Whitman's Yogic inclinations, O. K. Nambiar proposes a 'Tantric key'. Its physical site the 'body electric', 'through which', in Roger Asselineau's words, 'the "Superior Soul" [not Strindberg's hostile forces] invaded him, this 'Tantric' aspect of Whitman's poetry brings in 'nerves'.[41]

An enthusiast of the electro-magnetic revelation like Poe, Goethe maintained that 'Electricity is the pervading element that accompanies all material existence', calling it 'the soul of the world'. Indeed, 'electricity, energy, and life were synonymous', such that an electromagnetic 'energy model constitutes the background against which the deterioration of the consistent ego makes its appearance, in precisely the moment in which [the 1880s] a practical application is beginning to be found for electricity'. Hence 'if fatigue was the disorder of energy, electricity had the promise of restitution': Beard's reasoning in his electrical cure for neurasthenia.[42] In the guise of his revitalized 'body electric', to develop this train of thought, reconstituted 'nerves' would be the conduit through which Whitman's electro-magnetic counterpart of *Kundalini* (Asselineau's 'Superior Soul') flows to revivify himself and depleted humankind. Whitman's 'body electric', with its importance for modernist body-culture (naturism, gymnastics, dance), is a cross between Romantic energetics and borrowings from Yoga.

Whitman experiments with urban-industrial allusion, his technological vitalism portending Futurism's rupture with Decadence. The Belgian poet, Emile Verhaeren, was another harbinger of this break. With his paeans to modern industry in his 1895 *Les Villes Tentaculaires*, 1902 *Les Forces Tumultueuses* and 1906 *La Multiple Splendeur*, Verhaeren devised a 'social, dynamic, and energetic' Symbolism, where one critic detected the rattle of 'scrap iron'. Equally, the French Whitmanian, Jules Romains, 'celebrated the collective soul of large city crowds' in his 1908 collection, *La Vie Unanime*.[43] No longer menacing as in Decadence, modern technology's electro-magnetic forcefield, a correlative of modern man's 'electrical' neural network, thus led to collectivist absorption of 'New Men' into a mass-modernity that, of itself, served as a tonic for nerves. Foreshadowing what Constant Lambert called the 'mechanical romanticism' of the twenties, in post-Decadent quarters like these, suspicion and evasion of modernity finally yielded to its embrace.[44]

Idolized by Russian Futurists and Blaise Cendrars, Whitman's cosmic Self is a multitudinous, modernity-compatible way of salvaging the microcosmic 'I' from the instability afflicting it from mid-century onwards. Capable of 'unselving the object' as well as this 'little I', his *Atman–Brahman* identification is also a source of the blurred subject–object mergers that mark the 'cosmically conscious' varieties of modernism.[45] Traceable to the 1855 first edition of *Leaves of Grass* (a time when Baudelaire was cultivating the 'disintegrative' Poe), the American roots of 'wholesome', anti-Decadent modernism consisted of a revitalized vision of urban-industrial modernity, combined with an optimistic, Hinduizant view of humankind's ability to embrace the modern condition within an expanded self and mind.

Amid allusions to a 'new gnosis' and 'renovated consciousness', further marks of catastrophe ceding to utopia, the Teens saw a 'maximal' inflation of manner, followed by 'minimal', reductionist emphases on the 'elemental origins of art'. Finally able to envisage a mind on the mend, cognitive debility was tackled in Germany by artists and writers dedicated to what, in his 1917 proclamation of a *neue Gnosis*, critic Julius Hartlaub called the 'atavistic yet totally self-willed recall of ancient states of consciousness'. Enlisting Steiner and the Theosophists to recommend a retrieved 'atavism' as an aid to restored cognition, Hartlaub evokes the quest for new, post-Schopenhauerian foundations (Ball's 'essential' and 'spiritual', below) as pursued by Expressionists. Less tolerant of modern transience than Imagism and Dada, Expressionism's anguished heroes sought what Ball called an 'augmented nature' to counterbalance modernity's flux.[46]

In Russia, too, the impulse towards a new post-Decadent art laid claims to redeemed cognition. This is tacit in Matiushin's Ouspenskyite additions to his 1913 translation of Gleizes and Metzinger's *Du Cubisme*, in Ouspensky's own Superman prophecies of 1911, and Malevich's reworkings of Vivekananda. Combining machine-age dynamism with claims to be the 'primitives of a completely renovated consciousness', the Italian Futurists, and even more so their Russian disciples, trumped Hartlaub, to arrive at a vision of an electro-mechanical/superconscious New Man. The Teens saw a much changed climate of thought about a relationship between aesthetic culture and cosmos/cognition that 20 to 30 years earlier had been less hopeful than 'accursed'.

Ouspensky's 1911 *Tertium Organum* (subtitled *The Third Canon of Thought: A Key to the Enigmas of the World*) and 1914 *A New Model of the Universe* proved popular with Russian avant-gardists, and, translated by Claude Bragdon, in interwar America. A mainstay of Malevich's Suprematism, Ouspensky's assertion that 'limitation is a characteristic that belongs only to the human "Euclidean" mind' found man about to 'pass out of the field of vision of positivism and logical understanding'. Anticipating Yeats's 'Descartes, Locke, and Newton took away the world, and gave us excrement instead' (1930), logic, Euclid and positivism belonged to an old world order marked by a 'sense of three-dimensional space … philosophical division of "I" and "Not I". Dogmatic religions and dualistic spiritualism. Codified morality. Division of spirit and matter … Mechanical universe.'

In contrast, Ouspensky's new canon entailed 'a feeling of four-dimensional space. A new sense of time. The live universe. Cosmic consciousness. Reality of the infinite. A feeling of communality with everyone. The unity of everything. The sensation of world-harmony. A new morality. The birth of a superman.'[47]

For Ouspensky, intuition, not information, was the point of

> science, philosophy, religion, and art [which] serve true knowledge only when they … manifest intuition … The aim of even purely intellectual … systems, is not … to give … information, but to raise man to a height of thought and feeling where he … can pass to the new and higher forms of knowledge, to which art and religion are closest.

Like atonality and the absurd, the last shared by Dada and the 1913 Cubo-Futurist 'opera', *Victory over the Sun*, intuition was another path to 'higher realities'. Such claims to a new cosmology and cognition (compare Cabalistic 'restoration' again) bolstered the wonder-working self-image, if not the clarity, of post-Decadent avant-gardes.

In industrially backward Russia, where the electro-mechanical New Man was preferred to the *Naturmensch*, translations of Carpenter, the Theosophists, the American mystics, Yogi Ramacharaka, and Vivekananda supplemented Ouspensky.[48] But not, in Vivekananda's case, without gross bowdlerization. In his *Raja Yoga* (Russian translation 1906) Vivekananda wrote,

> No books, no scriptures, no science, can ever imagine the glory of the Self, which appears as man – the most glorious God that ever was, the only God that ever existed … I am to worship, therefore, none but my self. 'I worship my Self', says the Advaitist. 'To whom shall I bow down? I salute myself.'

With Malevich, that becomes:

> This is how I reason about myself and elevate myself into a Deity saying that I am all … and all that I see, I see myself, so multi-faceted and poly-hedral is my being … I am the beginning of everything, for in my consciousness worlds are created. I search for God, I search within myself for myself.[49]

The 'new gnosis' could clearly lead to a grandiosity surpassing Whitman's.

Similar claims to have merged with the cosmos are found in Musil's 1906 *Young Torless*. A Theosophical *Ubermensch* here asserts that 'people like Basini … signify nothing; they are an empty, chance form. Real human beings are those who are able to penetrate themselves, cosmic human beings who are capable of submerging themselves until they reach their correspondence with the great global process.'[50] The solipsism of Malevich's 'in my consciousness worlds are created' had Schopenhauerian and Symbolist precedents too, like Scriabin's 'I am all that I create. All that exists, exists only in my awareness', Strindberg's 'the world is a reflection of your interior state', or Fyodor Sologub's 'I am the god of a mysterious world, the entire world is my dream alone.'[51]

Conveniently overlooking such continuities from Symbolism, and substituting anomic-utopian, messianic time for secular time, Russian avant-garde art posts a cognitive elect to take charge of an entirely new world model, subsuming science, machines and technology within the new canon of thought.[52] The 'alogical' prophecy of a fourth-dimensional utopia in *Victory over the Sun* – for which Malevich designed the costumes and sets, and where new space-time coordinates resulted from the New Man's triumph over the old solar order – epitomizes distinctions between the visions of the political vanguard and the avant-garde. Including an 'Aviator' and 'Time-Traveller' in its cast, the 'opera' was a compound of millennialism, occultism, technics and Wellsian science fiction, a recipe doomed to political failure. Nothing deterred, as an apocalyptic matrix for figuring the impact of science and technology on peasant life, in modernist Russia the Dr Who-like 'shock of the cosmic' was inseparable from the 'shock of the new'.

In industrially advanced Germany, prior to Dada's advent, priorities differed, the *Naturmensch*, or an improved second nature, proving more attractive than an Americanized modernity or an electro-mechanical New Man. Ball's demonic picture of the machine age in his 1917 lecture on Kandinsky accentuates the difference: 'the mass culture of the modern megalopolis' is 'destructive, threatening with its desperate search for a new ordering of the ruined world'. In this inferno, 'Individual life died out … Machines … replaced individuals … Power was measured in tens of thousands of horsepower. Turbines, boiler houses, iron hammers, electricity, brought into being fields of force and spirits that took whole cities and countries into their terrible grip.'[53] Worlds apart from Futurism,

Ball follows Strindberg in ascribing to 'spirits and powers' (compare his 'anarchy of liberated demons and natural forces' from the same lecture) a destructive modern force-field like the one in Ludwig Meidner's depictions of a Promethean modernity imploding upon itself.

Nature alone is insufficient antidote in the anguished, Steiner-inspired quarters which Ball describes:

> The artists of *these times have turned inwards* … They are … *prophets of a new era* … Their works are … *philosophical, political, and prophetic*. They are … forerunners *of an entire epoch, a new total culture* … *They dissociate themselves from the empirical world*, in which they perceive *chance, disorder, disharmony* … They *seek what is essential* and *what is spiritual* … *the background of the empirical word* … They become creators of *new natural entities that have no counterpart in the known world*. They create images that *are no longer imitations of nature but an augmentation of nature by new, hitherto unknown appearances and mysteries*.[54]

I italicize Ball's 'cosmic', 'new gnosis' and 'third spiritual age' materials: reminders that, as an inspiration to abstraction, the images of auras in Leadbeater's 1902 *Man Visible and Invisible* came into their own during the Teens, as did the illustrations to the 1905 and 1908 studies, *Thought-Forms* and *Occult Chemistry*, by Leadbeater and Besant.[55]

In contrast to the haiku-like simplicity and transparency of Pound's 1913 *In a Station of the Metro*, Theosophy's cultic milieu encouraged turgidity, intoxication, floridity, irrationality. Expressionist art and pronouncements exude a breathless maximalism, distorting the Sublime. Noting shared obscurities in Steiner and Buber, Bahr remarked how Expressionists 'like to talk in a fog'. Harlaub's comparison of Marc's 'cosmic animal world to Steiner's experiences in the ethereal and astral plane' exemplifies this murkiness; or, even vaguer, 'The aura of Munch's and Kokoschka's spiritual portraits, the astral colour world of Klee and Muche, Chagall's mythical dreams, the way a Kandinsky experiences elementary aspects of water, air and earth in inner colour – all … this must seem clairvoyant in the occult sense of the Theosophist.' Theodore Daubler's 'with Kandinsky a Mongolian cloud envelops us in a mystically coloured chaos or defines a cosmos' (1916) further illustrates such excess.[56]

Unlike the *Japonisme* of Pound and Amy Lowell – sister of Percival Lowell, author of *Occult Japan* and later astronomer, who described

Japanese art as 'a glimpse of the soul of nature by the soul of man' – the Hartlaub–Daubler aesthetic is flabby and lush.[57] One sign of objectivist reaction was Ball's 1916 praise for Arp's emphasis on precision, reduction and order:

> Arp speaks out against the bombast of the gods of painting … He would like to see things more ordered and less capricious, less brimming with color and poetry … When he advocates the primitive, he means the first abstract sketch that is aware of complexities but avoids them … A love of the circle and the cube, of sharply intersecting lines … he is concerned not … with richness [but] simplification … He wants to purify the imagination and to concentrate on … opening up not … its store of images but what those images are made of.[58]

Related to Kandinsky's 'search for a common denominator' in the arts, some Expressionists believed in irreducible, and functionally interchangeable, arts-minima. Destruction/decomposition here operated as preliminaries to finding a foundational Something (contrast Strindberg's Nothing) beyond the veil of Maya. Jelena Hahl-Koch notes the correspondence between the 'dissolution of the … object' and 'the dissolution of … tonality in music'; between 'the emancipation of colours and forms' and 'the emancipation of dissonance', as well as 'the dissolution of grammar and syntax' found in Expressionism, Futurism and Dadaism. The common factor was

> the will to express the primordial, to get past the impediments of artistic tradition in order to discover … the elemental origin of art. This explains why so many artists were interested in the reduction of artistic means to their smallest components, and the return to primary forms, with a predilection for the archaic, primitive, and anarchic.[59]

Apropos early modernist music, Glenn Watkins agrees: its ideal was a new language 'constituted from the most basic conceivable elements'.[60]

Cut adrift from their conventional syntactical moorings, the arts' individual creative units – sound in music, Kandinsky's 'reduction to primary forms, and … primary colours' from 1922, the 'transrational' tradition's phonemes, the image as poetry's 'primary pigment' (Wyndham Lewis) – were now at liberty, as 'creation' followed 'destruction', to act as building blocks for a new world. Visible in Poundian *Imagisme*, Cubo-Futurist *zaum*, Varese's call for new sounds, and Arp's reductionism, this visual, imagistic, phonemic and sonic primitivism leant towards the Oriental-archaic, as a source of 'non-degenerate', revitalizing idiom. Other emancipations had to await the forties: the idea of 'primal markings', for instance, and, with the advent of 'Zen *écriture*' and calligraphy, the final liberation of line.

Ordinary Magic: Dada

Dadaists tend towards a metaphor- and image-free procedure: questioning art's necessity, this implies that alert presence to life's continuum reveals a Tao or ordinary magic, quite different from the 'higher vibrations' and 'cosmic I am' of the Whitman- and Theosophy-influenced succession. As primitivists, Heracliteans and 'Taoists' (ciphers, partly, for Bergsonism), Dadaists shun order and reaction, adhering to a pared-down Romanticism of sorts. True to Smith's formula, Dadaists despised the classical West: 'we want to continue the tradition of Negro, Egyptian, Byzantine and Gothic art, and destroy ... the ... sensibility bequeathed ... by the detestable era that followed the quattrocento' (Tristan Tzara 1917). For Richard Huelsenbeck, Dada offered 'the most primitive relation to the surrounding reality', being an 'image and index of collapsing, post-classical bourgeois culture'.[61]

Founded in Zurich in 1916 – the publication year of Pound's *Certain Noble Plays of Japan* – Dada distinguished Buddhism from Theosophy, conflating it with Buber's 1910 Taoist translation, *The Sayings and Parables of Chuang Tzu*.[62] Like some Americans, other German-speaking modernists travelled a similar route: Arthur Doblin read Chinese philosophy, 'incorporat[ing] Taoist ideas into his [1915] pacifist novel ... *Wang Lun's Three Leaps*'; Georg Lukacs 'corresponded with Buber from 1911 to 1921', turning to Jewish, Christian and Hindu mysticism to alleviate his 'despair at being trapped in the ... ['iron cage'] of bourgeois modernity'. Brecht and Hesse were equally attracted to Taoism, while Kafka knew 'Cabbala, Taoism and ... Kierkegaard'.[63] In its 1929 English translation, Wilhelm's *The Secret of the Golden Flower* influenced the Abstract Expressionists. Rexroth, Bynner and Eugene O'Neil were also drawn to Taoism: after discovering Schopenhauer, Max Muller, the Sinologist James Legge, Coomaraswamy and Mead, O'Neill travelled to China via India in 1928, to christen his Californian residence 'Tao House' in 1937.[64]

Shunning German Expressionism's 'soul-tapestries' (Georg Grotz), Dada links the metaphysical absurd of Decadent ironists like Alfred Jarry, Laforgue, Satie and Raymond Roussel to the 'Zen vaudeville' of Cage and the Fluxus group.[65] Affinity between Zen and absurdism is assumed in Wilson Ross's lecture on Zen Buddhism and Dada, delivered in late thirties Seattle and heard by Cage; also in Breton's 1952 question to Francis Picabia: 'Tell me, was not Dada perhaps … a flake of Zen, wafted as far as ourselves?' Breton was right: Dadaists commonly utilized Buddhism to signify paradox, flux, impermanence, ontological indeterminacy and non-differentiation (the 'indifferent': see below).

Dismissing abstraction as irrelevant to the modern 'world of forces' (Raoul Hausmann) – and anticipating Hartlaub's turncoat 1925 warnings against Expressionism's 'intoxicated ecstasies … cosmic swirls … and incomprehensible abstractions' – Dadaists favoured an activistic monism which identified the old soul-sphere with modern flux. Its purpose to assist a 'contemporary world, which is … in a state of disintegration and metamorphosis' (Wieland Herzfeld, 1920), Dada's embrace of a no longer 'anti-modern' vitalism was a more pragmatic response to crisis than was the Expressionist drive to utopia, 'with its intuitions and prophecies, its immersion in the Self or the All'.[66] 'The Dadaist is opposed to the idea of paradise in every form', wrote Huelsenbeck in 1920. Long before Cage's interest in random procedures, Dada envisaged 'reality as unending process', based on 'the creative flux of the universe' and 'the laws of chance'.[67]

Though scorning Expressionist excess, Dadaists did not eschew mystical syncretism altogether. More, they devised a modern myth out of Buddhism, Taoism, Bergson and the German mystics: a gnosis close to Benjamin's view of Surrealism as 'profane illumination'. Despite his 1920 rejection of Theosophy, magnetism, occultism, 'inner necessity', Expressionism, Futurism and Cubism, and his assertion that *Geist* was unnecessary in 'a world that runs on mechanically', Hausmann, assiduous reader of Whitman, still toyed with East–West syncretism.[68] As he wrote to Johannes Baader, their writings would 'have a future meaning, as had Brahmanism, Buddhism or Christianity'. Besides 'claim[ing] that from … the age of sixteen he had read the pre-Socratics, Lao-Tzu, Buddhist texts …

Eckhart, and Angelus Silesius', Hausmann also drew on Haeckel, Mach, Freud, and Wilhelm Fliess.[69]

East–West syncretism, with emphasis on the German mystics (read aloud at Dada soirees in Zurich) marked most Dada spirituality, an anti-hysterical mutation from Expressionism. Thus in Otto Flake's 1920 Dada novel, *Nein und Ja*, the part-time Asconan Arp who had illustrated the *Bhagavad Gita* in 1914, and longed for the 'unencumbered ground' of the mystic Johannes Tauler, was portrayed as a follower of Boehme and Lao Tzu.[70] Ball, who shared Arp's tastes, compared Thomas Munzer's Anabaptists to contemporary 'mystics and enthusiasts', proclaiming, 'I shall be reading poems that … dispense with conventional language … Dada Johann Fuchsgang Goethe. Dada Stendhal. Dada Dalai Lama, Buddha, Bible, and Nietzsche … It's a question of connections, and of loosening them up a bit'.[71] Ball's initial god of the Teens, the Siva of Wilhelm Jahn's *Saurapuranam*, a 'translation … of texts dealing with … Shiva that appeared in Strasbourg in 1908', had been an altogether fiercer figure.[72]

Taoism, the East's nearest counterpart to Bergsonism, was the most important ingredient in Dada mystical syncretism.[73] In Flake's novel, the Ball character reads 'section 29 of the *Tao Te Ching* to Hans (Arp) and Lisbao (Tzara)'; Hannah Hoech owned copies of Buber's Taoist translations and (a 1916 gift from Hausmann) of Alexander Ular's 1912 edition of the *Tao Te Ching*; the last's 28th chapter was quoted by Huelsenbeck in the 1920 *Dada Almanac*; while Michel Seuphor, a Belgian writer close to the Dadaists, later recorded youthful interests in Chuang Tzu. In 1923, soon after his Dadaist phase, and 20 years before his 1943 book on Buddhism, *The Doctrine of Awakening*, Evola published his Italian translation of the *Tao Te Ching*. Finally, combining Taoist with Hindu and Buddhist allusion, Hausmann wrote in 1919, 'Dada is the only savings bank that pays interest in eternity. The Chinaman has his tao and the Indian his brama. Dada is more than tao and brama … Gotama thought of entering Nirvana and after he was dead, he stood not in Nirvana but in dada.'[74]

Other Dada Buddhist allusions have a strong Taoist resonance. This gives them a ring of Zen, itself a Buddhist-Taoist hybrid, even if Zen's modernist debut still lay some years ahead. Thus Huelsenbeck's 1920 assertion that 'Dada is the American side of Buddhism, it raves because it knows how to be silent, it acts because it is in a state of rest' evokes the *Tao Te Ching*'s reconciliation of opposites and, through 'American', the era's fashionable machinism. In similar Taoist/Buddhist vein, noting that Chuang Tzu was 'as dada as we are', in 1922 Tzara asserted 'Dada is not all modern. It is more in the nature of a return to an almost Buddhist religion of indifference.'[75] The implications of 'indifference' are clarified by Salomo Friedlander's 1913 *Der Sturm* essay, 'Prasentismus'. Reversing Malevich's Vedantic 'I am', an extract reads,

> I am no man. I am no one and everyone. Indifferentist. If people wish to understand me they must die, be destroyed like me, undifferentiated ... I am indifference ... I am present ... I am the living nothing ... I have annulled all the opposites within me ... I am no reason, but therefore everything: because I am the indifferent centre of all reason, the neuter of all logic, the logical null! ... I am.[76]

Friedlander's 'indifference' implies universal acceptance, impersonality, non-differentiation, neutrality: qualities very different from a shrug of the shoulders. Interpreted in this light, Tzara's 'Buddhist religion of indifference' suggests a refusal to differentiate, synoptic neutrality, anonymity, acceptance. The Taoist/Buddhist colour of Friedlander's 'logical null' is reflected in Tzara's 'Always destroy what you have in you. On random walks. Then you will be able to understand many things.'[77] This koan-like pronouncement implies gnosis in self-annulment, plenitude in vacuity, paradoxical consequences of a degree-zero, non-differentiating stance. Outright 'destruction' is not involved; nor again utopian 'creation' – more, a point of genuinely a-nomic balance between the two. Finally, there is Hausmann's 'the partial inexplicability of Dada is refreshing for us like the actual inexplicability of the world – whether one calls the spiritual trump Tao, Brahm, Om, God, Energy, Spirit, Indifference or anything else, the same cheeks still get puffed out while one does so'.[78]

An 'ordinary' immanentism, objectivism and impersonality akin to that of the otherwise very different Imagists, and an unconditional acceptance of modern flux and contingency: these emphases distinguish Dada from Expressionism, with its intolerance of 'chance', 'disorder', 'disharmony' and longing for a second, improved creation. Along with a wish to be through with art's auratic interposition between acts of perception and their objects in everyday life, the qualities of irony, detachment and ordinariness also attach to Duchamp's ready-mades. The most famous of these, his *Fountain* of 1917 (a urinal signed 'R. Mutt'), was dubbed the 'Buddha of the Bathroom' by Louise Norton in *The Blind Man*, a New York Dada review. Repeated by Carl van Vechten, who wrote to Gertrude Stein that 'the photographs make it look like anything from a Madonna to a Buddha', Apollinaire picked up the allusion, writing that Duchamp had 'ennobled' his theme 'by transforming a hygienic object of masculine toilet into a Buddha'.[79]

Though Duchamp remained silent, ordinary Enlightenment's 'direct pointing to reality' had arrived in modern art by 1917. 'A urinal, too', wrote Huelsenbeck, 'is a thing in itself'.[80] The episode announces the 'let the world be' philosophy of Cage's Zen/neo-Dada alliance where, amid similar weariness with 'tourism in the house of images', similar reinstatements of life's more unassuming, even trivial faces were (less skilfully) promoted in the name of Dada and Zen. As the transcendental pretence's attractions waned, the 'extraordinary' Enlightenment of Lawrence, Kandinsky, Malevich and company ceased to be the main contender on the modernist spiritual front. The older cosmicist tendency had acquired two major rivals: Dada's anti-transcendental 'profane illumination', and the Imagists' epiphanic aesthetic, with its location of perfection, not in supersensible archetypes, but in everyday life.

Particularly in Dada, Buddhism and Taoism were instrumental in deflecting attention to quotidian 'ordinary magic', away from 'occult puzzles beyond'. This equilibrated mood-swings between 'destruction' and 'creation', craving for the nomic and despair at its absence, apprehensions of disaster and utopian hopes. As Hesse, another Taoist, wrote in his 1922 *Siddhartha*, 'meaning and reality were not hidden somewhere behind things, they were in them, all of them'.[81] Like Ad Reinhardt's 'no reality behind reality', Hesse's sentiment crystallizes the differences between the older transcendentalism (also its *neantiste* complement), and the new East Asia-inspired objectivism which, with some interesting, non-Western implications for the well-springs of 'call to order' (Babbitt, Pound, Confucius, Pali Buddhism, the later Yeats and Zen), had emerged by the end of the Teens. Already visible in Dadaist anti-Expressionism, twenties 'spirit-wars' were imminent, based less on an East–West than a classical–Romantic divide. Provided it was 'orderly' and 'classical', the East was welcome to several reactionary modernists who sought to keep neo-Romantic chaos at bay.

4

CALL TO ORDER, OCCULTIST GEOPOLITICS, SPIRIT WARS

Out of Asia: Prophecy and World Politics

Early twentieth-century utopias were built on the old order's ruins. From 1911, traditional empires like Manchu China, Tsarist Russia, and the Austro-Hungarian and Ottoman empires fell to the upheavals of modernization and mechanized war. In a physical sense, this brought the 'long middle ages' to a close. But at an inner mythico-occult level, it reinvigorated the *longue durée*'s prophetic-gnostic forms of knowledge. The pattern which developed – one of the forces of politico-cultural modernity wedded to the atavistic power of apocalyptic and myth – was repeated, briefly, in the (sub-modernist) countercultural sixties, and on a grander scale with the Soviet Union's fall. When the phoenix rises from the ashes, its support is the 'mythopoetic function', to redeploy Myers's term. Modern revolutions are scarcely secular events: their prime, mass-mobilizing need is to lodge their programmes in the mind's 'oldest strata' (Ball), and to that end, like modernism, they enlist prophecies, myths, magic, invented traditions, all to legitimate or glamourize the new.

Ancient myths and prophecies came to mind when, on the Great War's outbreak, Serusier wrote, 'It seems … I am reading a page of the *Apocalypse* or … the *Bhagavad-Gita*. I often think of discussions with Ranson on the battle of nations.'[1] Musil tried to make more secular sense of twenties turmoil:

> Malaise. Swarms of sects in Germany. Anxious looks towards Russia, the
> Far East, India. We blame economics, civilization, rationalism, nation-
> alism; we imagine a decline, a slackening of the race … [Some say] we
> have lost all morality. Others … that we … lost our innocence when we
> swallowed … the demon of intellectualism. Still others that we ought to
> transcend civilization and get back to culture as the Greeks knew it.[2]

No consensus, just unease: a perfect breeding ground for occultist
sects – with leanings East. As Georg Fuchs boasted (1931),

> The occult fashion of the time after the first world war had its origin …
> in Schwabing! Theosophists … mystics, Gnostics, Taoists, Mazdaists,
> Buddhists, … Zionists … Nihilists, Collectivists, Syndicalists, Bolshevists,
> Pacifists … and other world-reforming fanatics … Here everything
> impossible to man was jumbled together with all human possibilities.[3]

Nazism's occult roots, traceable to Bohemian Munich-
Schwabing, are well known, less so early Soviet occultism.[4] Mixing
old with new, one Soviet faction geared ancient Central Asian
prophecy – the myth of Shambhala, with its Buddhist world ruler –
to the cause of Bolshevizing the East.[5] Its Western counterpart
Joachim of Fiore's Third Kingdom of the Holy Spirit, a proph-
ecy known in modernist circles and source of the term 'Third
Reich', the Shambhala myth was also central to the 'World Plan' of
Nicholas Roerich and his wife Helena, as instructed by Blavatsky's
'Master Morya'.[6] Roerich was a globe-trotting Russian White who
had designed the sets for Stravinsky's *Rite of Spring*. An ambitious
Theosophist who played off the Soviets and Americans, he mas-
queraded as a reincarnation of the fifth Dalai Lama to win over
Buddhist Central Asia: a similar, collectivist goal to that of the 'Red
Shambhala' gang. Lenin as chakravartin/Buddha Maitreya – or a
loner, theocratic Theosophist, bent on maintaining his lavish Silver
Age lifestyle? Hard for a proto-nationalist Central Asian nomad, hat-
ing any form of centralized rule, to choose between the two.

These inner Asian intrigues captivated Europe. Citing a 1921 book
by the Polish-Russian engineer Ferdinand Ossendowki – who joined
the rag-tag Mongol army of Roman Ungern von Sternberg, another
player in the Shambhala game – Lawrence effused (1928),

> The … mysterious barrier has fallen … the … leaning of the Germanic
> spirit is once more eastwards, towards Russia, towards Tartary. The strange

vortex of Tartary has become the … centre again … Western Europe is broken … all Germany reads *Beasts, Men, and Gods* … [Ossendowski had revived Saint-Yves D'Alveydre's fiction of an advanced underground civilization in the Kingdom of Agartha, itself integral to the twenties Shambhala myth]. Returning … to the fascination of the destructive east, that produced Attila … Back … to the savage polarity of Tartary … away from … civilized Christian Europe … Students the same, youths with rucksacks the same … These … Young Socialists … with their non-materialistic professions, their half-mystic assertions … strike me as strange. Something primitive, like loose, roving gangs of broken, scattered tribes … [T]he … southern races are falling out of association with the northern races, the northern Germanic impulse is recoiling towards … the destructive vortex of Tartary.[7]

Poetic embroidery, at basis, on Musil's 'swarms of sects' and 'anxious looks towards Russia, the Far East, India', but with a gloating menace.

The prophetic and programmatic yoke the atavistic and futural together in such a way that the 'rational' mind assents to what the unconscious/second self has already agreed, given its susceptibility to the Lawrence/Roerich style in magic. Similar psychagogic sleight-of-hand, a mix of the atavistic and futural, marks the new, cosmic-Promethean art of the earlier Teens, particularly German and Russian, as well as the recipes for millennial revolution which matured soon after. Apocalyptic time is different from historical time: turn-of-the-century politicized occultism, like that of the folk-soul's poets and seers, who overstepped regular history to arrive at history-as-messianic-phantasmagoria, had laid foundations and drawn up blueprints.[8] Now, with the old order's collapse, the time of the unscrupulous adventurer visionary, of the *grand magnétiseur* feared by the crowd-psychologists, had eventually come.[9] Magnetic command – or as Nietzsche wrote of Wagner, 'persuasion by means of the nerves' – becomes the key to the early twentieth-century utopia, whether political or aesthetic, though the dividing line is blurred.

Fixation on 'Nazism's occult roots' ('the CIA and mind-control' is the post-Second World War equivalent) has sidelined the comparable, political paradigm-changing role of other axe-grinding sects and secret societies in the years around the Great War and the old order's collapse. Espionage, occultism and prophecy were related activities, and illuminated opinion was that the historical epicentre was deserting the modern 'West' for the more intriguing 'rest'. Occultist Afrocentrism began in these watershed years, as did other new nationalisms and indigenisms, often grouped in 'pan-'movements. Their tenor could be violent, or folkish and frivolous – a form of ethnic fancy dress, or play-acting for 'rich white folk'. I deal with the frivolous and folkish first ('folk' were still magical), then with the more substantial 'Germano-Asiatic offensive against the West'. A foretaste perhaps of 'culture wars' between poststructuralists and humanists, the last was a relative and continuation of France's 'Bergsonian controversy': apostle of 'flux' and 'energy', Bergson terrified stasis-craving French conservatives.[10] Touching on Tantra in Bloomsbury (the occultism of 'rich white folk'), I conclude with the dance of Ruth St Denis, who arrived at her own, syncretic form of colonial *moderne*, without it becoming an overt body-politics, as in Mary Wigman's case.[11]

My choice of themes will hopefully emphasize that when the arts and/or politics suddenly jump tracks, from one paradigm or spectrum of possibilities to another, the results cannot but fascinate: together with its 'meta-world', modernism was strange and ex-centric enough, without striving after Shklovsky's 'defamiliarization'. Aesthetic criteria alone cannot explain modernism's glaring, phantom-haunted departures from 'art's known and standard forms'. Along with the Roerich/Lawrence brand of occultist geopolitics, Mythos, Cosmos and Psyche, as I called these paradigm-shifting factors in Chapter 2, must be brought into the picture too. As a mythic, post-positivist modality for construing a far larger and less certain world than the Victorian, that means taking the occult as a symbolic, articulative idiom, not as something weird or wantonly obscure.

Indeed, from a supply-and-demand perspective, occultist sects arguably only proliferated as they did (Musil, Fuchs) because of the ghostly, cryptic and liminoid nature of this transitional phase of modernity. As an idiom of the 'in-between', another term for 'transitional', the occult, which thrives on political laxity or chaos, could plug the gap between irreparably damaged *ancien régime* 'throne and altar' and unfolding, not-yet-fully secular modernity, in ways that positivism and normative religion could not. During this phase of modern experience, the range of the actually mysterious, uncertain and uncanny was vast: but so was the range of 'irregular', mythico-occult knowledge (a precondition of 'swarms of sects'), with its capacity for remodelling, if hardly stabilizing, a no longer 'known and standard' world.

Pan-coloured Exoticism: The Rest against the West

I begin with the neo-aristocratic, pan-coloured uprising of *Dark Princess*, a 1928 novel by W. E. B. Du Bois, African American author of *The Souls of Black Folk* (1903), and a Germanist who met anthropologist Franz Boas in 1906. The novel's reactionary revolutionaries could come from a page in the annals of empire, at their atavistic best. Intent on 'arming all the Coloured Peoples, in Asia, America, and Africa against the Whites', one 'H.R.H. The Princess Kautilya of Bwodpur, India' conspires with Matthew Towns, 'a negro medical student from New York'. With other 'coloured leaders', they discuss 'expressionism, cubism, Futurism, vorticism', the Princess (like Smith on anti-classical reaction) noting of *art negre* that 'the Congo is flooding the Acropolis'. A convention occurs, where

> I [the Princess] and my Buddhist priest, a Mohammedan Mullah, and a Hindu leader of Swaraj, were India [note the emphasis on race and religion]; Japan was represented by an artisan and the blood of the Shoguns [nobility meets Arts and Crafts]; young China was there and a Lama from Thibet [religion again]; Persia, Arabia, and Afghanistan; black men from the Sudan, East, West, and South Africa; Indians from Central and South America, brown men from the West Indies, and – yes, Matthew, Black America was there too.[12]

Qua myth-making expression of the 'aristocratic-folk ideology' as transferred to anti-colonial nationalism, but on a pan-coloured scale, the passage's *hauteur* is more 'Toryentalist' than left-wing – despite Princess Kautilya's recent visit to revolutionary Russia. In line with period primitivism, Du Bois deals in the romantic coinage of culture, religion and status, not economics or class. This is Smith's Elgin Marbles-dethroning exoticism with a vengeance, its focus not the materially new but the spiritually pre-modern. As an instance of the modernist 'political poetic' – of Benjamin's hated 'aestheticizing' style in politics – the passage goes an anti-liberal 'pan-'step further than, say, the educated atavist, John Laputa, reactionary revolutionary hero of Buchan's 1910 *Prester John*: not as a plea for empire, but as an *ancien régime*-inflected attempt, like that of the obscurantist branch of Indian nationalism, culturally to be free of its shackles. Indeed, the novel romanticizes Indian opposition to the British, concluding with the Princess's delivery of Towns's child 'Madhu', a future king messiah. Mystic invocations of ancient Indian deities and the great Mauryan emperor Chandragupta surround the birth of this avatar: a 'shock of the old' finale of which the average Theosophical romancier and Buchan could have been proud.

Dark Princess has its (less all-inclusive and less mythic) parallel in sensationalist scares like the 'pan-Oriental' menace brought to the attention of a twenties 'committee on Eastern unrest' by the 'gentleman spy' Norman Bray. Bray was convinced that the British Empire was threatened by the spread of Mahdism and Wahhabism in Nigeria, and by the financing of pan-Islam by German, Russian and Turkish monies passing through Switzerland. (To defend the Berlin–Baghdad railway, Wilhelmine Germany had tried to stir up an anti-British Islamic jihad during the First World War.[13]) Not that Du Bois sounds so threatening – he disliked Marcus Garvey's racial separatism, and judging from *Dark Princess*, his main objective (perhaps shaped while studying in myth-conscious Berlin from 1892–94) was to create a pan-coloured 'new Mythos'. The anti-Western thrust of twenties 'spirit-wars', apparent in this non-Afrocentric, cosmopolitan fantasy, calls for further exploration.

Wild Jews and Muslim Pretenders

In a study of Lev Nussimbaum, member of the Weimar counterculture and an 'impostor' Jewish Orientalist who struck a Muslim warrior stance, Tom Reiss deals with the element of self-glamourizing auto-exoticism just seen in Du Bois. Nussimbaum's Café Megalomania brand of Orientalism attracted Else Lasker-Schuler, 'the Prince of Thebes' as she, a Jewess, called herself, her poetry, according to Eric Muhsam, alive 'with the fire of Oriental fantasy'.[14] A friend of Oscar Kokoschka, she professed to speak 'Asiatic', the language of the biblical Hebrews, 'Wild Jews' in her parlance. Arrested in a Prague church for preaching in 'Asiatic' (meta-language again), her revitalizing 'Wild Jew' Mythos was meant to counteract two thousand years of Diaspora. Her outfit, according to Kokoschka, included 'harem pants, a turban … long, black hair, with a cigarette in a long holder'. An Arabophile, she hated the Holy Land when she tried to live there: 'Even King David would have moved on.'[15]

Despite its High Bohemian flamboyance and disregard for 'new sobriety', Lasker-Schuler's 'Jewish Orientalism' had a serious side, dedicated to East–West synthesis and Jewish–Muslim alliance. 'Some … [Weimar Jews and Zionists] were reviving an older tradition', writes Reiss, 'an Orientalism that … linked Judaism and Islam … East and West, in a common harmonious past, and sought … a common, harmonious future'. Nussimbaum's vision evoked multi-ethnic, syncretic empire after the aristocratic-military model: in the Caucasus, he maintained, 'the descendants of crusader knights and Muslim warriors not only live in harmony with Jews but … almost merge with them as well'. Liebersohn's 'modernist myth of merging with the primitive' (Chapter 1) was perhaps becoming a cliché. But not least because of the value of (even 'faux tribe') ethnographic diversity as a check to homogenization, the 'atavistic/folkish' party to twenties spirit-wars should not be ignored.

Reiss observes that Victorian Orientalist Jews like Arminius Vambery, William Gifford Palgrave and Disraeli had deliberately '"gone Oriental", in Muslim mufti', to counteract the over-assimilation of their fathers. Of their Weimar successors, he notes that other Jews set 'esoteric Orientalism' against modernity's harsh political realities, citing Eugen Hoeflich, a pan-Asianist who wanted 'Jews, Muslims, Buddhists, Confucians' to form 'a united front against … European mechanization and mass warfare'. Like the Theosophists, such figures saw the Orient as an alternative to 'brutal modernity'.[16] That had been equally true of turn-of-the-century pan-Asianists, like Okakura, Fenollosa and Tagore, also of T. E. Lawrence, not to mention the opponents of 'Civilization and Enlightenment' in Meiji Japan.

Some of the Jewish embrace of what, in 1905, the English liberal Charles Masterman deplored as the 'ancient barbarism' may have resulted from imitation of 'German *völkisch* thought'.[17] But in spite of the modern idea of a 'self-ancestral' or 'cultural-racial soul' – which Buber, for one, shared not just with *völkisch* 'pre-fascists', but also with Celtic revivalists, Russian 'Scythianists' and Calcutta neo-Romantics like Havell and Coomaraswamy – the ghost of *ancien régime* and old empire, where a reasonably harmonious coexistence (or syncretism) of cultures and religions was not uncommon, lingers on in this style of thought.[18] Ironically, too, if the not so politically correct 'German *völkisch*' (better, 'racial romantic') Zionists and Jewish Orientalists had been more successful in their plans to reconcile Jew and Muslim, much carnage could have been spared.

The Western Islamic vogue of the day is equally instructive. While researching Nussimbaum, Reiss found 'countless copies of magazines like *The Muslim Review* and *The Light*, to which Baron Omar-Rolph Ehrenfels [the Austrian convert to Islam and Nussimbaum's friend] … contributed articles on prospects for world Islamic revival, the state of Muslim women, and interfaith healing between Muslims and Jews'. With a hint of Marx on the repetition of history, as tragedy first, then as farce (though farce has priority here), Reiss found in this literature

> a whole world of Orientalists and converts with names like Lord Headly al-Farooq, Major Abdullah Battersbey, and her Highness the Dayang Muda of Sarawak, 'the daughter of the late Sir Walter Palmer of Reading.' There was Muhamud Gunnar Erikson from Sweden, Omar Mita from Japan, and Ismail Wieslaw Jazierski from Poland.[19]

With its Lord Snooty-type personnel (compare Du Bois's liking for aristocracy, and contrast IS), this looks like another *Dark Princess*-style insurrection against heartless modernity. Even allowing for radical chic, high-imperial-age globalization appears to have opened up new vistas and viewpoints for anti-modern/anti-Western spirit-wars, the 'best' (*hoi aristoi*) throwing in their lot with the spiritually superior 'rest'.

Engaged as they were in what *Action française* member Henri Massis called a 'germano-asiatic offensive against the West', others among Reiss's characters, like the followers of conservative revolutionary Artur Moeller van den Broek, flirted with violence. 'A translator of Dostoyevsky', Moeller was assured of 'the coming triumph of "the East", from bolshevism to Islam over the bankrupt cultures of the West'. Like Spengler, Moeller thought the West was finished, convinced that a German–Russian alliance, reinforced by other 'Asiatic' powers (compare Lawrence's Tartary), was to wage 'cosmic' war against 'bourgeois liberalism'. Germany and Russia were 'searching, experimental nations', with barbarian origins (the primitivist myth of the 'rest' again). Hence Russia was a 'false enemy. The real enemies … were the victors of Versailles.'[20] The West their common foe, one and the same extravagant, atavistic/neo-Romantic (and catastrophic-utopian) way of regarding the world could lead to serioludic *jeu d'esprit* (Nussimbaum, Lasker-Schuler) or to 'Jihadi cool' (Lawrence, Moeller).

The full spectrum of modernist 'Asiaticist' positions, if mythically phrased, fraught with occultist geopolitics and wildly histrionic, was evidently rich and varied. Doubtless sniffing apocalypse, Blavatsky herself had discussed the Mahdi's revolt in Egypt with Jamal al-Din Al Afghani, Masonic anti-imperialist, a founder of neo-Salafist, modern Islam and something of an 'adept' – a case of heterodoxy put to the service of subverting the status quo ('old Islam') so as to replace it with neo-orthodoxy.[21] Though the Holy War against Western civilization (or bourgeois liberalism) took many forms, the idea of a regenerated Asia that was in turn to regenerate or replace the West was popular, even commonplace. In dissemination of this 'sacred' anti-imperialism, Theosophy played a major, mystical imperialist role.

The Theosophical brand of modernism, an active force in spiritwars, specialized in art's experimental fringes – non-objective film, colour-music, merger of the arts (what Adorno called the 'blurred boundary aesthetic'). This went down better in America, another 'experimental nation', than in 'call to order' Europe, where Johannes Itten's proselytizing for Mazdaznan, a harmless neo-Persian sect, created a rift in the Bauhaus. Two German-American Theosophists, Katherine Dreier and Hilla Rebay, were major patrons of 'non-objective' art in the USA. The *Societe Anonyme*, an association to promote new art, was created by Dreier with Duchamp and Man Ray in 1920; while in 1939 Rebay, disliked by MOMA supremo Alfred Barr for turning modernism into a religion, founded The Museum (or 'Temple') of Non-Objective Painting, precursor of the Guggenheim Museum. Anti-Theosophical, and by implication anti-experimental and anti-exotic, conservative reaction had set in by the mid-twenties, to oppose figures like Dreier and Rebay.

Germano-Asiatic Offensive against the West

Its nearer targets 'Moellerian' Germany and Russia, the twenties turn against Theosophy and neo-Romanticism, though picked up in England and America, began life in French hostility to Spengler and Bergsonism. (Bergson's sister, Moina, was married to MacGregor

Mathers, leader of the Golden Dawn.) Massis threw down the gauntlet in a 1924 article in *Le Journal Litteraire*, entitled 'L'offensive germano-asiatique contre la culture occidentale', followed by a 1927 book, *Défence de l'Occident*, a neo-Catholic, *rappel a l'ordre* reply to Spengler's 1918/1922 *Decline of the West*.[22] For the reactionary French right, 'Asiaticism' was metaphysical Bolshevism, akin to Leninism, the 'yellow peril', Bergsonism and German counter-philosophy. Chaotic and irrational – in Massis's words, 'une vision catastrophique de l'univers' – the Germano-Asiatic faction's world-view was the antithesis of the *Action francaise*'s orderly vision. In the February/March 1925 issue of *Les Cahiers du Mois*, entitled *Les Appels de l'Orient*, the Eastern threat to the *moi* was debated. Joining the fray, the Surrealists sided with the anti-classical cause of Germany, Russia and Asia, for association with which the neo-Vedantist Romain Rolland had been lambasted by the right. As with the Moellerians, political violence attracted the Surrealists.

With its uncanny premonition of the 9/11 attacks on America, a 1925 outburst by Louis Aragon (not in fancy dress) ventilates a violent anti-Westernism:

> Western world, you are condemned to death. We are Europe's defeatists … Let the Orient, your terror, answer our voice at last! We shall awaken everywhere the seeds of confusion and discomfort. We are the mind's agitators … Jews leave your ghettos! … Rise, thousand-armed India, great legendary Brahma! It is your turn Egypt! … *Let distant America's white buildings crumble among her ridiculous prohibitions*. Rise, O world![23]

The law-court testimony of a teenage recruit to Barindra Kumar Ghose's Swadeshi training centre in Calcutta bears on Aragon's vision: 'In the garden [ashram] Upen Babu [taught] Upanishads and politics and Barindra Babu [taught] Gita and History of Russo–Japanese war and Ullas Babu delivered lectures on explosives.'[24] Such 'radical ashrams' (*plus ca change*) were modelled on the 'Abbey of Bliss' in Bankim Chandra Chatterjee's 1882 novel, *Ananadamath*. Anti-British organizations like these attracted support from Fenollosa's associate Okakura and Vivekananda's pupil 'Sister Nivedita', the Irishwoman Margaret Noble, who wrote a book about Kali and corresponded with Kropotkin. But that particular pan-Asian 'offensive against the West' was 20 years earlier: for Massis, 'Europe' (meaning France) was being besieged by barbaric neo-gnostic forces, corrupted by unholy coalitions struck between Aragon's 'thousand armed India' and the West's treasonable clerks.

My aim in this section is to elucidate the ways in which, amid a millenarian attempt to revitalize the West by appeal to a synthetic Asia, the occultist, vitalist and Orientalist initiatives introduced in Chapter 1 impacted on the twenties modernist scene. Mythic and esoteric by nature, a case of occultist geo-politics, not real-politik, this question cannot be resolved by appeal to the familiar left–right polarities of the thirties and Cold War. As elsewhere with 'disorderly' modernist myth-making ('order' had myths of its own), an intricate anti-classical and anti-liberal mosaic of factors, including *Lebensphilosophie*, Bergsonism and occultism, needs consideration. As for the 'Orients' (plural) involved in the quarrel, Massis's main target was the product of a 'maximalist' or 'cosmic-utopian' mentality, drawn, like Scriabin, Malevich and the Expressionists, to what Yeats called 'vague Asiatic immensities'.

By the twenties, these 'immensities' entailed a mix of syncretic India, Whitman's 'I, me monomania' (Lawrence), Theosophical cosmology and Bergsonism, all of which dissolved the *cogito* in the 'second state' or the cosmos. Opposed to such cosmic mergers and 'outpours of me', a new, anti-Romantic/anti-Theosophical ingredient in the twenties controversy was a static eternalist Asia. Of Guénon's Traditionalist devising, this was the quasi-Platonic Orient favoured by Coomaraswamy and Eliot, the first with his friendships in neo-Catholic circles, the second with his post-conversion admission of the *Bhagavad Gita* into his canon, alongside Dante's *Paradiso*. Like Eliot's, Coomaraswamy's political ideal was a deferential neo-feudalism, based on the priority of caste and social loyalty or *bhakti*.[25] Political apocalypse and worldview, not spiritual practice, being the dominant focus (as likewise with Du Bois and Nussimbaum), Coomaraswamy shared his anti-dynamic Orientalism with other Guénonians, including Fritjof Schuon and Marco Pallis.[26]

Scaremongering akin to classic sorcery accusations continued to dog modernity's fortunes in the twenties, portraying the new condition as a diabolic and illegitimate departure from preordained right. This was in the 'masonic plot' line of conspiracy theory of Abbe Barruel and his pro-*ancien régime* successors, one of whom, 'Leo Taxil', had horrified 1890s France with tales of feminist Satanism in high places.[27] Along with neo-Barruelian tracts like ex-Theosophist

Nesta Webster's 1924 *Secret Societies and Subversive Movements*, the anti-Semitic conspiracy theories of the *Protocols of the Elders of Zion* raised the post-war political temperature.[28] Hysteria duly mounted, as anxieties about what Eliot called 'the futility and anarchy of contemporary life', and Eliade 'the terror of history', fuelled speculation about the working, not of worldly historical causes, but of the catastrophic-utopian extremities of millenarian thought.

Julien Benda apart, 'professors of civilization' (aka liberals) are notably absent from this alternatively 'reactionary' or 'revolutionary' modernist quarrel about East and West. With a view to shoring up or tearing down the tottering edifice of privilege and tradition – preservation of the nomic for conservatives, an unavoidable 'destructive' prelude to 'creation' for radical right and left – myths and fictions (not liberal rationality) flew from nascent fascism, revolutionary left and conservative right. Radical and reactionary, dynamic/Bergsonian and static/Platonic versions of the Orient competed here, less as workable substitute sacralities than as ciphers for opposing cultural political aims. Favoured since prewar times by vitalists, neo-pagans, Theosophists, *völkisch* occultists, Asconans and Expressionists, the Nordic-Asian Mythos, with its 'poetic political' ramifications and affinities with Bergsonism, was regarded by conservatives as on a par with 'Judaeo-Bolshevism' and masonry, qua diabolic model for the new.

Modernist syncretism was now more fissiparous than before the war. A static or classic version of the Orient could accordingly be espoused without contradiction by the more cosmopolitan 'reactionary modernist' defenders of the pre-modern, pre-democratic and pre-materialist West. Rejecting Vivekananda's and Aurobindo's neo-Hindu revivalism, and dismissing Theosophy as 'counter-initiatic', Guénon enlisted 'traditional' Vedanta to support a strict *ancien régime* conservatism. In like vein, Eliot, his Harvard mentor Irving Babbitt, Coomaraswamy and Pound savaged modern heresy, Romantic subjectivity, Theosophy and Taoism respectively, while idealizing the Indian classics, Pali Buddhism, Brahminism and Confucianism.

Though he shared Massis's anti-Bergsonism, Lewis described *Défence de l'Occident* as the defence of a 'corpse'. But he, too, admitted a 'classical' Guénonian Orient into his version of 'call to order':

'Classical' is for me anything which is nobly defined and exact, as opposed to … fluid – of the Flux – without outline, romantically 'dark', vague, 'mysterious', stormy, uncertain … The opposition … is … universal; and the seeds of the naturalist mistakes are … to be found precisely in Greece … we should use the Classical Orient (… in the sense of Guénon) to rescue us … from that far-reaching tradition.[29]

On the conservative as opposed to the revolutionary right (the last preferred yoga and Tantra), selective appeal to purist or authoritarian forms of Eastern religion, again as a meta-political cipher, was as common a response to the current crisis of tradition and modernity, as the outright rejection urged by Massis. Ignoring bourgeois liberalism, spirit-wars were three-cornered in this particular fight: two quasi-religious, arch-conservative forms of the would-be nomic, one Eastern, the other Christian, set against the prophets of a brave new Theosophical syncretism-derived world.

Against the tastes of patricians like Eliot, Guénon and Coomaraswamy, we could range the mystic enthusiasms enumerated by Fuchs ('Theosophists, Gnostics, Taoists' and so on). Too radical, dynamic and populist for Traditionalists, these relatives of the cosmic-utopian prewar Orient were proto-New Age fashions, affected as much by some early Nazis as by the left-wing sects specified by Fuchs. Close to the 'magical eclecticism' of the Expressionists, these fashions involved countercultural roving, *Wandervogel* antics and Atlantean speculations, like those of 'savage pilgrim' Lawrence. Among English modernists, it was Lawrence, Eliot's bugbear, who came closest to the spirit of Munich-Schwabing and its outlet at Ascona.[30] Bearing on this 'left-bank' quarter of Munich, Hermann Rauschning traced Nazism to a prewar 'hysterical romanticism' which 'flourished especially in Vienna and Munich'.[31] This suggests a Dionysian romanticism like that of Fuchs and Lawrence, the last with his countercultural German wife Frieda, and first-hand acquaintance of Ascona and Taos.

What most offended twenties Traditionalists were these populist, post-war variants on Schwab's 'Nordic–Asian axis of thought'. With its labyrinthine counter-cosmology, extended Self, trance-accessed imaginary, and 'politics of myth and the unconscious' (Thomas Mann), this type of Orientalism was a companion of Rauschning's 'hysterical romanticism'. For Guénon, such 'counter-initiatic' affiliates of Theosophy lacked respectable Asian prototypes. More, they superimposed a superficially Orientalist lexicon on a Western occultist deep grammar, concerned with *anima mundi*, the 'self-ancestral', the 'astral light', the 'second state' and so forth (the themes of Chapter 2). Nevertheless, by the twenties, a remagicalized world-picture akin to the New Age's 'new paradigm' was well entrenched. Indeed, with its anti-Judaeo-Christian, anti-Cartesian and anti-Newtonian rhetoric, the New Age (listlessly) contests much the same 'Latin-Christian' certitudes as were dear to Massis.

Before detailed consideration of Massis's objections to Asiaticism, it could be helpful to expand on the then-current metapolitical associations (occultist geopolitics again) of the primitivism and Orientalism he decried. Reverting to Lawrence's 'Russo-Asiatic' embroidery on Germany's 'return to Tartary', the extract's wild meta-geographical sweep gives some measure of how Massis contrived to portray German Buddhism, Slav mysticism and Bolshevism as threats to Europe's Latin-Christian inheritance.[32] In messianic vein, Lawrence proceeds to offer a 'mystic socialist' Tartary as 'the father of the next phase of events', and, giving an Asiaticist twist to a Northern primitivism hallowed in Tacitus's *Germania*, as the 'ancient spirit of pre-historic Germany coming back, at the end of history'.[33] His neo-Aztec, 'dark god' novel, *The Plumed Serpent* (1926), had likewise envisaged an international return to the old gods, including Asia's, hoping that 'the Teutonic world would once more think in terms of Thor and Wotan, and the tree Igdrasil'.

Lawrence's Tartary is a perfect anti-Western symbol, attuned to the myth-historical, Spenglerian mood of the post-war radical right. The Central Asian travelogue cited by Lawrence – Ossendowski's *Beasts, Men and Gods* (Eng. trans. 1923) – had introduced the *Kalachakra Tantra*'s figment of a *chakravartin*, or millenarian 'king of the world'. As popularized by Saint-Yves d'Alveydre, this cosmic 'leadership' motif, with its promise of a new historical cycle, was strangely adopted by the otherwise circumspect Guénon, and, less surprisingly, by his fascist admirer Evola.[34] Already touched-on forms of acting-out were Roerich's 1925–28 expedition to the edges of Tibet, looking for Shambhala, and the White pan-Mongolist *imperium* planned during the Russian civil war by the Baltic warlord, Ungern-Sternberg, relative of Count Keyserling, Buddhist enemy of Reds and Jews, and, for his lamaist entourage, a reincarnation of Tamerlane.[35] As told by Ossendowski, the mad baron's story, with its *Freicorps*-like plans for an 'Order of Military Buddhists', matches German mystical militarism (*virya*, as Evola called it) in its post-war state of suspension from normative nationalism and conventional state structures.

Like Lawrence, the nominally Marxist Surrealists welcomed the darkly Gothic notion of Germany, Russia and Asia rising against Europe. In the Anglophone world, the opposing conservative view was voiced by Eliot in his 1934 'primer of modern heresy', *After Strange Gods*, and by Lewis in *Paleface*, a 1929 attack on primitivism, including Lawrence's 'fetish of promiscuity and hysterical paeans to all that is "dark and strange"'. This was the era, too, when, not without controversy, the Central Asian theosophy of Gurdjieff, another son of Tartary, was making inroads into modernist circles. This influence calls for further study, running as it did to figures like Katherine Mansfield, Orage, Ouspensky (whose lectures were heard by Malcolm Lowry), Olgivanna Lloyd Wright (the architect's wife); a lesbian circle in Paris including Jane Heap, Margaret Anderson and Djuna Barnes; Diaghilev (fascinated by Gurdjieff's dances); Harlem renaissance figures like Jean Toomer and Zora Neale Hurston; Huxley, Heard, Isherwood, Dodge, John Cowper Powys, Daumal and possibly Brancusi.[36]

Not all 'anti-modern vitalism' had been 'dark and strange'. Algernon Blackwood's 1911 *The Centaur* (MacMillan) is a for once attractive piece. A mildly programmatic, anarcho-communitarian compendium of prewar mythology relating to the Simple Life, the *Urwelt* and *Naturmensch*, this non-extremist fantasy is set in a Caucasus like Gurdjieff's, offering a Russo-Asiatic variant on the Tartary motif, long before that became contentious. Intent on a new Dionysian account of consciousness and cosmos, the author exhibits the mindset which sent early twentieth-century spiritual seekers 'in search of the miraculous', to quote an Ouspensky title. Blackwood – a figure not usually classed as a modernist, who never visited Ascona, though he did belong to the Golden Dawn – reveals the extent to which, as a provocation to future advocates of 'order', neo-Romantic syncretism, however polite, had become the common currency of anti-civilizational renewal. *The Centaur*'s sources are openly advertised: constant references to Gustav Fechner's psycho-physics and James's pluralistic universe; to Myers's concept of the subliminal self and Flournoy's *imagination creatrice*; to Bucke's 'cosmic consciousness' and Carpenter on the shortcomings of civilized life.

The novel's mood is neo-pagan, with Orientalist touches thrown in. In the shape of an anonymous, primordial 'Russian', Blackwood's hero encounters a fragment of *anima mundi* during a sea voyage to the Eastern Mediterranean. Of his Celtic hero Blackwood writes,

> Over the cities of the world he heard the demon of Civilization sing its song of terror and desolation ... Its music of destruction shook the nations. He saw the millions dance. And mid the bewildering ugly thunder of that sound few could catch the small sweet voice played by the Earth upon the little pipes of Pan ... the fluting call of Nature to the Simple Life – which is the Inner.

Besides the world-soul of late Romantic *Naturphilosophie*, the work enlists other by now familiar motifs like the Earth's 'vast collective consciousness', the racial unconscious, the second self or double, and the Vedantic Self. Like the nymphs and satyrs of Arnold Böcklin, Franz von Stuck and other *Jugendstil* painters, Blackwood's Pan (otherwise the 'Russian', and the Centaur of the novel's title) is the pantheistic 'all' of 'cosmic consciousness', an emblem of primal energy, the ensemble adding up to a life-reforming riposte to over-civilized modernity.

Prewar neo-Romanticism of this type, where a world grown so much bigger under high-imperial globalization was most readily imaged in terms of myth, offered raw material for the animation of 'Strange Gods' galore. (New gods had likewise arisen from the Hellenistic globalization: Greco-Babylonian, Indo-Greek, Greco-Egyptian and so on.) Adding the era's tribal and Asian borrowings, a multi-lateral 'changing of the gods', its function one of breathing 'life' into depleted 'civilization' – a Dionysian rebirth – was arguably afoot from the turn of the century. Like Theosophy, the anti-Western movements involved had an international reach, pooling their resources. Thus, the Decadent poet Jules Laforgue took his Buddhism from Germany, and, like Carpenter in England, was drawn to the American Whitman, whom he translated into French. Granted the contagious attractions of a neo-Romantic imaginary where peasants, natural aristocrats, chivalry, mysticism, the middle ages, pagan Europe, sexuality, nature, children, Asiatics, *Urmenschen* and American Indians were accredited with redemptive and restorationist power, it is hardly surprising that the pre-First World War counter-cosmology saw a global diffusion, inspiring 'new' men and women to radical change.

Shared desiderata were exalted accounts of identity and community, also a glamorously rewritten past and millennial future, both semi-pagan or folkloric in colour. To supply these needs, which were felt with equal acuteness in Tagore's 'real' (no longer Anglicist) India and Yanagita's 'mountain' (no longer modern) Japan, much the same resources were enlisted, regardless of the precise local 'folk-soul' involved (Chapter 2). Along with the *Natur-* and *Lebensphilosophie* movements and their art-world reflections (Arts and Crafts, *Jugendstil*, Art Nouveau), these included Celticism (not just Irish) and a Theosophy that flirted with medieval heresy, socialism, feminism, mystical racialism, vegetarianism and 'secret' (outlandish or outlying) Europe. Fuelling attempts to forge a new auratic idiom for a new post-liberal and post-European order, the pre-modern repressed was certainly returning – even if its roadmap corresponded less to recognizable, empirical realties than to apocalyptic meta-worlds (and auras) beyond positivism's reach.

By the twenties, far-reaching distinctions between the old and new worldviews had emerged. On the side of the threatened world-picture – a 'regular', but for neo-Romantics outmoded, nomos that was later caricatured in 'from Plato to NATO' terms – stood Latinity, Descartes, Newton, orthodox Christianity (answered, among Traditionalists, by eternalist Asia), Renaissance humanism, *ancien régime* hierarchies and proprieties, Aristotelian mimesis, Euclidean geometry, 'synthesis', a limited fortress Europe and rationalist common sense. On the side of the new consciousness and its remagical-ized though unpredictable cosmos (an 'irregular', futural nomos) stood Nietzsche, Bergson, Freud, Einstein, the 'fourth dimension', Cubism, Expressionism, German and Russian irrationalism – and the Nordic-Asian Orient – conspiring against structure, order, sanity, reason, a three-dimensional universe and what remained of the Christian heavens. One sign of pro-Western resilience in France was a spate of neo-Catholic conversions between 1890 and 1914. Including Claudel, Ferdinand Brunetiere, Francis Jammes, Ernest Psichari, Charles Peguy and Jacques Maritain, this development, not far from Massis's own position, spelt ostensible opposition to (but sometimes complicity with) the Nordic-Asian Mythos and the *nouvelle gnose.*[37]

Related to Guénon's 'exoteric' recommendation of Catholicism (not his preferred 'esoteric' Sufism or Vedanta) as the only practicable source of a Traditional religion for the benighted West, such prewar tergiversations match Coomaraswamy's journey from neo-Romantic anarchism towards Tradition. They also anticipate Eliot's late twenties conversion to Anglo-Catholicism (at which point he disowned *The Waste Land*, reviewed on publication as a 'Theosophical tract'), as well as Berdyaev's trajectory, from Silver Age Marxism and Theosophy to post-war Russian Orthodoxy. The complaint on the Traditionalist and neo-conservative right was a variant on Nordau's: the 'degeneracy' charge, aimed at neo-Romantic 'hysteria' and 'mysticism', mixed with the older, Barruelian accusation of anti-throne and altar conspiracy. As voiced by Massis, this complaint was levelled at the neo-Romantic Orient's threat to any coherent picture of man and the world.

The *Défence*'s roll-call of enemies includes Rolland, Hesse, Keyserling, Tagore, Gandhi, Okakura, Confucius, Lao-Tzu, Dostoyevsky and Tolstoy, the last for his correspondence with Hindus, Buddhists and Muslims. His conservatism notwithstanding, Coomaraswamy is also attacked. Hostile to the type of syncretism attested by Lawrence and Fuchs, Massis scorns attempts to dress up St John of the Cross and St Francis as Oriental *bhiksus*, or to find a *Bhagavad Gita* in Aquinas's *Summa*. Heresy is detected in the 'semi-gnostic cosmogony' of Russia's 'godmanhood' sects, which are compared to the Self-worship of 'Oriental theosophy'. Max Stirner's anarchist nihilism is dismissed by association with Buddhist Madhyamaka, and a Taoist taint is found in Bergsonism, Haeckelian monism and Herbert Spencer's evolutionary philosophy. Special contempt is reserved for Spengler's 'catastrophism', with its determination to substitute healthy, life-affirming barbarians for an enervated West on the world-historical stage. From the above, Confucianism in co-option and Guénon's correspondent Coomaraswamy ironically stood for an anti-modern orderliness close to the reaction Massis personally craved.

The Jewish liberal, Julien Benda, who invented the term 'treason of the clerks' and characterized Bergsonism as 'intellectual Boulangisme' (a radical right species of subversive energetics, that is to say), denigrated the same mystical intuitionist and political vitalist trends, calling them 'Carthaginism' or 'Belphegorism', the last after an obscure Carthaginian god. But liberals in general seem to have been uninterested in 'defending the West'. Indeed, Massis would most likely have teamed up with his enemies in any campaign by bourgeois liberalism to claim the West as its own.

During the French debate, in a 1924 review of Rudolph Kayser's *Die Zeit ohne Mythos* (*L'Époque sans mythe*) the slogan of a 'New Myth' was discussed. This led to talk of the 'New Man', a prime example of which was Rolland's neo-Vedantic 'total Self', matched by Malevich's recasting of Vivekananda (Chapter 3). The theme of this Self's primal energy led back to Bergsonian vitalism and Nietzsche's hyperactive *Übermensch*. In sum, conservative horror was left to contemplate a primordialist threat to the classical/Christian underpinnings of its worldview, from quarters which claimed proximity to the energetic matrix of the universe at large. Indeed, even if the rebellious party had no single spokesman for its 'new paradigm' in the shape of some period Fritjof Capra, its physicists Asiaticized themselves, turning to Taoism, Tagore or Vedanta, to corroborate their new, 'processive/nonsubstantialist' model of the world.[38] Nomos was not only subject to modernity's shocks, it also fell hostage, among modernists, to competing, backward- and forward-utopian views.

Nor were the adherents of the 'catastrophic' Nordic-Asian mythology merely content with overturning the once predictable outer world. Adding Cartesian insult to Newtonian injury, they also bypassed the rational *cogito*, to equate their new 'unconscious' with the atavistic mind of primitives or the oceanic all-consciousness of Asia. After hailing 'our magnificent Buddhist renaissance', with its pagoda near Berlin, three reviews, and 2500 publications in one year, a German Buddhist character in Paul Morand's 1927 novel *Bouddha Vivant* says of his compatriots, 'we alone, who invented the unconscious, can understand the Orient, "this unconscious of the world"'.[39] Morand's irony implies that Asia was not so much a proud imperial possession of Britain and France as a colony of a Romantic German ideology that was intent on settling scores with the West. Though Germany never had an empire to speak of, this had not deterred the *furor orientalis* of German Indology and *Orientalistik* under the Kaiserreich.

Four points arising from the Asiaticist offensive against the West, all relevant to the contested modelling of the universe, could be stressed. First, there was the perceived Eastern threat to autonomous individuality (the *moi* of the twenties debate); second, a comparable threat to the common-sense structure, or 'self', of the universe at large; third (arising from these two points), a pranasophical/neo-mesmeric tendency to rewrite the self and universe in terms of unseen energies and forces; fourth, a related tendency to represent those energies in terms of 'daimonic images', drawn from a colonial syncretic reconfiguration of the imaginal realm.

Taking all four points together, it could be said that, having established a kind of 'emptiness' of self and other on the first two 'Cartesian' and 'Newtonian' counts – in relation to the current crisis of subjectivity and cosmo-conception, that is to say – the 'extraordinary' Asiaticist mythology went on to promote the idea of a second, subtle-energetic reality, not unlike what, on Enlightenment, becomes the *Sambhogakaya* realm (a purified 'in-between' space) in Tibetan Buddhism. It could also be argued that, much as New Agers now invoke the quantum energy world against the Newtonian universe, this concept of a second, Dionysian or Saktist, energetic reality was tactically deployed by neo-Romantic modernists to overturn the first, more orderly and structured, classical world and self as a 'catastrophic' prelude to utopian rebirth. Albeit purloined and refigured, sacrality was now a thoroughly polemical and political matter: not that acute politicization and subordination to apocalyptic agendas was likely to induce any 'withdrawn', hide-and-seek god to reveal his face.

Tantra in Bloomsbury

As the novelist Mulk Raj Anand's reminiscences show, Tantra, a forbidden subject for Victorian Indologists, was known to the Bloomsbury group.[40] A Romantic drawn to the 'repressed', Anand conflated Tantra, Lawrence and Freud:

> Reason, I felt, led to abstractions as in the old classical arts. Romanticism led to the unconscious as in the new vital works of … Lawrence, where the depths were being plumbed … I wanted to liberate the unconscious via … Tantric thought and dig down into the depths.[41]

As he explains to Catherine Carswell and Nancy Cunard,

> there are quite a few diggings down of our sages which anticipate what Freud has found … And Lawrence's search for the man–woman connection in the ecstasy of sex was already practiced by … secret cults. An Irish judge in Calcutta, Sir John Woodroffe [who had an Indian Tantric guru], has gone into these practices – called Tantra. He has written a book, *Sakti-Sakta* … Seems the Hindus seized upon the power of woman as a fountain of fire in the Kundalini – at the base of the spine … In the

man–woman union … Tantra seeks to lift the relationship above the egos of the couple. Of course, Lawrence is questing his own way.

So was Jung, who based his 1932 Kundalini Yoga seminar on Woodroffe's works.

At a comment by Cunard about 'phallic consciousness', Carswell resorts to early psycho-babble: 'Lawrence seems both fascinated and repelled by the mystique … He wants to displace the ego and get to a new centre. A kind of higher circle which may include the whole unconscious … To be immersed in obscure channels.' Sounding like a mix of Conrad's *Heart of Darkness* and Du Bois's *Dark Princess*, Cunard then remarks, 'This exhilaration my dear – and horror – of Lawrence is almost everywhere amongst us! … He likes the natives and is yet frightened of their myths.' Carswell's 'I know he is against our small-minded white ego … And he wants to turn his back on the West', is followed by Cunard's 'maybe, he too retains the fear of the dark gods like his enemy T.S. Eliot'.[42]

The talking points in Anand's conversation with the Woolfs show some Orientalist learning – Leonard had been a colonial officer in Ceylon – foreshadowing sixties interests: Shakti, Kundalini, Kali, the erotic sculptures at Konarak, 'yogic hocus-pocus', Tibetan yabyum, Indian androgyny, the reconciliation of opposites, Virginia's own *Orlando*, and 'the Regent's Park Ashram of Doctor Ramji', a one-time terrorist like Aurobindo who can raise the serpent-fire.[43] With its allusions to the 'surrealistic' myth of Kali, Shiva's phallus, Picasso and voodoo, Frazerian ghouls in Arabia, 'the bull on the Mohenjodaro seal', 'gargoyles in Christian art', images 'charged with intense feeling', folk magic, cave-paintings, yantras and Mondrian, Anand's conversation with Herbert Read and Eric Gill reads like a compendium for modernist myth-makers.[44] A case of the colonial syncretic gone mad, no tricks were missed in this exoticist foraging. Anti-assimilative indigenism like that of Du Bois and Nussimbaum figures too: Uday Shankar (Ravi's brother) notes how 'Our parents despised our ancient culture because the English said it was obscure.' Agreeing that 'European style choreography' can be blended with that of 'the old cultures', he suggests that 'we have to become Indians first'.[45] The same had been true of Aurobindo and Gandhi.

Sporting a new imperial-syncretic self at odds with 'the small-minded white ego' – Anand notes Woolf's venom about the 'tables, chairs and haberdashery' of Arnold Bennett, John Galsworthy and

H. G. Wells – Bloomsbury Orientalism involved play-acting for what Lewis called the 'revolutionary rich'.[46]

> She [Waley's companion, Beryl de Zoete] sat on a dais with crossed legs like … Buddha. Arthur Waley sat on a cushion, Japanese style, on the floor. 'I would like to sit Hindu fashion on the floor', Mr Keynes said … 'Though I can't sit like a yogi – cross-legged'. 'Shankar will teach you', Beryl de Zoete said, 'Tea'.[47]

Along with a very British Dundee cake, 'tea', or lunch at Schmidt's with T. S. Eliot, figures in most of Anand's politically anodyne adventures in Bloomsbury. As for period Orientalism's less aristocratic echelons, de Zoete cattily remarks, 'I have been to Madras and seen middle-class ladies dancing Bharat Natyam [a Kathakali-like form of dance] in the Theosophical Society. They are very exalted people and one of your great women, Annie Besant [who 'radicalized' Anand], is the presiding deity there.'[48] If haberdashery was the loser in Bloomsbury spirit-wars, the winner is less clear: possibly tea and Dundee cake.

Genuine Fake: The 'New Jersey Hindoo' Ruth St Denis

Outside spirit-wars and colliding worldviews, phantasmagoria, sex and syncretism added up to a successful and entertaining formula – not just in privileged quarters. Soon after Loie Fuller's invention of skirt-dancing, the American danseuse 'Little Egypt' modelled her 'hootchy cootch' on belly-dancing seen at the 1893 Columbian exhibition, next door to the World Parliament of Religions. Profane happily mingled with sacred. With a succession of 'Salome dancers' and vamps like Theda Bara (allegedly an anagram for 'Arab Death'), exoticist dancing caught on: even the Buddha became an accessory of the 'Chinese Virgin' act of Lili St Cyr, a 1940s stripper.[49] Equally, 'high' met 'low' in 'no-brow' with the Literary Stripper, Gypsy Rose Lee, the aristocratic act of her thirties heyday leading to house-sharing in Brooklyn with W. H. Auden, Benjamin Britten, Carston McCullers, Paul and Jane Bowles, as well as cultural chit-chat with Aaron Copland, Salvador Dali and gamelan enthusiast Colin McPhee.[50]

Eileen Garret, 'medium of the modernists', was similarly well connected. So was Ruth St Denis (1879–1968), a dancer less well known than Wigman, Isadora Duncan and Martha Graham, all of whom, unlike St Denis, danced the secret dimensions of their local folk-soul (Duncan visited Ascona; Graham, who believed that 'dance is the hidden language of the soul', was drawn to Amerindian mysteries). Intent on dancing her own Orient, St Denis knew the right people and read the right books. She was also a shameless vulgarian. Fascinating for her mix of sources, one woman's plausible, non-axe-grinding syncretism, St Denis ingeniously conflated 'high' and 'low'. The Denishawn troupe she formed with husband Ted Shawn featured in early silent movies, not least the lavish Babylonian sequence in D. W. Griffith's 1916 *Intolerance*. Where does modernism end and the early twentieth-century vernacular begin? Given their shared exotico-occult, high-imperial background and histrionic flair, that question is not easily answered.

With her New Thought-affiliated form of dance, the gifted *bricoleur* and autodidact in St Denis subscribed to the occult beliefs of the pre-First World War 'mystic movements' and the 'twenties' 'ultramoderns'. These were intermixed with a garish Coney Island exoticism. Some early sights and travels left a deep impression: an 1880s visit to Imre Kiralfy's Neronian extravaganza, *The Burning of Rome*, staged at a Manhattan Barnum and Bailey Circus; a trip to see *Egypt through the Centuries*, a pageant mounted in 1892 by the same Hungarian-born impresario (a poor man's Wagner or Diaghilev) at the Jersey Palisades amusement park; a visit to the 1900 Paris Exposition, where, besides the usual 'native villages' and South East Asian entertainments, St Denis saw performances by Loie Fuller and her Japanese associate, Sada Yacco, so acquiring a taste for *Japonaiserie* and vitalist Art Nouveau dance.[51] As an inspiration for her 1910 *Egypta* (by then she had read Wallace Budge and James Breasted on ancient Egypt), in the Buffalo of 1903 she became spell-bound by a poster with a picture of Isis, advertising 'Egyptian Deities' cigarettes. Finally, in 1904, there came the Coney Island episode: her beguilement by a mocked-up 'Streets of Delhi', complete with snake charmers, fakirs and nautch girls.[52]

Where her dance suggests 'myth and ritual' – a meeting of 'sex, art, religion, and spectacle' – it reflects that fascination with the Dionysian, orgiastic and daimonic which pervades the dance and drama criticism of figures like Nietzsche, Jane Harrison and Havelock Ellis.[53] A devotee of her mother's Christian Science beliefs, St Denis read Kant and Baker Eddy at an early age, along with Mabel

Collins's *The Idyll of the White Lotus*, a Theosophical romance. With its combination of Swedenborg, yoga and Francois Delsarte's theories, the vitalist/Symbolist dance system of one Genevieve Stebbins, who equated 'life' with the 'ether' and, like MacGregor and Moina Mathers, devised a pantomime called 'The Myth of Isis', was an early inspiration as well.[54] A reader of Hearn and acquaintance of Carpenter and Ellis, St Denis was introduced to Vedanta in England by Swami Paramananda in 1908. Claude Bragdon, translator of Ouspensky and Theosophist architect (he produced designs for a Denishawn colony), was also a friend.[55]

The purist Inayat Khan, after accompanying her on tour in the USA in 1911, refused to grant St Denis a certificate of proficiency in Hindu dance. 'Caruso of India no longer with Ruth St. Denis', read the headlines, when the Sufi sage (perhaps disillusioned from accompanying Mata Hari a couple of times as well) refused to play second fiddle to one who, granting all was not 'theologically accurate', admitted that 'at no time ... have I been sufficiently the scholar or sufficiently interested [!] to imitate or try to reproduce any oriental ritual or actual dance'.[56] As true of Gauguin or Artaud as St Denis – who, like the Salome dancer Maud Allan and the *Ballets Russes* artiste Anna Pavlova before her, blithely introduced the East to the East in 1925 – the 'fourth world remake' principle is clear from this remark, with its assumption that the Orientalist imagination is free to devise its own rules.

Although St Denis visited the Ramakrishna Math near Calcutta during her 1925 tour of the East, Theosophical interests predominated: a trip to the Society's headquarters at Adhyar, and, presumably knowing in advance what the Orient betokened, assiduous group-study of Ouspensky's *Tertium Organon* with her troupe. In line with the Ouspenskyite interests of such coevals as Waldo Frank, Hart Crane, Rexroth and Gordon Onslow-Ford, further readings of Ouspensky (and Eddy and the *Gita*) followed during her tour of South East Asia. During the thirties, her estranged (and yet more eclectic) husband having now joined Katherine Dreier's cultural empire, St Denis founded a 'Society of Spiritual Arts' for her dancers, at which Swami Nikhilananda spoke once or twice. She went onto an affair with the Chinese poet Sum Nung Au-Young, who taught her the rudiments of Taoism from 1934. Despite his Traditionalism, Coomaraswamy was an ally, Hofmannsthal and Count Harry Kessler friends, Rilke's occultist patroness, Princess

Marie von Thurn und Taxis, an acquaintance: natural or titled aristocrats all.

For all its provincial origins, St Denis's cosmopolitan, syncretic/ spiritual trajectory, which spans prewar and interwar, is similar to that of other neo-Romantic modernists. Like Nijinsky – in 1900 a dance troupe from Bangkok visited St Petersburg, whence a photograph of Nijinsky in 'Siamese' pose – she also displays a typical attraction to spectacular, Imre Kiralfy-like, exoticist pastiche.[57] Equally, being carefree if not careless about her use of sources, her work ignores highbrow–lowbrow distinctions, such as were crucial to theorists like Adorno. Nevertheless, granted 'lifestyle' modernism's lionization of Chaplin, music hall and Josephine Baker, this most likely mattered less to the average modernist than our overly solemn and theory-laden histories make out.[58] Add that the plebeian punter could presumably see the joke when Kiralfy's sometime collaborator, P. T. Barnum, exhibited a white elephant called 'The White of Asia', and the Orientalist vernacular starts to look very similar to the exoticism of the *beau monde*.[59] By comparison with St Denis's effortless 'no brow' syncretism – in contrast to Europe's fussy secret societies and esoteric orders, this had the advantage of being able to mimic older American meta-religion's 'magic worldview' – the countercultural sixties look unreflective and 'posy', and the New Age like a bad joke.

Eventually to appear onstage with Tagore in a Broadway theatre in 1930, after being invited during her Indian trip to teach at that bastion of the aristocratic-folk ideology, Santiniketan, St Denis discovered her 'real' India among the native villages on show at Coney Island, along with the roundabouts and big wheel. With the *Ballets Russes* designer Lev Bakst, dubbed an 'Egyptian-Persian-Assyrian-Nordic plagiarist' by the Futurist Enrico Prampolini – like Gauguin, Bakst is a myth-maker of the 'interchangeable Other', in so many words – the sources of his exoticism may have been more learned and less demotic.[60] But religio-cultural signs having worked loose, in transit, from original signifieds, and fancy from reality, the point to be stressed is that simulacra of the colonial periphery's seductions were now at a premium, as an enhancement to a generalized, 'aristo-plebeian' culture of ornament and display. Without such a context, the imperial occult-exotic could only wither away.

In *Soaring*, a memoir of her experiences during the Denishawn Indian tour, the 18-year-old dancer Jane Sherman shows touching naiveté, at odds with St Denis's high-minded determination to create a genuine fake. From a Sinhalese Theosophist persuaded of the truth of Besant and Leadbeater's 'fancies' about Indian religion, she hears of a spooky 'Krishna-somebody' who is to act as the mouthpiece of Christ; of a bust of Zarathustra seen at Adhyar, she writes to her mother, 'who was he?'; of St Denis's 'virtual' Indian dance, she records the regret of the *Lahore Sunday Times* that 'the soul of the East' has been captured better by foreigners than Indians; Tagore and the Nizam of Hyderabad are both convinced of the authenticity of St Denis's dance, the first to the point of inviting her to lecture at his university; the said Nizam and the Sultan of Java are *much* more interesting than ordinary locals; fancy-dress primitivist fashion, the troupe takes to wearing Indian dress; Ted Shawn and dancer Charles Weidman strike up 'little Buddha' postures for the camera at Borobodur; Miss Ruth is (unnecessarily) nervous about presenting her Indian dances, never having seen the real thing.[61] With her finger-on-the-pulse mix of showbiz extravaganza and 'serious' art, and, after Smith on modernism, combination of exotic form with occult content, Adorno would have scorned St Denis. But like Ball's 'Grand Hotel Metaphysics', modernist syncretism had many mansions, each with its own décor – politically neutral for once (or 'Hollywood liberal' at most) in St Denis's case.[62]

Taoism and Buddhism apart (Chapter 3), modernism's Japan–China axis has yet to be discussed. Together with forerunners from the 'Pound-era' vogue for Chinoiserie and Japonaiserie, the 'second' post-Second World War Japonisme, with its reinvented Zen, will be my next theme. Though Theosophical syncretism continues to provide a baseline, another change of décor set in with this Japanoid turn.

5

'ZEN' IN THE SECOND ABSTRACTION

Pacific Axis Art

Zen stands in a similar relationship to late modernism as Theosophy to early modernism. Like its European counterpart, *Art Informel*, American Abstract Expressionism was a mutation from Surrealism, itself an esoteric movement with Decadent/Symbolist roots.[1] Their syncretism more Jungian and Theosophical than that of their source, Americans adapted Surrealism to their own needs. New England Transcendentalism, Melville, Frazer, Campbell, 'Oriental thought', cosmogenesis (a Blavatskyite, not a 'Buddhist' category), Amerindian primitivism, 'early man': frequently encouraged by Mellon/Bollingen patronage, all figure in the Abstract Expressionist Mythos.[2] The artists involved, John Cage apart, were alienated from modernity, politically anarchist 'modern men in search of a soul', inclined to set 'myth' to impossible redemptive tasks.

Surrealism was less earnest: and where it displayed a typical early modernist concern with the 'the forest of symbols', the new abstraction attempts to pass beyond that into the 'ground of being'. In this it was aided by Zen – and by Meister Eckhart, an honorary Oriental, thanks to co-option by Coomaraswamy and Suzuki. Added to the new art's other 'polymythic' resources (primitivism, Jung and so on), the persistence of older Theosophical/Indianist ideas led to overblown syncretic fusions, at odds with Zen's simplicity. The result was a reinvented Zen based on modernizing lay sources, and rife with preconceptions drawn from earlier myth-making. Largely without assistance from fussy 'esoteric orders', the early modernist 'mystical' had found a new disguise.

Where New York faced Europe, and eventually India across the Atlantic, America's West Coast, a truly 'new world', looked across the Pacific to Japan and East Asia. The first, post-1860 *Japonisme* had been international, its adaptation of *Ukiyo-e* ('floating world') prints matching the era's sense of flux. Against this cosmopolitanism, there are signs of experimental West Coast culture striking up a 'special relationship' with Pacific Rim Asia – in 1907 Fenollosa contributed to a periodical intriguingly entitled *Pacific Era* – such that, by the fifties, a 'Pacific school' of art could be canvassed, the engine of a second *Japonisme*.[3] Anglo-American Imagism, which included Chinese models thanks to his widow's 1913 bequest of Fenollosa's papers to Pound, was transitional between the two *Japonismes*. So was Arthur Wesley Dow, an art teacher who systematized Fenollosa's writings on East Asian art, to influence Georgia O' Keeffe.[4]

By 1946 Mark Tobey was eyeing up East Asia and Zen as elements for an 'indigenous style': 'America … is placed geographically to lead in this understanding [of Asia], and if … she has constantly looked towards Europe, today she must assume her position, Janus-faced, toward Asia.'[5] Tobey's Pacific axis, perhaps traceable to Fenollosa's day, infuriated Clement Greenberg, the New York king-maker critic:

> [Franz] Kline's apparent allusions to Chinese or Japanese calligraphy encouraged the cant, already started by Tobey … about … Oriental influence on 'abstract expressionism'. This country's possession of a Pacific coast offered a handy … idea … to explain the … fact that Americans were at last producing a[n] … art important enough to be influencing the [Europeans] … .[N]ot one of the … 'abstract expressionists' … has felt more than cursory interest in Oriental art. The sources of their art lie entirely in the West.[6]

Greenberg's 1955 claims are false. Pre-eminently usable for (supposed) 'starting from scratch' with Cage, the zero-point of Zen's 'ordinary' Enlightenment offered a *tabula rasa* on which a new, postwar American cosmogony could be built. In rivalry with Europe, too, the 'Suchness' variety of Enlightenment, with its 'collapsed', single-state worldview (no labyrinthine 'planes') could bolster 'you get what you see' claims to a simplified monism and unmediated perception, such as older 'forest of symbols' modernisms were too convoluted to allow.[7] Not that Abstract Expressionism necessarily wore East Asian influences on its sleeve, whatever its conceptual debts. Of these, Bert Winther writes, 'The Oriental Thought generation ... sought to pump meaning and profundity into abstract art by drawing on ideals ... associated with East Asian culture such as detachment, passivity to nature, spontaneity, the void, transiency, chance, and ... rejection of rationalism.'[8] Like Theosophical 'secret doctrine', the aegis under which, with some influences from Transcendentalism and America's older 'magic worldview', Zen was largely received, the 'profundity' was a syncretic hybrid.

Countering the trans-Atlantic prospect from New York, in 1951 Tobey spoke from Seattle of 'my land with its great East–West parallels'. In 1957, as European influences ebbed, he noticed 'the growth of "an indigenous style" and ... increasing awareness of "the Japanese aesthetic"'. Of Zen's contribution to this, Tobey disingenuously stated, 'What hold this philosophy will have on our national culture, how indigenous it might become as part of our aesthetic remains to be seen.'[9] America's 'possession of a Pacific coast' *had* entailed the growth, since the twenties, of an experimental/non-European 'indigenous style', with Janus-faced West Coast / East Asian characteristics, including awareness of Zen. Several American artists and musicians had undertaken an East Asian *voyage en Orient*; and Frank Lloyd Wright's architecture was imbued with the 'Japanese aesthetic' that had captivated the turn-of-the-century world.

At odds with such earlier, spontaneous and non-chauvinist intercultural activity (see Bernard Leach as quoted in Chapter 1), Tobey's East Asia looks like a pawn in an American game. Though 'anti-imperialist' America could not openly boast an Asian jewel in its crown, thanks to military occupation lasting until 1952, Japan was effectively a US colony. Like British India or French Indo-China under high empire – albeit without the ornamental trappings (graduated cosmologies, initiatic pecking order, World Plans) of old empire's Indo-Tibetan extravaganzas – Japan was accordingly open to low-key waves of cultural appropriation by the imperial power. Amidst increasing US cultural separatism, some innocence was lost, especially as the Cage-influenced, neo-avant-garde art modes of the 'American (half) century' supervened on those of the older, high-imperial globalization.[10] After 1960, assimilation of the new counter-knowledges propagated by that globalization became erratic and trivialized: forfeiting an earlier interdependence, scholarship went one way and the arts and spirituality another.

East Asian Influences on Pre-forties Modernism

Within earlier twentieth-century *Japonisme*, overtones of sudden Enlightenment's doctrine of 'original face' were absorbed through literary and artistic, if not philosophical, channels. Pound's 1915 *Cathay*, a collection of Chinese translations, was a landmark for modernism's sudden Enlightenment-related 'epiphanic' strain.[11] Though the story of Pound's discovery of a 'new Greece in China' is well known, it only acquires its true, bookish significance when related to Arrowsmith's British Museum 'reading-room modernism', as introduced in Chapter 1. Standing in a similar relationship to the early modernists' picture of East Asia as Whitman and Theosophy to their image of India, Pound's source, Fenollosa, also inspired Yeats's Noh plays. France and America were rich in this East Asian exoticism too. Besides 'Yankees in Japan' (Edward Morse, Bigelow, Lowell, Hearn), Claudel, Debussy, Victor Segalen and the now forgotten French imitators of haiku detailed in 1927 by William Schwarz deserve note.[12] So do Hans Bethge's 1907 translations from Judith Gautier's 1867 *Le Livre de Jade*, Mahler's source for *The Song of the Earth*.

The 'Fenollosa–Dow' art method and vague mysticism aside, little in this exoticism resembles the second, strongly masculinist *Japonisme*. Prefiguring the Zen vogue, there were a few interwar stirrings – some even older, to go by the 1909 and 1915 'discoveries' of Zen by Bernard Leach and Yeats. These included Theosophist Nancy Wilson Ross's 1938/9 lecture on Zen and Dada in Seattle; Leach and Tobey's 1934–35 East Asian tour; Julius Bissier's calligraphic and Orientalist studies from 1927 with Sinologist Ernst Grosse (Bissier met Tobey at Ascona); Rudolph Otto's 1934 preface to a book of Zen extracts; and Andre Masson's 1930 introduction to Zen through Kuni Matsuo, organizer of the first, 1932–33 Surrealist exhibition in Japan. In Masson's words, Matsuo 'came to see me in 1930 … he remarked … "I would like to speak to you about Zen because I think it would interest you." I had never heard of it. I was only aware of Buddhism in general terms.'[13]

Masson's response harks from a time when Far Eastern exoticism, however 'fairy-tale' and otherworldly, still lacked any 'profound' metaphysical thrust (Winther, above). Prior to Suzuki's missionary efforts, Zen's profile was insignificant: from the East Asian systems, Taoism, Shinto, Bushido and Shingon most attracted earlier modernists. Suzuki wrote an essay, 'The Zen Sect of Buddhism', in 1906: but his national messianic identifications of 'universal' Zen with the 'Japanese genius' only began with his first, 1927 series of *Essays in Zen Buddhism*. With its literary, pictorial and animistic-folkloric emphases, the earlier Far Eastern exoticism, both European and American, was more ornate than the Zen vogue, a sign of cultural exuberance in an 'old imperial' age.

Suzuki Zen

The leanings of the Kyoto School to which Suzuki belonged were modernist (Jamesian, Nietzschean, Heideggerian) and right-wing. Many Kyoto School members studied in Nazi Germany with Heidegger, who never acknowledged his Eastern debts, while one of them, Kuki Shuzo, introduced Heidegger's works to Sartre.[14] The ensuing existentialist fashion accordingly had the stamp of a right/ left crossover, as did the later poststructuralist vogue. Another crossover, Suzuki's hyper-nationalist version of Zen, as popularized by the neo-Theosophical Jungian Eranos circuit, was adopted by late modernists who, like Sartre, professed to be left-wing.

Suzuki's career spans Gilded Age America (1897–1909), a Japanese interwar and wartime period and the American fifties and sixties (1950–66). His early American phase, marked by Swedenborgian interests, shows no designs on exporting Zen to the West. Redolent of the mystical racialism seen in Chapter 4, his middle, Japanese period saw the publication of his *Nihonjinron* ('unique Japanese national character') study, *Zen and Japanese Culture*, in 1938. Finally, he taught the complex interdependencies of the *Avatamsaka Sutra* in fifties New York, while further promoting 'Zen'. Suzuki was a philosopher layman, not a Zen master. His welcome in post-war America is best compared to that of other rightists, like Eliade and Stravinsky: in the academy and art world, semi-formalist appeals to 'music as music' and 'timeless' myth or Zen served to cover politically suspect interwar tracks.

Cage's co-option of Suzuki was one thing, that of the Beats and Abstract Expressionists another. Developing David Doris on the 'big, fast and unshaven' gestures of 'American-Type' painting as 'the automatic writing of the American unconscious, vast and spontaneous, but always bound to its territory', the initial, pre-Cage construction of Zen arguably represented a wedding between two 'folk-souls', the American and the Japanese.[15] Some such fusion between two forms of national romanticism/indigenism is a potentially useful key to Zen's role in Abstract Expressionism and Beat writing: 'Oriental mysticism' could anyway consort with 'Amerindian mysteries', as we saw in Chapter 2 (the same combination is found in Lawrence's *The Plume Serpent*). 'Folk-soul' mergers had in fact long been an option, thanks to the interchangeable, trans-ethnic wisdom-lore carried by the 'extraordinary' Nordic-Asian Mythos: prior, that is, to any designs by that Mythos on 'ordinary' Japanese Enlightenment. Hence the addition of one more wisdom culture to that myth's prismatic spectrum of possibilities – whereby, as it were, Emerson's originally Indianist all-seeing eyeball came to wear Japanese spectacles – could be just another tactical syncretism, unlikely to offend in a folksy climate where Zen purism was yet to be born. Ad Reinhard's anti-'neo-Zen-Bohemian', mid-fifties drift towards a dark and obscure form of some such purism paralleled Cage's debunking of Abstract Expressionism's transcendental and gestural leanings: by that stage an easy target.

This is to suggest that Zen's initial American reception was not attended by austere and minimalist pieties: more by an expansive transcendentalism, related to the 'Asiaticism' decried by Massis. The last was part of a larger 'Bergsonian controversy', where a world driven by 'process' and 'flux', forces central to neo-Zen cosmology, enraged classicists and conservatives: but not fascists or countercultural leftists, who often swapped ideas. Here, then, we might have expected to find, if not a sequel to the twenties East–West quarrel, at least accusations of 'un-American activity', as voiced by US conservatives in the related field of Jungianism. The longer background to Zen's reception in Emerson's and Whitman's 'respectable' Orientalism perhaps explains silence on this score. There was, admittedly, the 1948 scandal of the 'guru-letters': correspondence between the then presidential candidate, Henry Wallace, and his former Theosophist teacher, Roerich.[16] But neither Zen nor Suzuki provoked any immediate anti-Oriental outcry: equally, Woodrow Wilson's daughter had headed for Aurobindo's ashram in 1938, apparently without disgrace (Wilson himself consulted the psychic Edgar Cayce in the White House in 1918 or 1919).

Conservative outrage on Pound's 1949 receipt of the Bollingen Prize for Poetry was more vociferous. Here, the trail led to the 'fascist' Jung through his pupils, Mary and Paul Mellon, friends of the Dartington Elmhirsts and Wilson Ross, who introduced Suzuki to the Eranos circuit.[17] Including a new *Golden Bough* in Campbell's 1949 *The Hero with a Thousand Faces*, post-war America had all the right ingredients for another round of Massis-like fulminations about mystical infiltration from traitors and alien lands. Perhaps luckily for Zen, McCarthyite anti-communism cornered the infiltration theme. Jewish intellectuals like Norman Podhoretz, Gershom Scholem and Arthur Koestler later queried Zen's political record, and a Beat irrationalism reminiscent of *Wandervogel* 'blood and soil'. But most liberals and conservatives remained silent, until Doris's American unconscious ran amuck in the 'Sixties Great Awakening', as a result of new trance-zone experiments aided by LSD.

Coinciding as it did with Japanese shame about Zen's manipulation (akin to Nietzsche's abuse by Nazism) during the war and its militarist prelude, America's left-countercultural co-option of Zen was ironic.[18] True, Samurai ethic writings like Nitabe Inazo's 1905 *Bushido the Soul of Japan*, and Nukariya Kaiten's 1913 *The Religion of the Samurai* (where this lecturer at Harvard praised General Nogi's recent ritual suicide) once answered high-imperialist liking for the middle ages, 'martial races', caste and so on. Not unlike Evola with his *kshatriya*-ideal, Baden Powell had equated European chivalry with the Samurai code. Soyen Saku, author of *Sermons of a Buddhist Abbott*, the first English book on Zen (1906), likewise struck a feudal/warlike note by approving the Russo–Japanese war, rejecting Tolstoy's request for a pacifist declaration, and claiming that poverty is a karmic dessert.

There are troubling moments in *Zen and Japanese Culture* (reissued by Bollingen in 1959), like Suzuki's promotion of an amoral 'no-sword' obscurantism, its implication that, as 'compassion', Zen, and by extension Japanese, killing is not killing at all. Eugen Herrigel, author of *Zen in the Art of Archery*, an offshoot of this 'no-sword' genre which became a textbook in post-war American art schools, was a Nazi, as was Karlfried von Durckheim, another Black Forest sage like Heidegger, who combined Zen with psychology.

In line with Heidegger's counter-philosophical ploy of *Destruktion*, Suzuki insisted on Zen's 'destructive' capability: identifying Zen with 'will-power', his target was 'degenerate' China and Chan.[19] Suzuki's 'negative Orientalist' image of China arguably stands in a similar relationship to a would-be youthful and vital Japan, as the cultural burden of Europe to avant-garde post-war America. As a way of levelling the ground, Zen certainly suited the iconoclastic ambitions of Americans intent on a distinctive cultural profile – complete with atemporal all-seeing eyeball – and on breaking with a Europe whose extremity had become their opportunity. Unlike the rest of the world, mainland America was untouched by the war, hence in a position to claim supremacy on multiple fronts. But Abstract Expressionism aside, whose founders still looked to Europe, American arts-hegemony proved elusive.

Echoing the Bergson vogue, Zen myths of immediacy, fluidity and spontaneity flourished in their new home. These myths of pure experience and unmediated perception furthered the demolition of cultural and philosophical defences already damaged by earlier Orientalist/primitivist (and Bergsonian) fashions. American art soon became one vast experimental *tabula rasa*, where, without a clear successor iconography, earlier modernism's myth and symbol imaginary was discarded. Particularly with Cageans, pretences to direct *kensho*-style perception and intuition of 'Suchness' sufficed for 'making it new' in the arts. As 'timeless mysticism' and 'freedom', Zen also assisted Doris's 'automatic writing of the American unconscious', alias the rebellious and increasingly aniconic American Sublime. The Zennist *tabula rasa* further accorded with the 'experiential' and 'creedless' dimensions of what Harold Bloom calls 'the American Religion', with its anti-institutional/anti-European, and folkish/magical roots.[20]

This very religion helped the Kyoto School package its Zen in terms of the 'rhetoric of immediacy' that became central to Abstract Expressionism. In a 1904 essay, 'A World of Pure Experience', William James had pondered the existence of a zone of unmediated experience, a haven of pure perception beyond culture's sullying reach. Invoking experience devoid of 'thinking and discrimination' and knowledge based on 'abandoning the artifices of self', Nishida Kitaro, Suzuki's Kyoto School friend, adopted James's idea, giving it a Buddhist twist. The 'experiential' post-war artists and Beat poets bought a Jamesian myth that had been Orientalized in Japan, and reimported by Suzuki. In Robert Sharf's words, 'like Narcissus, Western enthusiasts failed to recognize their own reflection in the mirror being held out to them'.[21] This in itself was nothing unusual: 'mysticism East and West' had long since merged into a free-for-all, metaphysical no-man's land. That such enthusiasts also bought a demilitarized version of fascist vitalism and 'imperial-way Zen' is another possibility, argued by Gustavo Benavides, from similarities between Giovanni Gentile's Fascist 'pure act' (*atto puro*) and the energetic/gestural discourse of Zen, as forged in Kyoto, then transplanted to America.[22]

In contrast to monastic Zen, the Zen of post-war art, whatever its aesthetic achievements, is just as factitious as the 'pure experience' which it boasts. A case of American naiveté or deliberately turning a blind eye? Zen's role in the cultural Cold War, another case of the 'esoteric' tracking of historical turning points, awaits fuller exposition.[23] It has been argued that, as a Cold War weapon, prizes at art exhibitions like the Venice Biennale were rigged by the CIA.[24] Associated with imported Zen, 'freedom' was part of the new art's propaganda. Mellon and Elmhirst's patronage of modernist myth-makers has already been touched on. The Rockefeller Foundation sponsored Suzuki's move to America.[25] And Fowler McCormick, son of Edith Rockefeller, treated by Jung and his patroness thereafter, had accompanied Jung on his 1937–38 Indian tour.[26] Mysteriously, too, Rauschenberg and Graves worked with NASA for a time. Millionaires, myth, high politics, intrigue: Roerich would have found a 'world-plan' in this thought-provoking jig-saw. As John de Gruchy notes, modern Westerners 'have found in Japan what they wanted, and what they needed, ignoring that which they chose not to see'.[27]

What the post-war American art world wanted was a recognized world-class art of its own. As a 'transmission outside the law' – and in the absence of genuine masters, anyone's guess – 'Zen' (in Griffin's terminology) offered a new nomos without any rules. Not the same as 'meaningful order', that was a recipe, without adequate guidance, for American modernism falling apart, which it did in the sixties. Tired, perhaps, of borrowing myths from Europe's empires and middle ages, most late forties-to-fifties American artists adopted the 'Pacific axis' path outlined by Tobey: but its 'Zen' component, particularly with lawless (or anomic) Cageans, proved a double-edged sword.

The Second Abstraction: A Synoptic Approach

In an essay on the impact of '*soi-disant* Zen' on post-war American art, Winther summarizes D. J. Clarke's researches into the matter:

> A fad for 'Oriental Thought' swept a whole generation of American art-ists from the mid-1940s to the mid-1960s ... [Its] intellectual compo-nents ... were culled from ... a limited library of works about Asian culture by such authors as ... Coomaraswamy ... Herrigel ... Waley ... Jung, Alan Watts, and ... Suzuki. Artists such as Morris Graves, Stanton Macdonald-Wright, Isamu Noguchi, and Mark Tobey resumed ... their prewar interests in Oriental Thought. They were joined in the middle or late 1940s by others such as ... Cage ... Kline, Ibram Lassaw, Richard Lippold ... Still more artists joined the bandwagon during the 1950s: Carl Andre, William Baziotes, Philip Guston ... Gordon Onslow-Ford ... Pollock ... Reinhardt, and Theodore Stamos.[28]

The list could be much extended.

But how, precisely, did the second (apparently) post-Theo-sophical abstraction originate? Suzuki's open classes at Columbia University from 1952 – attended by Lassaw and poet Jackson Mac Low (class notes from both survive), by Guston, Cage, Reinhardt, Noguchi, composers Earle Brown and Morton Feldman, critic Arthur Danto, psychologists Karen Horney and Eric Fromm, and gallery owner Betty Parsons – are too late to explain beginnings.[29] Other, already touched-on interwar pioneers (Tobey, Graves, Bissier) link the first and second *Japonismes*, or the older Theosophical syn-cretism and 'Zen'. Tobey's 'Pacific/indigenous style' was not a virgin birth, nor without European parallels. Theosophy's ongoing con-tributions to the art world (diminishing with Indian independence) have also been overlooked: an early modernism much influenced by Vivekananda, 'the American mystics' and Theosophy is thereby falsely isolated from a post-war milieu increasingly pervaded by Taoism, the *Avatamasaka Sutra* and Zen, but still Theosophical in its substrate.

If we include Europe, and other arts besides painting, a more accurate picture emerges. A synoptic account would ideally include interwar Kandinskyism;[30] the New Mexico Transcendental Painting Group;[31] Pollock's and Henry Cowell's experimentalist California; the Krishnamurti circle and Hollywood neo-Vedanta; Seattle as an incubation ground for 'Zen'; and lines of transmission (literary and musical, not just visual) from the first *Japonisme*, as mediated by Rexroth's poetry or Sino-Japanese influences on interwar music.[32] Themes and techniques as old as Symbolism and Art Nouveau, like synaesthesia, 'allover' brushwork, vitalist art–life merger and syn-thesis of the arts are picked up, respectively, by Yves Klein, Tobey and Masson, and Cagean 'intermedia'. Again linking the two mod-ernisms, late Surrealism explored affinities between (originally spiritualist) 'psychic automatism' and Far Eastern calligraphy, already known by the turn of the century.[33] Finally, from late for-ties Europe, French *Art Informel*, the German *Zen Gruppe 49* and the North European Cobra group (another mutation from Surrealism) need adding to the picture, which turns out to be less exclusively American, and more residually Theosophical and Indianist, than standard accounts imply.

The most important art-historical factor for the rise of the new abstraction was late Surrealism, a repository of turn-of-the-century arcana, which midwifed the 'psychic improvisations' of European informal abstraction and a 'tragedy'-prone Abstract Expressionism. (Much of the tragedy was real, as witness Pollock's alcoholism and the suicides of Arshile Gorky and Rothko.) Drawing on a Jungian unconscious, and what Pollock's occultist guru 'John Graham' (Ivan Dombrowski) called the 'primordial racial past', the new abstraction leant initially towards a familiar recipe of self-ancestral, Nordic-Asian Orient, Romantic supernaturalism, and transcultural symbol and myth. By the fifties, a more confident liaison between psychic automatism, calligraphy and Far Eastern cosmologies had sidelined such emphases, creating a relatively self-sufficient art domain for 'Zen'.

Less porous to the Jungian fauna and Theosophical 'glyphs' and 'graphs' of the mid-forties Pollock, and more adept at gesturalist encodings of the rhetoric of unmediated perception, this extension of the new abstraction was still subjective and expressive, thanks especially to its calligraphical base. Nonetheless, in the shape of Reinhardt's and Guston's self-cancelling brushstrokes – deliberately hesitant painterly correlatives of Zennist 'no self' – anti-heroic, ane-goic or objectivist alternatives to the 'unshaven' vitalist/gesturalist ethos soon arose. But it was Cage, above all, with his mechanical 'nobody at home' interpretations of 'no-self' and 'chance operations', who set an unprecedentedly impersonal East Asia at odds with all earlier models of the metaphysical East.

The questions of change and continuity in the new art could be tackled in terms of three main developmental stages. The first entails the subjectivist/visionary interwar and Forties Orient, prior to 'Zen dawn' at that decade's end. The second involves Zen's role in the still subjective, calligraphic or (near) monochromatic abstractions of figures like Masson and Sam Francis (or Tobey and Reinhardt, apropos of whom, respectively, Helen Westgeest writes of an 'art of the calligraphic gesture' and an 'art of the empty field'). The third relates to the 'selfless' impersonality of the would-be Zennist Cage aesthetic (capturing only its aspect of art–life merger, Westgeest calls this 'living art').[34] These three stages in turn suggest three rough taxonomic categories – oneiric-visionary, calligraphic/cosmosophical, and conceptual/epiphanic, as I shall call them – as a criterion for grouping the different art styles involved.

The first two categories have a background in the way the old turn-of-the-century 'reality behind reality' could present itself in one of two ways. The first was as a 'storehouse of images'; the second, as a reservoir of occult forces, like Golden Dawn member J. W. Brodie-Innes's 'ocean of *prana*', or Symbolist Jean Delville's 'great magnetic reservoir of undefined forces'. Where the 'storehouse of images' option entailed an oneiric-visionary manner akin to the Symbolist, the 'strange forces' approach encouraged a vitalist, cosmosophical art like that of the abstract pioneers. As for my third, epiphanic category, this too has an early modernist background, less in visionary/energetic soul-culture, than in Symbolist art–life merger and the 'objective' insights into the soul of man and nature afforded by the first *Japonisme*. 'Oriental Thought', like chop suey, was ladled into pre-existent Western containers.

The oneiric-visionary approach privileged India, retaining a penchant for myth and symbol, the 'second self' and trance. Anticipating Zen dawn, however, as a result of pioneering interwar efforts on the Sino-Japanese front by figures like Tobey, Noguchi and Bissier, a (largely calligraphic) East Asian veneer becomes visible in some art quarters by 1940. My second and third categories – a sometimes calligraphic, sometimes monochromatic, cosmosophical abstraction indebted to Taoism, Zen and the *Avatamsaka Sutra*, and the similarly based, but formally very different, perceptual epiphanies of the Cage aesthetic – are best regarded as parallel post-war outcrops from this tentative interwar turn to the Far East. This scheme is only provisional, but it could help the reader with what follows.

Among others, Richard Pousette-Dart and Pollock represent the first, oneiric-visionary group. The Orient in question here is the one that Massis detested: primordial, supernaturalist, a host to 'alternate consciousness' and the mythopoetic function. Transitional to my second, vitalist/energetic or monochromatic grouping, we encounter artists like Wols, Henri Michaux and Onslow-Ford; and, more firmly within it, the calligraphers, 'writerly' painters and gesturalists – Bissier, Tobey, early Robert Motherwell, Bradley Walker Tomlin, Masson, Pierre Tal-Coat, Georges Mathieu, Jean Degottex and the Belgian Cobra artists, Christian Dotrement and Pierre Alechinsky. The process-continuum sculptors, David Smith and Lassaw, belong here too, as do the metaphysical monochromaticists: Reinhardt, Yves Klein, Sam Francis, later Motherwell, Brice Marden and Agnes Martin. More than Jung and Theosophy (the first detested by Reinhardt, but still fancied by Tal-Coat and Francis), Taoism, Zen and the *Avatamsaka Sutra* provided the metaphysical basis for the calligraphic 'Zen *écriture*' or monochromatic energy-cosmos visions of artists like these.

Though their conceptual sources differed, Colour-Field painters like Barnett Newman and Mark Rothko were cousins of the 'Oriental' monochromaticists, 'experimental transcendental', with its emphasis on cleansing the doors of perception (most mystical systems agreed on this goal), being common to both groups. Rothko was influenced by Patristic accounts of the restoration of perception and appearances in a final '*apokatastasis*' or palingenesis, and Newman by Lurianic Cabala, traces of whose doctrine of the fracture (*zimzum*) and restoration (*tikkun*) of the soul-sphere were still carried by modernist occultism.[35]

My third 'epiphanic', alternatively 'conceptual Oriental', category covers the Cage group (this includes Merce Cunningham, Jasper Johns and Rauschenberg), as well as Cage-inspired neo-Dada, notably the Fluxus movement. This category is distinguished by impersonal and objectivist tendencies shared with the self-inhibiting Guston, and (though he abhorred the Cage aesthetic) the anti-expressive Reinhardt. With an emphasis on origins, my aim is to enlarge on this ground-plan, developing my three categories in a sometimes comparative, sometimes chronological way. Conventional art criticism's formalist '-isms' become redundant once we focus less on 'look' than on the mysteriosophic and counter-cosmological underpinnings of turning points (1910–20, 1940–50) in modernist history. Late modernist

'Zen' art is underpinned by an Orientalized form of counter-cosmological occultism, a modified continuation of the Theosophical, Nietzschean and Bergsonian impulses which, in-house quarrels aside, gave the post-1910 '-isms' an inner cohesion of sorts.

American Pioneers

As shown by the earlier careers of Noguchi, Tobey, Graves, Pollock and Cage, Orientalist affiliations between 1920 and 1950 wavered between old and new, the predictable and the experimental. Noguchi read Okakura, studying Max Muller and Coomaraswamy in the British Library in 1927. Apprenticed to Brancusi, he met Michio Ito, who danced in Yeats's Noh-plays. Travelling to China and Japan in 1930–31 and discovering Zen, he dabbled in Surrealism, to work with the Jungian Martha Graham, then collaborate' with Cage and Cunningham on their Coomaraswamy-inspired 1947 ballet, *The Seasons*. With a Bollingen grant, Noguchi revisited Japan in 1950 via India and South East Asia, to become increasingly attracted to Zen, meeting Suzuki several times. An early exposure to Swedenborgianism having sensitized him to universal analogy and myth, like Cage he was a friend of Joseph Campbell and Buckminster Fuller.[36] But for Rothko, there were still 'too many images' in Noguchi's art.

After attending the 'Monsalvat School of Comparative Religion' at Green Acre, Maine, Tobey joined the Baha'i faith in 1918.[37] The school was an originally neo-Vedantic foundation, the brain-child of Vivekananda's pupil Sarah Farmer, who transformed it into a Baha'i colony in 1901. Tobey's introduction to the shape-shifting 'mystic East' was followed by experiments with Chinese calligraphy, an interest from 1927 of Bissier, the German East Asian pioneer. He began his famous 'white writing' series in 1935, after his China/Japan trip, characterizing its manner in 1946 as 'fourth-dimensional' and symbolic of 'higher states of consciousness' – not in terms of Zen.

Thirties Seattle hosted an Orientalism that lay on the cusp of the older Indianism and new Zen fashions to come. Originally a Vedantist, Graves, an off-beat artist who defies categorization, travelled East in 1928 and 1930, then paid regular visits to a Seattle Buddhist temple from 1935, living as a Thoreau-like recluse in an offshore retreat.[38] With his mystical cult of the wild and Dadaist leanings, Graves, a West Coast experimentalist, is an important intermediary: but where the Buddhist temple visits are concerned, his five months spent at Father Divine's Vivekananda-influenced Harlem mission in 1937 suggest nomadic sampling of the older syncretism, not an 'American Buddhism' that lay 20 years ahead.

Graves formed 'The Northwest School of Visionary Art' with Tobey, Kenneth Callahan and Guy Anderson in 1938–39.[39] Cage joined the Seattle group in 1938, to hear Ross lecture on Dada and Zen soon after. With their insistence on the Ruskinian doctrine of mediaeval/Oriental analogy (axiomatic for Tobey since 1925), Coomaraswamy's writings, later much cited by Cage, were popular in Seattle. Prior to meeting him in 1947, Graves echoed Coomaraswamy in 1941 by speaking of the 'spiritually-realized form' of Asian art, with its movement from 'partial consciousness to full consciousness'.

The Ross lecture on Dada and Zen, and Tobey's white writing, arguably situate the prototypes of the epiphanic/Suchness and cosmosophical/Zen *écriture* schools in late thirties Seattle. Tobey's 'writerly' approach to painting was prefaced by a 1923–24 course in Chinese brushwork, taught by Teng Kuei, a Washington university student. Other, Japanese contacts and influences played their part in his graduation towards a post-painterly style. Tobey spent a month in a Zen monastery during his Elmhirst-sponsored 1934–35 visit to Japan and China with Leach; returning to Seattle in 1938, he then studied with Zen-master Takizaka, learning the flung-ink *sumi* technique from Japanese artists Paul Horiuchi and George Tsutakawa.[40]

Given that Leach refers it to Tobey's experience of Hong Kong street life, the origins of the white writing which ensued on the Eastern trip (in his 1935 *Broadway Norm*, initially) are apparently less Orientalist than mundane. In 1946, furthermore, Tobey, as noted, characterized his signature style in fourth-dimensional, not Zennist terms.[41] Nor was his travelling companion any more purist: prior to embracing Baha'i like Tobey, Leach, with Watts and Orage, had been a student of occultist Dimitrije Mitrinovic who wrote for Orage's *New Age*.[42] For all that his white writing might evoke limitless space and energy in an *Avatamsaka Sutra* fashion, the dissolution of mass into a continuous line acting as an image of cosmic process, Tobey's roots were in the older syncretism more than 'Zen'.

Like Pollock, Tobey was once classified as a 'Pacific School' painter. Despite its aptness for the worldview and provenance and of so many in the 'Oriental Thought generation', thanks doubtless to New York chauvinism, this idea of a Pacific School has vanished into thin air. Along with consignment of Francis, another West Coast wanderer (interested in Jung, alchemy, Ouspensky and after 1955, Zen), to the less influential tastes of Europe and Japan, where Tobey enjoyed favour too – not to mention critical blindness to cosmo-conceptual and formal parallels in Europeans like Bissier and Masson, who also practised a form of 'Zen *écriture*' – this led to Tobey's exclusion from the post-war American canon. (Greenberg's hostility to Tobey has already been noted.)

At art school in Los Angeles (1928–30), Pollock, with class-mate Guston, was introduced to Theosophy by his teacher Frederick Schwankovsky. Inspired by a Krishnamurti summer camp, in 1929 he considered a career in 'occult mysticism', then moving to New York in 1930, he wrote, 'I am still interested in theosophy and am studying a book'. Following current fashion for Amerindian art and 'mysteries' (Indian burial mounds had long since been co-opted by occult America), he purchased several ethnological volumes (1930–35). A source of Picassoid drawings and his 'second self'-related claim to 'paint straight from the unconscious', Pollock's Jungian analysis with Joseph Henderson – friend of Cary Baynes, translator of Wilhelm's *I Ching* – began in 1939. The earlier forties saw his Surrealizing phase, indebted to Jung and Theosophy, and dense with 'mystic figures and signs'. With its calligraphic affinities, the 'whole body *coulage*' signature style that followed took Surrealist psychic automatism to a physical, 'body electric' extreme.[43] Not to forget Schwankovsky, who back in the twenties had introduced Pollock to the idea of poured and dripped paintings.[44]

Acquiring a copy of Herrigel's *Zen in the Art of Archery* in 1955, and producing numerous abstract ink drawings, Pollock was nonetheless closer to yogic India, and a cosmosophical vision of nature and the unconscious drawn from Emerson, Theosophy, Campbell, John Graham and Jung. Still, granted the momentous nature of his signature style, Schwankovsky's lead was arguably as fruitful for post-war art as those (white writing, Ross's lecture) of Tobey's Seattle. Interestingly, Cage's pre-Zen relationship to Cowell and Oscar Fischinger parallels Pollock's to Schwankovsky. With its background in the 'cosmic/vibrational' ambience of Theosophical Halcyon (below), one legacy of the musical teacher–pupil relationship was Cage's prepared piano. Another, encouraged by Fischinger, a Kandinskyite Californian émigré from 1936, was visits to junk-yards, looking for used brake-drums and other detritus, with a view to releasing their trapped 'vibrations'.[45]

Fischinger's 'absolute' films were shown at the Guggenheim Museum of Non-Objective Painting, becoming familiar to Pollock during his 1943 spell there as an assistant.[46] Owner of a book on yoga and a copy of the *Bhagavad Gita*, Pollock, who had two Indian friends, Nataraj and Pravina Vashti, with whom he discussed Indian philosophy, also visited Thomas Wilfred's colour-organ studio during the thirties.[47] A response to the 1915 New York premiere of Scriabin's *Prometheus: The Poem of Fire*, Wilfred's silent clavilux organ of 1921 (acclaimed as 'fourth-dimensional' by critic Sheldon Cheney) crowned the synaesthetic ambitions of Bragdon's circle of Prometheans.[48] Intra-modernist syncretism proved particularly fruitful for Pollock's career.

Symbolist musicalism graces the title of Richard Pousette-Dart's 1942 *Symphony Number 1, The Transcendental*.[49] (The 'absolute' Symbolist musical analogy originated in Schopenhauer's view of music as a 'copy' of the Will.) A painter with affinities to Pollock, and another reader of Jung, Pousette-Dart mixed calligraphic and myth and symbol modalities to 'cosmic' effect. Besides his wife's Theosophical poetry, he read Krishnamurti, Bucke, Eckhart, the *Gita*, the *Upanishads* and Lao-Tzu: pre-Zen favourites, mostly from 'mystic movement' days. Reverting to Smith's account of modernism, his formula, like Pollock's, was occult content in exotic form.

In his 1971 ancestry of the Zen-vogue, Rexroth, a California resident since 1927, cited Hollywood neo-Vedanta (Huxley, Auden, Heard, Isherwood), the Orientalism of Graves's and Tobey's Seattle and the Krishnamurti milieu.[50] Krishnamurti's immediate circle included Stravinsky, Mann, Chaplin, Bertrand Russell, Huxley, Isherwood, Anita Loos, Greta Garbo and Bertold Brecht. Through his writings, Krishnamurti's ideas were known to Tobey, the artist Louise Nevelson and maybe Graves, and through his lectures, to Pollock, Guston and Cage.

A choleric nonconformist, Rexroth later dismissed Jack Kerouac's Buddhism as a 'dimestore incense burner' imposture, Chogyam Trungpa as a 'counter-Buddha', and Zen as being for 'white people' or militaristic. His earlier interests were Theosophical and Taoist: besides Ouspensky, he read Waley's 1935 translation of the *Tao Te Ching*, a text rendered into Emersonian idiom by Witter Bynner after the war, and owned by Pollock. Including a liking for Boehme, he shared these interests with Vivekananda enthusiast Henry Miller, a friend from 1942. In publishing two neo-imagist translations from East Asian poetry in 1955–56, thus planting the standard of 'Pound era' modernism in a decade that was otherwise setting new trends, Rexroth showed where his true, palaeo-modernist allegiances lay. Visiting Japan five times from 1967, he affirmed this conservatism by embracing Shingon, the Japanese form of Tantra practised by Fenollosa and Bigelow. Rexroth, who like Kerouac died a Catholic, weighs up two very different Orientalisms, and ultimately opts for the more old-fashioned. Not simply the choice of an angry old man at odds (like Watts) with the hooligan Beats, where it scorned incipient New Ageism, the preference showed discernment too.

Surrealism was represented in California by the poet Philip Lamantia and émigré artists Wolfgang Paalen and Onslow-Ford.[51] A British friend of Watts from 1949, Onslow-Ford discovered Zen by way of the fourth-dimension, alias 'the unconscious beyond dreams'. Older esoteric interests persisted: Robert Duncan, a Bay-area poet acquainted with Golden Dawn magic since childhood, brought a note of *fin de siècle* literary occultism to the forties scene. Equally, Malcolm Lowry's 1947 masterpiece, *Under the Volcano*, written from 1934 in Canada, is packed with Cabalistic and Indological allusions. Present by virtue of an encounter with the Crowleyite 'Frater Achad' (George Stansfield Jones) Lowry's interests in Golden Dawn Cabala, later shared with Kenneth Anger, show how Symbolism-era occultism, if not its 'orders', continued to flourish.[52]

Accompanied by increasing perceptual didacticism – along the lines of his 1952 'silent piece', 4'33" – Cage's career embraces three phases – Theosophical, Indianist and Zennist – the third of which overshadows the other two. Fischinger's theory of 'souls' locked up in matter (an influence on the 'brake-drum aesthetic' of Cage's and Cowell's late thirties percussion pieces) was one Theosophical influence; others were forthcoming from Cowell, who prior to teaching Cage Eastern musical systems in 1933 had courted a rogue Theosophist, the Irish West Coast American, John Varian.

Meeting Varian in 1913, Cowell set his Celticist writings to music from 1914–26. One of Varian's dottier schemes at the Theosophical community of Halcyon involved a 'harmonious speaking cave': a hollow dug out in the shape of a throat with an Edisonian electric tongue.[53] Another was a 'Harp of Life', to which Cowell got as close as he could with his famous tone-clusters, or by strumming the strings inside his piano. The strumming technique's eventual progeny was Cage's 'prepared piano': perhaps a poor man's gamelan, but also a response to period calls for new instruments and sounds. True, Cage did not participate in these strange events at Halcyon, with their shades of Yeats's Celtic twilight and the turn-of-the-century techno-occult. Nevertheless, he learned from Cowell that any aspiring experimentalist should look East. The basic idea was expressed by Varese, reader of Polish occultist Hoene Wronski, when he called for 'a new mode of expression ... for the new era of higher thought'.[54] For 'higher' read 'Oriental' as we approach the forties.

A likely inspiration for the 'detritus aesthetic' behind Rauschenberg's fifties *Combines* – in 1990 Rauschenberg asserted 'somehow a bone, or a piece of rag that has been run over by several trucks has another soul' – Fischinger's doctrine, in Cage's words, was 'that everything in the world has a spirit which is released by its sound': a notion close to Kandinsky's 'the world sounds ... it is a cosmos of spiritually effective beings. Even dead matter is living spirit.'[55] The trapped 'spirit' of Cage's sonic theology in his eccentric percussion pieces is a cousin of Kandinsky's *innere Klang*: the occult virtue or vibration celebrated in his 'total artworks' and non-objective paintings. Theosophy's post-Euclidean cosmology entailed a new 'astral/vibrational' dimension which the virtuosos of expanding consciousness (like Beuys and Stockhausen later) were eager to explore.

Hindu interests occupied Cage from 1946–51. Coomaraswamy contributed to this phase, as did Gita Sarabhai, a music student who gave Cage a copy of *The Life of Ramakrishna*. Cage frequently quotes Sarabhai's 'music sets the soul in operation', its task to 'sober and quiet the mind, thus rendering it susceptible to divine influences'. Add his debts to Fischinger, and one wonders if Cage was a latter-day animist with a mystical reverence for sound. Other forties influences were Joseph Campbell and Huxley's *The Perennial Philosophy*. Heralding a major 1951–56 change of aesthetic – the more pronounced if we consider that his austere, Tarot-aided *Music Of Changes* of 1951 appeared not long after Messiaen's 'maximalist' *Turangalila Symphonie* (1946–48) – Cage's next destination was an aggravated perceptual didacticism based on 'thinking' but not 'sounding' Zen. To this, distinguishing his wilfully non-relational cosmology from that of the still syntactical 'allover' painters, he added (neither Taoist nor Buddhist) 'chance operations' drawn from a mechanically reimagined *I Ching*.[56]

Cage's substitute for 'meditation', this use of the *I Ching*, like his talk about 'silence' (a Maeterlinckian, not a Buddhist category) exemplified an ingrained modernist tendency to rewrite the metaphysical East. Like the Theosophists, Cage, suspected of charlatanry from early on, clearly felt happier with a synthetic, Westernized remake of 'Oriental Thought'. An example of something similar was the 1928 plan of another experimental composer, the Scriabinite Dane Rudhyar, for reacquainting modern India with a Theosophical symbolism (itself a guarantee of an 'Aryan' musical rebirth in America) which its benighted musicians had lost. Innocent of the actualities, sounds and beliefs of the East, and allowing laborious, programmatic epiphanies, 'conceptual Oriental', à la Cage and Rudhyar, amounted to carte blanche.

European Intermediaries

The bridge-building activities described above show the importance of Symbolist / earlier modernist mysticism and West Coast experimentalism as filters for post-war understandings of 'Zen'. Granted so many survivals from older, occult counter-cosmology, what Cage promoted as 'starting from scratch' was more rehash than *tabula rasa*. Less prone to gild the Eastern lily, bridges between early and late modernist Orientalism were being built in Europe too. By the early fifties, fashion here, as in Japan, had turned towards what Michel Tapie called 'new art for a new era': otherwise *Art Informel* or *Tachisme*, another Surrealist derivation, much concerned (Michaux, Degottex, Alechinsky: compare the American Tomlin) with the interface between writing and painting.[57]

Unlike Greenberg, Tapie had studied Eastern philosophy, cultivating an extensive network of American and Japanese contacts. Concerned with energy, not matter, hence scorning the old 'Euclidean' figure-ground format, European informalists enlisted the same process-continuum, Zen/Tao universe as the Americans. Much as its US counterpart, but less 'heroic' and prone to deny Eastern debts as suited (Kline, the later Motherwell), the late Surrealist East Asia of 'allover' painters like Wols and Masson promised an existential liberation to a recently war-torn West.

Equivalents of Americans like Tobey and Noguchi, who sought a simplified, post-myth and symbol modality from the Far East, pioneers of Europe's new abstraction like Bissier and Wols merit recognition. A reader of Bachofen and later member of the Rebay-affiliated *Zen Gruppe 49*, Bissier turned Eastwards after meeting the Freiburg sinologist Ernst Grosse in 1927.[58] Drawn towards abstraction through friendship from 1929 with Baumeister and a 1930 meeting with Brancusi, Bissier was associated with Bauhaus artist Oscar Schlemmer from 1933–45. After the war, this painter of 'psychogrammes' and 'miniatures' met Tobey, Arp and Ben Nicholson, moving to Ascona in 1961. From 1929–33, at Freiburg, where Heidegger was pursuing his own interests in Zen and Taoism, Bissier taught composition and drawing.

Befriended by Grosse, who had written on Far Eastern painting, in 1931 Bissier took up ink brushwork monochromes, a manner that was to last around five years. Calling his profession 'a monkish business' (compare the 'black monk' Reinhardt), he wanted to avoid the extremes of *Beaux Arts*-style *peinture* and too much 'Japanoid entanglement'. Adopting a small-format, colourist manner like Klee's after 1945, Bissier rejected formalism: 'The quest for a sacred, ritual art becomes more and more clear, firm, and unequivocal through intensive engagement with it. What good to me is the pursuit of a formalistic aesthetic without content?'[59]

The 'cursed' visionary Wols was a major force in Tapie's thinking about *Art Informel*. Relying on semi-accidental effects, Wols combined interests in Taoism and biosophical 'natural history' with Surrealist automatism. Proving the durability of modernist trance-modes, Wols's self-designation as a 'somnambule' anticipates Jean Degottex's talk of 'gestural trance' (Degottex's 'Zen' calligraphy was related to earlier, soul-code-style attempts to create a 'universal language').[60] 'Somnambule' recalls Schopenhauer, as quoted by Schoenberg in the *Blaue Reiter Almanac*: 'The composer reveals the innermost essence of the world ... he is like a mesmerized somnambulist who reveals secrets ... that he knows nothing about when ... awake.' Originally a student of ethnic music with Frobenius in Germany, Wols was befriended in Paris by Surrealist Camille Bryen, Mathieu and Sartre. He quoted his favourite Oriental and Symbolist authors in a mid-forties exhibition catalogue: but by 1951, apparently without discovering Zen, he had drunk himself to death.

Rene Daumal, Wili Baumeister and Yves Klein show affinities, respectively, with Rexroth's Vedantists, the early Abstract Expressionists and the Californian occultists. Suzuki's French translator and author of *Mount Analogue* (1944), the Guénonian, Gurdjieffian and quasi-Surrealist Daumal taught himself Sanskrit, an interest shared with Simone Weil. A cousin of Hollywood's wayward Vedantists – notably Huxley, with his attraction to psychedelics – Daumal, a self-styled 'anarchist of perception', was fascinated by bizarre cognitive states, the origin of his 1944 experiments with carbon tetrachloride.[61] Acquainted with Zen since 1939, Baumeister painted abstract Surrealist 'ideograms' from 1937–41, wrote a Zen-inspired book, *The Unknown in Art* (1947), and read works on prehistory and *The Tibetan Book of Dead*.[62]

A 1925 French translation of Max Heindel's 1909 *Rosicrucian Cosmo-conception* (a Californian tract) led Klein and his fellow Nicois artist Arman to a 1948 'initiation' into the Rose + Croix.[63] From 1947 Klein studied Judo, becoming a vegetarian. He 'meditated' in a cave on the property of Arman's parents, where he painted one wall blue. In 1949, he wrote a minimalist *One-Note Symphony*, proceeding in 1951 to the Scriabinist conceit of monochromes surrounded by fountains of fire and water, with musical accompaniment. In 1952, Klein followed up these experiments in synaesthesia with a trip to Japan. One result was a 1954 book on Judo: another, some knowledge of Buddhism and Japanese. A 'Conquistador of Space', his true interests lay with 'spiritual evolution', levitation, telepathy and so on. His anti-gravitational 'Blue Age' was to see the usual 'non-objective' dematerializations, an 'architecture of the air', and, recalling Scriabin's ambitions, 'aerial men' able to fly. His magical counter-cosmology still basically that of 1910, Klein was snubbed by Rothko at an art event.

Unlike Artaud and Aragon, Masson transcended interwar Surrealism's subversive-provocative or oneiric-visionary Orientalism.[64] An early inspiration was Georges Duthuit's *Chinese Mysticism and Modern Painting*, a 1936 study which likened Chinese calligraphy to Surrealist automatism. In 1942 Masson visited the Oriental collection at the Boston Museum of Fine Arts, curated by Okakura's successor Coomaraswamy. He settled at Aix after the war, pursuing East Asian art and philosophy from 1947. Reading Herrigel, Suzuki and Frazer, in *Quadrum* (vol. 1, 1956), now equipped with an 'allover' discourse about the 'fluidity of things', he wrote a text about Far Eastern painting, 'Peinture de l'Essentiel'.

Inspired by the new physicists' attraction to the East, Tapies, originally another Surrealist, discovered Watts and Huxley after reading Schopenhauer and Okakura's *Book of Tea*. Using breathing exercises learned during an illness as 'meditation', his eventual goal, like Michaux's, was a fusion of 'meta-painting' and 'meta-poetry'. (The 'interdependence of Japanese art and poetry' had been an article of faith with earlier modernists.[65]) The Scottish painter Alan Davie, drawn to Zen, was another Surrealizant myth-maker with a colourist flair for the mind-altering hues of the 'storehouse of images'.[66] In wild transcultural free-fall, the French Cobra painter Jean Michel Atlan felt 'very close to the Hasidim ... Moslem dervishes ... Buddhist dancers, the voodoo rites of Africa and America'. The trance-procedures and meta-linguistic soul-codes of such figures (including Pollock) prove the persistence, as a 'channeling zone', of the Symbolist intermediate state. Most importantly, though, none of this syncretic experimentation, whether European or American, would have been possible without the opening up of world art and world religion by high-imperial globalization.

From Myth and Symbol to the Ground of Being

Abandoning visions and dreams, late Surrealism progressed from a 'mesocosmic' to an 'absolutist' thematics. This transition towards a new, energetic-cosmogenetic, post-oneiric-visionary zone within the 'triple universe' spelt the end of symbol and myth. Eliciting techniques like those of Wols and the later Masson, this theo-ontological upgrade from the 'house of images' towards what Klee called 'the powers that do the forming' was written into Paalen's concept of the 'Dynaton' (Paalen practised Yoga and was interested in modern physics). The Dynaton – Greek: 'ability', 'capacity' – was a Zen/Tao-like continuum of pure potentiality, related to the Symbolist idea of a reservoir of occult forces, outside conventional time and space. However, a turbid fourth-dimensional syncretism confused the concept's formulation: thus the paintings of enthusiasts of Paalen's cosmology like Onslow-Ford lack distinctive status within a 'triplicate' order of things.

Including Rollin Crampton's Buddhism-inspired monochrome, *Premise*, of 1950–51, Dan Flavin's 1962 *Icon IV (The Pure Land)*, Klein's monochromes and Reinhardt's imageless icons, ground of being abstraction is less clearly defined than 'writerly' continuum art.[67] Straddling the two, Motherwell is more the process-continuum calligrapher in his 1955 *Je t'aime* series, but in his *Open* series, from 1967, he adopts a 'Zen-voidness' approach to space akin to that of Sam Francis. Motherwell shows better comprehension of Buddhism's 'form equals emptiness' doctrine than his coevals: that formula's 'emptiness' component (the 'voidness' half of the era's quasi-Eckhartian 'plenum-void' concept) is not interpreted in his art as indicating some static eternalist truth. In this, to take two affirmative and negative monochromatic extremes of his day, Motherwell differs greatly from 'Yves le monochrome' and the 'black monk' Reinhardt, for whom emptiness did not equal form, nor did *nirvana* equal *samsara*: rather, the absolute had priority over the relative, and emptiness over form.

Not easily classified, Reinhardt's real position is probably closer to contingency-shunning Vedanta than anything else.[68] This would align him with Traditionalists and classicists like Guénon and Eliot, his hostility to 'transcendental nonsense' and 'belief in a reality behind reality' maybe smacking, less of disenchantment with metaphysics per se, than of Traditionalist opposition to the 'wrong' spiritual world. Not that the Romantic supernaturalism he pilloried in Abstract Expressionism is entirely absent from his own record. His earliest models, Mondrian and Malevich (the relevance of whose 'zero of forms' to Reinhardt is clear) had been Theosophical neo-Romantics, no matter how later recast. Equally inescapable is the neo-Romantic halo surrounding Reinhard's frequent citations of Eckhart's 'Divine Dark', and Lao Tzu's 'dim and dark' Tao 'showing no outward form'.[69]

Reinhardt's hymns to blackness celebrate the quality-less dark Tao (or *nirguna*) into which manifest reality disappears in his art. His assertion that 'Art begins with getting rid of nature' is a key to his 'last paintings' (an eschatological tag), with their refusal to acknowledge the empirical world. In contrary affirmative vein, and attracted to the Monet of *Nirvana Jaune*, whose work he wanted to 'make pure', Francis asked of his virginal canvas 'are you the white from eternity?'[70] Reminiscent of Malevich's 'white beyond' (not his 'zero'), Francis's metaphysical axis is that of the world-creating calligraphers, not the anti-contingent Reinhardt or transcendental Klein. Congruent with calligraphical dynamism, too, Francis, unlike Reinhardt, pays spontaneous gestural homage to nature's 'manner of operation', as captured in the fields of colour that dance on his part-Zennist, part-Mallarmean cosmogenetic ground.

Pending focus, whether on ground of being alone (Klein and Reinhardt), or on ground and world-creating energy (Francis's colourist fields, the calligraphers' *chi*), we encounter the Orientalist monochrome proper, or a cosmosophical abstraction which is more dynamic (and still partly 'middle world') in scope. We could accordingly assign Marden's 'silent' monochromes to the first subcategory and, even though her traceries are more subtle than most 'writerly' art, Martin's Zen/Tao cosmogonies to the second.[71] More fully abstract, or aniconic, than their precursors due to diminished interest in image, symbol and myth, most of the above artists head for the transmundane, emptiness-only, or emptiness-and-cosmogenetic energy, 'no mountains' level of Zen Enlightenment: a level rescinded by the 'then there are mountains again' thrust of the Cage aesthetic. Tapies could be seen as an independent practitioner of the '*samsara* equals *nirvana*' – or return to the object – approach of the Cagean 'just as it is' or Suchness school.[72] Drawn to poor materials and distressed surfaces, Tapies, like Rauschenberg, refuses to discriminate beauty from ugliness, opting for forbidden themes like armpits and extracted teeth: no pious mystagogue of the sacred, one of his works is a sculpture of a molar inscribed 'Buda'.

Conclusion: A Turbid Transmission

Whatever the consequences for their art, the original 'Oriental Thinkers' were earnest and informed. Klein and Daumal studied Oriental languages. So did the Californian painter Stanton MacDonald-Wright, who discovered East Asian art in 1912 and calligraphy by 1923, living in Japan during 1937. From 1942–52 he taught art history and Eastern aesthetics at UCLA, then from 1958 spent five months each year in a Japanese Zen monastery.[73] Drawn to Eastern languages, the Belgian Christian Dotrement, initially a Surrealist poet, then a Cobra painter of 'logogrammes', took up Oriental studies and calligraphy after 1943; while Reinhardt became interested in Chinese and Japanese painting in 1944, to study Asian art history from 1946–52. As for visits to Japan, like those of Klein in 1952, Graves in 1954, Alechinsky in 1955, and Tapie, Mathieu and Francis in 1957, Noguchi and Tobey had set precedents, in 1931 and

1934 respectively. Though the museum was now 'without walls', this Oriental frenzy could be compared to the adoption of new models (Assyrian, Egyptian, Chinese, Japanese), as described by Arrowsmith apropos the British museum's anti-classical role in early Anglophone modernism. (No more 'hiding behind the Elgin marbles', in Roger Fry's words.)

Along with excessive busyness and *horror vacui*, time- and place-bound assumptions and projections undeniably muddy the story. When, around 1950, Zen stole up on Indianism, there was a long backlog of such baggage, which could bring a spurious air of cosmosophical profundity into the new art. In particular, continuities from Romanticism's spectacular-omniscient India gave a 'reality key' (more than a meditative) cast to Zen dawn, such that, retrospectively, late modernist Zen art can look like an outcrop from the old, Indianist 'new paradigm', as that headed towards the New Age. Indeed, after a decade or so of uncertain autonomy, much of the Zen universe was reabsorbed into Yeats's 'vague Asiatic immensities', thanks to the counterculture's neo-Theosophical/neo-Hindu (more than Buddhist) designs on cutting the cosmic cloth to its own needs.

Together with the more juvenile and anomic aspects of Fluxus and neo-Dada, the Beats were partly responsible for the countercultural trivialization of Zen. Thus, Peter Orlovsky, Alan Ginsberg and Gary Snyder travelled to the Himalayas to see, not a genuine Tibetan lama, but the German Romantic pretender 'Lama Anagarika Govinda'. Like interests at Esalen, Ginsberg's and Snyder's folkish and visionary proclivities, weakness for drugs and shamanism – and in Snyder's case, for frontiersmanship: the 'bearshit on the trail school of poetry', as Rexroth called it – suggest deep attachment to Romantic supernaturalism, despite its incompatibility with Zen. Though Cage and his followers took an anti-mythic stance on the Beats and Abstract Expressionists, superficially akin to that of Dada on German Expressionism, older Dadaists mostly stood off from their bastard child.

The ultimate lot of the tired Indianism of the Theosophists, 'American mystics' and Jungians was to merge with Leary's Indo-Tibetan psychedelia and the Esalen milieu ('rich white folk' again), then, with Beat defections from 'ordinary' Zen towards 'extraordinary' Tibetan Buddhism, to merge into the New Age. As formulaic

clichés about 'the spiritual' began to sideline older informed interests in the East (high empire's intercultural exchanges, libraries,
museums), the original promise of the 'Oriental Thought generation' was lost. In 1980s France, I asked the translator of an elderly,
Tibet-born lama, what, judging by questions asked, the most common misconception about Tibetan Buddhism might be: her deeply
resigned reply (central to this study) was, 'They all think it's about
Jung.'

6

OWNING, DISOWNING AND TRIVIALIZING THE OCCULT

The Downfall of the Modernist Culture of Soul

As a historian of travelling gods, I have developed Bernard Smith's insights about the role of the imperial occult and exotic in modernism's break with the past. The occult/syncretic, a keynote of old, multi-ethnic empires with their mutable and absorbent pantheons, is as crucial to modernism as Platonism and high magic were to the Renaissance. The second point is widely admitted, the first is not. Modernist studies have overlooked the transcultural, deity- and worldview-compounding, high-imperial milieu, and the potential for cultural enrichment, anti-Western revolt, and cognitive/cosmo-conceptual revolution offered by that. Romain Rolland captured the proto-modernist mood: 'The reason of humanity was exhausted. It had just made a gigantic effort ... The gate of dreams had reopened; in the train of religion came little puffs of theosophy, mysticism, esoteric faith, occultism to visit the chambers of the Western mind.'[1] Signalling changed directions within the occult, Strindberg stressed the Eastern contribution: from the 1880s, 'Vedanta, Buddhism, penetrated into Europe and religion returned under the designation of Theosophy and Occultism.'[2]

Oversight of modernist occultism is doubtless due to the fact that mystical syncretism is one of those rabbit holes in history – Buddhist Gandhara is another – the time-consuming exploration of which can badly upset received ideas. To broach such topics is to risk being seen as a maverick: but that did not deter Frances Yates and E. R. Dodds from exploring the occult in the Renaissance and Greco-Roman antiquity.[3] Modernist studies could learn from their example, accepting underground passage-ways and magical-syncretic untidiness as part of the course. To mix Grace Slick with Manley Hopkins, the mind has its Alice in Wonderland like rabbit holes as well as its mountains; and 'mysticism' and 'reason' are more of a Centaur than distinct entities. Regarded thus, modernism joins a succession of other heterodox chapters in cultural history – Romanticism, the Platonic-Hermetic Renaissance, Neoplatonic antiquity – when emphases on the 'a-rational' side of the Centaur predisposed, at its best, to what Joscelyn Godwin calls 'Theosophical Enlightenment': a state which assumes parity between imagination, mysticism and reason as faculties of an undivided mind.[4]

Returning to travelling gods: as the conquered took the conquerors captive with their dazzling wares, a kaleidoscopic range of mystico-theological encounters, transcultural interconnections, new hybrid artistic styles and countercultural circuits emerged under high empire. Because of the syncretism-prone nature of intellectual interaction between colonizers and colonized, felt needs for a revitalized modernity, and the speed with which high empire entered the cultural limelight, 'creative misinterpretations' – constants of religio-cultural interchange from antiquity onwards – affected the processing of the imperial occult and exotic, prior to their incorporation into art. Scores of now hardly remembered middle-men were involved in this redaction of religio-cultural backwash from the colonies, and a magic-hungry imagination was the agent of its translation into art. The mid-Victorian Indologist Max Muller had required 'sacred books', 'founders', 'creeds' and so forth of religions worth the name. Such 'Protestant' considerations were now redundant, upstaged by animism and cults of outré or badly behaved foreign gods. Writ large in D. W. Griffith's Babylon set and St Denis's dance, a magical worldview, with neo-Alexandrian touches, had returned to the West.

To recapitulate briefly: after 1880, stay-at-home domestic realism ceded to adventurous neo-Romanticism. With its associated culture of trance and Oriental, archaic, folkloric and occult revivals, this new romanticism – modernism's matrix – was prone to bipolar alternations of millennial hope and end-of-cycle despair. In their struggle (*agon*) between these two extremes, modernists failed to achieve any overall 're-enchantment', if indeed that was their single-minded goal. Because of an inherent dynamism, there is little frozen sacrality in modernism, even in 'classicists' like Eliot: rather, modernist resort to the occult and exotic (less so, 'the sacred') was largely to make sense of modernity, which now included empires, as a perplexing lived condition.

To cap this sense-making function of extra-canonical knowledge and borrowed alien idioms – like Impressionist adaptation of 'floating world' Japanese prints to capture modern transience – modernists revived an apocalyptic 'meta-world' of chiliastic and catastrophic possibilities, which mirrored the modern condition's extremes.[5] In all this, modernists arguably came closer to syncretic folk religion's unselfconscious goals, namely the practical management of a carefully mapped meta-reality (or 'lower mythology'), than those of 1890s occult revival.

Undermining traditional certainties and securities, modernity and modernization had expanded exponentially since Romanticism: Decadent catastrophism (collapse into nothingness, hell) was as logical a response to these changes as the millennialism (paradise, utopia) of some modernist groups. Doubtless aware of current equations between modernism, occultism and *fascism* like those drawn by T. H. Robsjohn-Gibbings in his 1947 *Mona Lisa's Mustache*, Greenberg tried to make modernism safe for democracy by exorcizing its meaning and meta-world – its interplay between overt and covert – as if they represented the very Devil himself. But myth, magic and apocalyptic, apolitical in themselves, proved more potent than his sanitizing formalism, as the countercultural sixties show.

True to the modernist pattern of see-sawing extremes, the 'mystic sixties', a coda to the millennial/eschatological impulses behind modernism, had their dark side, as well as utopian dreams.[6] Blind faith in the redemptive power of the 'house of images', as accessed, now, by LSD, led to self-deceptions like those depicted by Ball; and as among Teens avant-gardists, delusions about a cost-free, remagicalized utopia were fostered by some of the gurus involved. Indeed, folk religion usually makes a cleaner, functional job of syncretism than the 'initiatic' professionals and maestros of psyche who derive their living from it.

Attempts to take heaven by force, like Jim Morrison's, usually ended with a crash to earth. Instability was of the essence with modernist, and sub-modernist, ways of reframing the world. Modernism like empire now dead-and-gone, painless 're-enchantment' had to await the frivolities of the New Age. With its commodification of the 'spiritual', consumerist repackaging of fallout from the mystic sixties, and oblivion of its own roots, the culturally barren New Age is an offspring of the new, entrepreneurial world system, which, aided by poststructuralism and postmodernism, began its war on memory, history, meaning and intelligence with the onset of neo-liberalism around 1980. Henceforth, knowledge and (lack of) imagination reassumed the blinkered, utilitarian, edited-out and rabbit-hole free aspect which disfigured them under the mid-Victorian bourgeoisie.

To trace the degradation and downfall of the modernist culture of soul, for all its own weaknesses (and strengths), would need another book. Nevertheless, a few salient points stand out. As old empire receded and decolonization advanced, post-war culture forfeited direct exposure to the foreign influences that had made it so vibrant and truly multicultural in the earlier twentieth century. A trivializing, airport lounge 'been everywhere, seen nothing' is all that survives of modernist cosmopolitanism today. A few exceptions apart, notably lionization of older, African American bluesmen, together with the Kathmandu trail and discipleship to gurus like the Maharishi, ghostly, and probably unwitting, after-echoes of the older imperial culture take the place of the living exotic by the sixties. Always a mirror, the exotic, in this new context, reflected ideas and values that were soon to become trivial or stale.

In a study of Buddhist references in Conrad, Peter Caracciolo comments on later twentieth-century 'amnesia of empire', with its far-ranging knowledges of a more varied and magical world than our own.[7] (Perhaps those born after 1980 are the first truly secular generation.) Reviving their message for yet another transitional age, and encouraged by surviving modernists like Henry Miller, the hippies resurrected works by the Theosophists, Gurdjieff, Ouspensky and Evans Wentz, all mouthpieces of a cosmopolitan, high-imperial culture they had never known. The florid, sitar-assisted Indo-Tibetan psychedelia which resulted was a return to the neo-Romantic, Theosophical baseline that had temporarily made way for the inter-war's 'orderly' spiritualities (Chapter 4), and more recently for 'Zen'. Not simply invented tradition, some of the relevant Romantic and modernist ancestry figures on the 1967 *Sergeant Pepper* album sleeve. Though like Huxley and Ernst Junger he had experimented with mescalin in the fifties, the Oxford Orientalist R. C. Zaehner slated the hippy formula of 'pop Buddhism and LSD'.[8] As 'paganism' and pilfered 'shamanism' entered the melange, the scene was set, not for another Ascona (*pace* the Hesse and Lawrence revivals), but for a 'vulgarized elitism' that was ripe for commercialization, its only experience of rabbit holes the recreational use of drugs.[9]

One of the Colin Dexter novels describes the anthropological Pitt-Rivers museum in Oxford as 'the place where myths go home to die'. Though I confess to a weakness for the earlier *Indiana Jones* films (a latter-day form of imperial Gothic), my own graveyard of choice, after 1980, would be the entertainment industry and the New Age. Ironically, the devaluation of myths and symbols by the philistine bourgeoisie was one of the things modernism was reacting against – the threadbare, mid-Victorian mythologies (Gothic revival, pre-Raphaelitism) of the escapist, idle hour. Imperial-age magic now being, at best, a Merchant Ivory-like curio from the past, Harry Potter and *The Da Vinci Code* pick up from where Pugin's stained-glass windows and King Arthur left off: under a form of liberal ascendancy in both cases. With its Sibylline imagery (Tarot, cosmic cycles, Crowley), Bob Dylan's 'The Changing of the Guard' (or Gods?), from his 1978 album *Street Legal*, could be interpreted as an epitaph for a lost Eden: after the hopes of the later sixties – a repetition of modernism's restorationist impulses – Bahr's detested 'bourgeois rule' was back in charge of the arts.

Nordau's response to such hopes for a new dawn had been predictably deflating:

> In all countries … critics repeat … that the forms hitherto employed by art are henceforth effete and useless, and that it is preparing something perfectly new … Wagner first spoke of 'the art-work of the future', and hundreds of … imitators lisp the term after him … But all these talks about sunrise, the dawn, new land … are only the twaddle of degenerates … The idea that tomorrow morning at half-past seven o' clock a monstrous, unsuspected event will suddenly take place, that on Thursday next a complete revolution will be accomplished at a single blow, that a revelation, a redemption, the advent of a new age, is imminent – this is frequently observed among the insane; it is a mystic delirium.[10]

Millenarians preferred the bipolar, cyclical pattern of catastrophe and utopia. Thus, in an 1890 copy of the *Jugendstil* periodical

Moderne Dichtung, Bahr added the end-times of Decadent pessimism to Nordau's new dawns:

> It may be that we are at the end, at the death of exhausted mankind and that we are experiencing mankind's last spasms. It may be that we are at the beginning, at the birth of a new humanity and that we are experiencing … the avalanches of spring. We are rising to the divine or plunging … into night and destruction – but there is no standing still. The creed of *die Moderne* is that salvation will arise from pain and grace from despair, that a dawn will come after this … darkness … that there will be a glorious, blessed resurrection.[11]

Renewal or decay, cosmogony or catastrophe, ecstatic transcendence or nihilistic despair: as seen in Chapter 3, these palingenetic/eschatological poles of Bahr's dilemma (which excluded simple progress) were recurrent early modernist motifs. In 1910 Berdyaev remarked of Bely that 'his sensibilities are apocalyptic and catastrophic';[12] while Bely himself, much as Bahr, asserted, 'The failure of the old ways is experienced as the End of the World, the tidings of the new era as the Second Coming. We sensed the apocalyptic rhythm of the time. Towards the Beginning we strive through the End.'[13] Much in Bob Dylan's charismatic-prophetic oeuvre, with its quasi-Lurianic drive to gather up exiled soul-sparks in a *tikkun*-like restoration, plays on exactly the same 'catastrophic-utopian' (or destructive–creative) themes.

The Modernist Meta-world

Returning to modernist syncretism, as distinct from occult revival, there is a notable dearth in modernism, in contrast to Decadence and Symbolism, of occultist staples like vampires, ghosts, Sphinxes, apparitions and so forth. With its links to the Victorian vernacular (Varney the vampire, Spring-heeled Jack) and its afterlife in horror movies, Surrealists were exceptional in keeping this Gothic subcategory of the occult alive. At its most lurid in the '*sousrealiste*' schism led by Michel Leiris and Georges Bataille, this rehashed Decadence fetishized Voodoo, cannibalism, human sacrifice and sexual perversity – features of Lawrence's American fiction and the 'obsessional art', or *Ankoku Butoh*, of sixties Japan.[14]

Like Crowley's anti-social 'Magick' and seventies exploitation movies, such sensationalism says little about the underlying history involved. In particular, the occult's monomaniacs and exhibition-ists conceal the important truth that the 'instrumental reason' and 'positivism' responsible for modernization were unable to explain the part-disorientating, part-spellbinding *experience* of modernity. As creations of pre-modernity, their supernaturalist apparatus suffering from closure, orthodox religions could not explain it either. Hence the ransacking by modernists of orthodoxy's leavings – the raiding of pre-modern counter-knowledges, both foreign and domestic – in order to make sense of existence in a very strange new world.

Modernist supernaturalism was addressed to something out-side the purview of the 'carry on transgressing' school: namely, modernity's inherent ghostliness, a spirit-possession of its aura and energies that accounted for modern experience's strangeness, and permitted adaptation, furthermore, to the kind of millennial/eschatological thinking found in Bely and Bahr. I have argued else-where for correspondences between the post-materialist impulse towards modernism in the arts, and the age's new, energetic and interdependent cosmo-conception – the anticlassical work not just of 'new physicists', but also of occultists and 'advanced think-ers'.[15] Against a background of degenerationist gloom, concerns with sensory overload and the unstable perceiving subject, matter, in this universe, was apparently disappearing, yielding to strange energies and unknown forces. Christoph Asendorf, historian of art and perception, notes that 'invisible but very effective energies' were '*the* phantasm' of the 1880s and 1890s; and that with the grad-ual, post-1900 'death of matter', already implicit in Impressionism, the art world became fascinated by the notion of 'streams and radiations'.[16]

X-rays, radium, electricity, Mesmerism's 'fluidic revelation', Bergsonism, Futurist lines of force: all provided different perspec-tives for the reformulation of spirits, ghosts and powers, as this mag-ical metamorphosis of matter into energy taxed modernist minds. Both exemplars of the 'marvellous', science and occultism were still not clearly distinguished: whence techno-occult or science-fiction-like experiments in depicting the strange forces, 'vibrations' and force-fields by which modernists felt beset. Futurists resorted to spiritual-ism to explain this supernatural aura of the modern, while Gabriele Buffet-Picabia noticed that the idea of 'non-perceptible forces' haunted the art world of the Teens. But how to represent such forces in 'known and standard' art forms? The need for renovated consciousness and a new idiom (Chapters 2 and 3) re-enters the picture with this question. So do the irregular and outsider sources used by modernists to depict their 'processive, non-substantialist' universe, where solid matter, like Euclid's and Newton's theorems, had been replaced by para-Gothic, scientifically tricked-out spirits and ghouls. In Dylan's 'Visions of Johanna', electricity retains just such a 'ghost': another modernist survival, it would seem.

Not to forget that the rise of science and technology (one-time cousins of the occult) was intimately connected with the emergence of capitalist modernity. A cause for instability, for never-ending flux and loss of solidity, capitalism itself could be seen as instrumental in Asendorf's 'death of matter', with its vaporization of substance into 'streams and radiations'. In conservative, quasi-Traditionalist vein, Marx famously wrote of capitalism's consequences that 'everything solid melts into air, everything sacred is profaned'; like Baudelaire on the fleeting nature of modern experience, Hofmannsthal characterized modernity as the 'slippery, the sliding' (*Das Gleitende*); pinpointing an uncanny dynamism, Evola asserted that 'modernity, like a Golem, erupted into settled bourgeois space'; while, on top of assaults from 'spirits and powers', Strindberg suffered 'electrohysterical' attacks in tramcars: the unstable, cognitively disorientated subject, disappearing into modern flux.[17]

From a typically Decadent position of 'nothing to hold onto' – the vanishing of 'all fixed and fast frozen relations' (Marx) into a maelstrom of unknown forces and strange energies – the next step could be 'creative' transvaluation of what Asendorf calls modernity's 'oscillatory field', where much as in Bely's astral *Petersburg*, 'everything individual and bounded evaporates'.[18] Transvaluation entailed the recasting of hitherto unnerving forces as a source of 'electrovitalist' regeneration, after the pattern of Whitman, Verhaeren and Jules Romains (Chapter 3: compare Lawrence's 'power mode' and Evola's 'man as power'). The result was modernism's techno-occult New Man. On such a view, the Victorian bourgeoisie would have generated its own antitype: a modernist antitype, who, like G. K. Chesterton's anarchist professor in *The Man Who Was Thursday* (or Ernst Junger), delighted in the 'destructive' wreck of matter and its 'creative' release into energy, the subsequent vortical chaos serving as a crucible for new modernities.[19]

The capitalist bourgeoisie might have initiated 'world end' with it various afflictions: degeneration, neurasthenia, sensory overload, decay of cognition. But out of its ruins – represented as energy, alias unknown forces or 'streams and radiations' – the modernist 'occult cosmocrat', now a master of the universe like Malevich, not a victim of modernity like Strindberg, found himself empowered, particularly as 'the new model of the universe' internationalized during the Teens, to institute a new cosmogony, a world-beginning or cosmic spring.[20] Contrary to Nordau's mockery, new clients (natural aristocratic, repentant bourgeois irrationalist) could benefit from this new dawn, revitalized by their artist-initiate master's unseen sources of power. If capitalism dissolved the world (and victimized the Decadents), modernism and its Orient-backed occultism of vital force and energy regenerated it afresh.

Prior to any such utopian conjuring tricks, the non-imported modernist occult, on this argument, would have arisen in tandem with the overwhelming perceptual and existential fallout from modernity's new (im-)material culture, as a modality, like *Japonisme* or Gothic psychology, for recording the unanchored 'floating world'/'second state' types of experience generated by the modern condition. Modernism's 'meta-world' could, in other words, be seen as a gradual outcrop from, and complement to, modernity's new, hypnotic, bewitching and often threatening material culture. This meta-world shared features in common with the Gothic and the marvellous, like J. J. Grandville's 'compulsive-utopian' animation of the new commodity culture's trivia in his 1844, *Un Autre Monde*: dinner plates and teacups dancing to bourgeois modernity's beguiling tune.[21] On the darker, spook-ridden side of things, Gustave Doré's 1872 set of engravings, *London: A Pilgrimage*, could be cited, as well as much in Dickens.

Developing Daniel Pick, who stresses the commodity's 'invitation to ecstasy', as well as the unsettling role of 'irrational interpersonal forces and psychic contacts', modernity had arguably acquired its own magical or demonic, seductive or terrifying, meta-world (or 'next world') by the later nineteenth century.[22] This is best seen as a product of 'urban folklore', largely spontaneously arisen like traditional folklore, but doing new work. A compound, inter alia, of the 'electro-hysteria' emitted by Strindberg's tramcars or Ball's 'turbines, boiler houses, iron hammers, electricity', as they 'brought into being fields of force and spirits', modernity's very own ghostly 'next world', an epiphenomenon of modern *matériel*, proved invaluable, among modernists, as a substitute for tradition's otherworld, where river gods or tree nymphs, not the clamorous big city or glittering colonial exhibitions, were the forces powering 'god-creation'.

As modernity expanded, on such a view, urban-industrial and imperial-cosmopolitan supernaturalism would have dislodged the 'natural supernaturalism' of the Romantics, giving rise to a new 'lower mythology' and new, mystico-hypnoid states of mind.[23] As for the meta-world's non-domestic input, Schopenhauerian Buddhism aside (see Chapter 3 for its role in Decadent anomie and liquefaction), the 'magic and mystery' zones of the colonies, home to Eliot's 'strange gods' and Smith's occult and exotic, would have been later accretions within the above-adumbrated sequence, as impulses to revitalization and 'world-creation' gathered pace. Making modernity less daunting, religio-cultural backwash from the colonies could be argued to have offered modernists succour at a timely, post-Decadent and transvaluation-prone hour.

Subsequent to the 'death of matter', a hard and fast 'real world' was no longer an inspiration for art. Like their colonial opposite numbers, modernists were explorers in covert and potentially dangerous borderline regions that were either unknown or inadequately mapped. Like Ball's 'liberated anarchy of demons and natural forces', Strindberg's talk in such contexts of 'spirits and powers' could be said to represent an attempt, as unknown unknowns broke the surface of consciousness, to shape the shapeless, to form the formless, in a way that had affinities with 'trench religion'. Of this, one French observer noted, 'l'extraordinaire appel l'extraordinaire', the implication being that unprecedented modern conditions evoke equally unprecedented responses.[24] Or as an army chaplain put it, 'The British soldier has certainly got religion; I am not so sure, however, that he has got Christianity.' Another point of comparison, especially for modernist apocalyptic and messianism, might be the patchwork cosmologies of such forms of crisis-cult as the Ghost Dance, or the 'Vailala madness', a techno-shamanic cargo-cult that swept New Guinea from 1919.[25]

Like its twin the imagination, the 'daimonic' is clearly a shape-shifting bricoleur, able to supernaturalize new experiences at will; able, also, to dream up new models of the universe, new world-ends and world-beginnings, to keep the biological life cycle intact. This inventiveness on the part of what anthropologist Pascal Boyer calls the 'religion-making imagination', though a tactic of self-preservation, usually had tragic consequences for traditional religion: but that same imagination needed no pace-setting 'occult revival' to leave its mark on modernist history.[26] As a product of the mind's 'rational-scientific' faculties, modernization will doubtless continue to manufacture new modernities, the experience of which unintended consequences fashion, cannot but unleash the shadows, demons and occasional angels that specialized instrumental reason, ignoring the rest of the Centaur to which it belongs, has sedulously tried to suppress. Both being valid expressions of the human spirit, the historical clash, or pendulum swings, between the West's 'heterodox', magical-syncretic and 'orthodox', classical-rationalist traditions of thought has been disastrous. In a Cabalistic sense, the star-struck and the earth-bound need to be 're-paired'.

NOTES

1 Empire and Occultism

1. Eric Mahoney, *Religious Syncretism* (London: SCM Press, 2006).
2. Quoted from *Speech Genres*, 2, by Joseph Roach, *Cities of the Dead: Circum-Atlantic Performance* (New York: Columbia University Press, 1996), 187.
3. For magic and the marvellous, Gordon in Valerie Flint, Richard Gordon, Georg Luck and Daniel Ogden, *The Athlone History of Witchcraft and Magic in Europe*, vol. 2, *Ancient Greece and Rome* (London: Athlone Press 1999), 168ff.
4. Roger Griffin, *Modernism and Fascism: The Sense of a Beginning under Mussolini and Hitler* (Basingstoke: Palgrave Macmillan, 2007).
5. Griffin's introduction to Ben Hutchinson, *Modernism and Style* (Basingstoke: Palgrave Macmillan, 2011), xii; idem, *Terrorist's Creed: Fanatical Violence and the Human Need for Meaning* (Basingstoke: Palgrave Macmillan, 2012), 53, 73. Key terms from Griffin's work will intermittently recur in this study.
6. Suzanne Marchand, *German Orientalism in the Age of Empire: Religion, Race, and Scholarship* (New York: Cambridge University Press, 2010).
7. Ibid., 256 for the 'reconvergence' point.
8. Mahoney, *Syncretism*, 118.
9. Gary Lachman, *Madame Blavatsky: The Mother of Modern Spirituality* (New York: Tarcher/Penguin USA, 2012); Stephen Prothero, *The White Buddhist: The Asian Odyssey of Henry Steel Olcott* (Bloomington: Indiana University Press, 2012); Joscelyn Godwin, *The Theosophical Enlightenment* (Albany: SUNY Press, 1994).
10. Martha Shuchard, *Restoring the Temple of Vision: Cabalistic Freemasonry and Stuart Culture* (Leiden: Brill, 2002). There are Masonic 'survivals' and Cabalistic allusions in Theosophy, but these did not greatly impact on the art world.
11. Catherine Wessinger, *Annie Besant and Progressive Messianism, 1874–1933* (Lewiston, NY: Edwin Mellen Press, 1988); Gregory Tillett, *The Elder Brother: A Biography of Charles Webster Leadbeater* (London: Routledge Kegan Paul, 1982).
12. For Theosophical Neoplatonism, Michael Gomes, *The Dawning of the Theosophical Movement* (Wheaton, IL: Theosophical Publishing House, 1987).
13. Gerald Figal, *Civilization and Monsters: Spirits of Modernity in Meiji Japan* (Durham, NC: Duke University Press, 1999).
14. Eva Kuryluk, *Judas and Salome in the Cave of Sex: The Grotesque, Origins, Iconography, Techniques* (Evanston, IL: Northwestern University Press, 1987).
15. Paul Greenhalgh, *The Modern Ideal: The Rise and Collapse of Idealism in the Visual Arts* (London: V&A Publications, 2005), 118.
16. For 'the colonial syncretic', Joy Dixon, *Divine Feminine: Theosophy and Feminism* (Baltimore and London: Johns Hopkins University Press, 2001).

17. For Griffes, John Struble, *The History of American Classical Music: MacDowell through Minimalism* (London: Robert Hale, 1995), 79; for his Theosophy, Judith Tick, 'Ruth Crawford's "Spiritual" Concept: The Sound Ideals of an Early American Modernist', *Journal of the American Musicological Society*, 44/2 (1991), 224 n. 13; for Heyman's 1921 *The Relation of Ultra Music to Archaic Music*, Tick ibid., 22 and n. 27; for Flanner on Pound, Glenn Watkins, *Pyramids at the Louvre: Music, Culture and Collage from Stravinsky to the Postmodernists* (Cambridge, MA: Harvard University Press), 1994, 58; for Brancusi, Roger Lipsey, *An Art of Our Own: The Spiritual in Twentieth Century Art* (Boston and Shaftesbury: Shambhala, 1988), 242, 245, 256.

18. Paul Edwards, *Wyndham Lewis, Painter and Writer* (New Haven and London: Yale University Press, 2000), 4.

19. Paul Greenhalgh, *Ephemeral Vistas: History of the Expositions Universelles, Great Exhibitions and World's Fairs* (Manchester University Press, 1990).

20. John Mackenzie, *Orientalism: History, Theory and the Arts* (Manchester University Press, 1995); Greenhalgh, *The Modern Ideal*, 118ff.

21. Martin Green, *Dreams of Adventure, Deeds of Empire* (London: Routledge and Kegan Paul, 1980).

22. Richard Seager, *The World's Parliament of Religions: The East–West Encounter, Chicago, 1883* (Bloomington: Indiana University Press, 2009).

23. Quoted by T. J. Jackson Lears, *No Place of Grace: Antimodernism and the Transformation of American Culture* (University of Chicago Press, 1994), 309.

24. Paula Amad, *Counter-Archive, Film, the Everyday, and Albert Kahn's Archives De La Planète* (New York: Columbia University Press, 2010).

25. Margaret Jacob, *Living the Enlightenment: Freemasonry and Politics in Eighteenth-Century Europe* (New York: Oxford University Press, 1992); Paul Monod, *Solomon's Secret Arts: The Occult in the Age of Enlightenment* (New Haven and London: Yale University Press, 2013).

26. G. S. Rousseau and Roy Porter, *Exoticism in the Enlightenment* (Manchester University Press, 1989).

27. For Theosophy and pseudo-science, Linda Henderson, *The Fourth Dimension and Non-Euclidean Geometry in Modern Art* (Princeton University Press, 1983).

28. John Lester, *Journey through Despair, 1880–1914: Transformations in British Literary Culture* (Princeton University Press, 1969).

29. Gary Lachman, *Rudolph Steiner: An Introduction to His Life and Works* (Edinburgh: Floris Books, 2007); idem, *In Search of P. D. Ouspensky: The Genius in the Shadow of Gurdjieff* (Wheaton, IL: Quest Books, 2006).

30. Bernard Smith, *Modernism and Post-Modernism, a neo-Colonial Viewpoint*, Working Papers in Australian Studies, Sir Robert Menzies Centre for Australian Studies, Institute of Commonwealth Studies, University of London, 1992.

31. Rupert Arrowsmith, *Modernism and the Museum: Asian, African and Pacific Art and the London Avant-Garde* (Oxford University Press, 2011).

32. For some of these figures, Maurice Tuchman, ed., *The Spiritual in Art: Abstract Painting 1890–1985* (New York: Abbeville Press, 1987).

33. For Steiner's aesthetic, John F. Moffitt, *Occultism in Avant-Garde Art: The Case of Joseph Beuys* (Ann Arbor: UMI Research Press, 1988).

34. I owe the point to Tracy Thursfield.

35. Martin Green, *Mountain of Truth: The Counterculture Begins, Ascona, 1900–1920* (Hanover and London: University Press of New England, 1986); for Taos, n. 39 below.

36. Bennison, 'Muslim Universalism and Western Globalization', in A. G. Hopkins, ed., *Globalization in World History* (London: Pimlico, 2002), 74ff.

37. Billie Melman, *Women's Orients: English Women in the Middle East, 1718–1918* (London: Macmillan, 1995).

38. John Corbett in Georgina Born and David Hesmondhalgh, eds, *Western Music and Its Others* (Berkeley and Los Angeles: University of California Press, 2000), 163ff.

39. Lois Rudnick, *Utopian Vistas: The Mabel Dodge Luhan House and the American Counterculture* (Albuquerque: University of New Mexico Press, 1998).

40. Harry Liebersohn, *Aristocratic Encounters: European Travellers and North American Indians* (Cambridge University Press, 1998), 168.

41. Ibid., 1–2, 4.

42. Ibid., 167.

43. Stephen Hay, *Asian Ideas of East and West: Tagore and His Critics* (Cambridge, MA: Harvard University Press, 1970), 313–15.

44. Bernard Leach, *Beyond East and West: Memoirs, Portraits and Essays* (London: Faber and Faber), 74–5.

45. Marchand, *German Orientalism*; Joanne Cho, Eric Kurlander, and Douglas McGetchin, eds, *Transcultural Encounters between Germany and India: Kindred Spirits in the 19th and 20th Centuries* (London and New York: Routledge, 2013).

46. For the quotations, Jill Lloyd, *German Expressionism: Primitivism and Modernity* (New Haven: Yale University Press, 1991), 115–16.

47. Patrick Brantlinger, *Rule of Darkness: British Literature and Imperialism, 1830–1914* (Ithaca: Cornell University Press, 1988), 33ff.

48. Ibid., 12–13 (my italics).

49. Ian Buruma, *The Missionary and the Libertine* (New York: Vintage Books, 2001), 67ff.

50. Brantlinger, *Rule of Darkness*, 230, 240.

51. Lears, *No Place of Grace*, 100–2, 108–9, 117–18, 143, 222.

52. Benita Parry, *Delusions and Discoveries: Studies on India in the British Imagination, 1880–1930* (Berkeley and Los Angeles: University of California Press, 1992), 53 and n. 125.

53. Ibid., 131.

54. Kathleen Taylor, *Sir John Woodroffe, Tantra and Bengal* (Richmond: Curzon, 2001), 96.

55. Hugh Ridley, *Images of Imperial Rule* (London: Croom Helm, 1983), 108, 111, 114, 124.

56. Brantlinger, *Rule of Darkness*, 230.

57. Richard Fox, *Gandhian Utopia: Experiments with Culture* (Boston: Beacon Press, 1989), 108–9.

58. Leonard Gordon, *Bengal: The Nationalist Movement, 1876–1940* (New York: Columbia University Press, 1974), 112–13.

59. David Cannadine, *Ornamentalism: How the British Saw Their Empire* (London: Allen Lane, 2001), 12.

60. Bely, *The Emblematics of Meaning*, 1909.

61. Max Nordau, *Degeneration* (Lincoln: Nebraska University Press, 1993), 131.

62. Brian Stableford, *Scientific Romance in Britain 1890–1950* (New York: St Martin's Press, 1985), 40.

63. Brantlinger, *Rule of Darkness*, 251.

64. Lears, *No Place of Grace*, 172–3; Brantlinger, *Rule of Darkness*, 230, 232, 240.

2   Modernist Interworlds

1. For sensory decay, Jonathan Crary, *Suspensions of Perception: Attention, Spectacle and Modern Culture* (Cambridge, MA and London: MIT Press, 1999). For new optics and acoustics, Linda Henderson, *The Fourth Dimension and Non-Euclidean Geometry in Modern Art* (Princeton University Press, 1983).

2. Robert Pynsent, *Decadence and Innovation* (London: Weidenfeld and Nicolson, 1989), 111ff. Dion Fortune described the Sephira of Yesod on the Cabalistic Tree of Life as a 'treasure house of images': *The Mystical Qabalah*, 1935, 258.

3. Irena Paperno and Joan Grossman, *Creating Life: The Aesthetic Utopia of Russian Modernism* (Stanford University Press, 1994), 3.

4. Note the psychoses of Lautreamont, Nietzsche, Strindberg, Van Gogh, Artaud, and maybe Jung; also the alcohol or drug addictions of Munch, Malcolm Lowry, Pollock, Wols, Kerouac, Durrell and Burroughs.

5. For the reception of the *Gita* and *The Tibetan Book of the Dead*, E. J. Sharpe, *The Universal Gita: Western Images of the Bhagavad Gita* (La Salle: Open Court, 1985) and Donald Lopez, *Prisoners of Shangri-la: Tibetan Buddhism and the West* (University of Chicago Press, 1998), 46ff. Mircea Eliade, *Occultism, Witchcraft and Cultural Patterns* (University of Chicago Press, 1976), 47ff., reviews the 1960s occultist canon.

6. For Harvard Orientalism, C. McNelly Kearns, *T. S. Eliot and Indic Traditions* (Cambridge University Press, 2008). For Wagner's sources, Urs App, *Richard Wagner and Buddhism* (Rorschach and Kyoto: UniversityMedia, 2011).

7. Pynsent, *Decadence and Innovation*, 213–14 (my italics), apropos the Decadent 'fatal book'.

8. Pirandello, *The Late Mattia Pascal*, trans. N. Simborowski (New York: Dedalus, 1987), 117. For Pirandello's Theosophy, Ann Caesar in Peter Collier and Judy Davies, eds, *Modernism and the European Unconscious* (Oxford University Press, 1990), 132ff.

9. R. Schwab, *The Oriental Renaissance: Europe's Rediscovery of India and the East, 1680–1880* (New York: Columbia University Press, 1984). For Indian themes in German modernism, A. L. Willson, *Mythical Image: The Ideal of India in German Romanticism* (Durham, NC: Duke University Press, 1964), 241–2.

10. Catherine Albanese, *Corresponding Motion: Transcendental Religion and the New America* (Philadelphia: Temple University Press, 1977).

11. D. Michael Quinn, *Early Mormonism and the Magic World View* (Salt Lake City: Signature Books, 1998).

12. Richard Noll, *The Jung Cult: Origins of a Charismatic Movement* (Princeton University Press, 1994); Jeffrey Kripal, *Esalen: America and the Religion of No Religion* (University of Chicago Press, 2007).

13. Phil Cousineau, ed., *The Hero's Journey: Joseph Campbell on His Life and Work* (New York: Harper and Row, 1990).

14. William McGuire, *Bollingen: An Adventure in Collecting the Past* (Princeton University Press, 1989).

15. Charlotte Douglas in Maurice Tuchman, ed., *The Spiritual in Art: Abstract Painting 1890–1985* (New York: Abbeville Press, 1986), 192–5.

16. For Coomaraswamy's art ideals, Allan Antliff, *Anarchist Modernism: Art, Politics, and the First American Avant-Garde* (University of Chicago Press, 2001).

17. Quoted by John Lester, *Journey through Despair, 1880–1914: Transformations in British Literary Culture* (Princeton University Press, 1969), 89–90.
18. Alan Gauld, *A History of Hypnotism* (Cambridge University Press, 1992), 246, 504, 507.
19. For an example of the second transpersonal psychology, Ken Wilber, *The Spectrum of Consciousness* (Wheaton, IL: Quest Books, 1977).
20. R. L. Moore, *In Search of White Crows: Spiritualism, Parapsychology and American Culture* (Oxford University Press, 1977), 150.
21. Henri Ellenberger, *The Discovery of the Unconscious* (New York: Basic Books, 1981); Antoine Faivre, *Theosophy, Imagination, Tradition: Studies in Western Esotericism* (Albany: SUNY Press, 2000).
22. Adam Crabtree, *From Mesmer to Freud: Magnetic Sleep and the Roots of Psychological Healing* (New Haven: Yale University Press, 1993), ch. 16.
23. Stoddard Martin, *Orthodox Heresy, The Rise of 'Magic' as Religion and Its Relation to Literature* (London: MacMillan, 1989), 47.
24. Pynsent, *Decadence and Innovation*, 139–40.
25. S. M. Brown in Gay Allen and Ed Folsom, eds, *Walt Whitman and the World* (University of Iowa Press, 1995), 148ff.; Gary Lachman, *A Dark Muse* (New York: Thunders Mouth Press, 2005), 229ff.
26. *Studies in Classic American Literature*, 1923, ch. 6.
27. T. J. Jackson Lears, *No Place of Grace: Antimodernism and the Transformation of American Culture, 1880–1920* (University of Chicago Press, 1994), 36, 38.
28. Ibid., 232.
29. Tom Steele, *Alfred Orage and the Leeds Art Club 1893–1923* (Aldershot: Scolar Press, 1990), 75, 111.
30. Henry Summerfield, *That Myriad-Minded Man: A Biography of George William Russell, 'AE' 1867–1935* (Gerrards Cross: Colin Smythe, 1975), 48; J. W. Forster, *Fictions of the Irish Literary Revival* (Syracuse University Press, 1987), 76.
31. Noll, *Jung Cult*, 51–4.
32. Harry Harootunian in Stephen Vlastos, ed., *Mirror of Modernity: Invented Traditions of Modern Japan* (Berkeley and Los Angeles: University of California Press, 1998), 157.
33. Lears, *No Place of Grace*, 169.
34. For yogic-Tantric echoes in modernism, J. C. Bramble in Geoffrey Samuel and Jay Johnston, eds, *Religion and the Subtle Body in Asia and the West* (London and New York: Routledge, 2013), ch. 10.
35. James West, *Russian Symbolism: A Study of Vyacheslav Ivanov and the Russian Symbolist Aesthetic* (London: Methuen, 1970), 75 (my italics).
36. For mystical anarchist theatre, Beatrice Glatzer Rosenthal, ed., *The Occult in Russian and Soviet Culture* (Ithaca and London: Cornell University Press, 1997), 382ff.
37. For Tagore's 'aristocratic-folk ideology', Jon Lang, Madhavi Desai and Miki Desai, *Architecture and Independence: The Search for Identity – India 1880 to 1980* (New York: Oxford University Press, 1997), 120ff.
38. For Bergson, Noll, *Jung Cult*, 129.
39. For Pryse, Summerfield, *That Myriad-Minded Man*, 64; for Bynner and Orage, P. B. Taylor, *Gurdjieff and Orage: Brothers in Elysium* (York Beach: Weiser, 2001), 210.
40. Martin, *Orthodox Heresy*, 43.
41. Romain Rolland, *The Life of Vivekenanda and the Universal Gospel* (Almora: Advaita Ashram, 1931), 45, 83.
42. Lears, *No Place of Grace*, 175.

43. See Garrett's autobiography, *Many Voices* (Richmond: Time Life, 1991).

44. R. S. Ellwood, ed., *Eastern Spirituality in America, Selected Writings* (New York: Paulist Press, 1987), 125.

45. Ibid., 132–3 (my italics).

46. John Elderfield, ed., *Flight Out of Time: A Dada Diary by Hugo Ball* (Berkeley and Los Angeles: University of California Press, 1996), 108 (my italics).

47. Ibid., 112.

48. Ibid., 101, 109.

49. Ibid., 111.

50. Ibid., 104.

51. Ibid., 108.

52. Bruce Lamb, *The Wizard of the Upper Amazon* (Berkeley: North Atlantic Books, 1971).

53. G. R. S. Mead, *The Doctrine of the Subtle Body in the Western Tradition* (Shaftesbury: Solos Press, 1993), 70.

54. For *vis imaginativa*, Faivre, *Theosophy, Imagination*, 99ff.

55. Elderfield, *Flight Out of Time*, 73–5 (my italics).

56. John Bowlt in Tuchman, *The Spiritual in Art*, 178–9.

57. Elderfield, *Flight Out of Time*, 119 (my italics).

58. Ibid., 113, 69.

59. Lears, *No State of Grace*, 306–7.

60. Kathleen Rosenblatt, *Rene Daumal: The Life and Work of a Mystic Guide* (New York: SUNY Press, 1999).

61. Donald Gordon, *Expressionism: Art and Ideas* (New Haven: Yale University Press, 1988), 170.

62. Walter Benjamin, Eng. trans., *The Arcades Project* (Cambridge, MA: Harvard University Press, 1999), 543ff.

63. Robert Temple, *Open to Suggestion: The Uses and Abuses of Hypnosis* (Wellingborough: Aquarian Press, 1989), 62.

64. For Machen, Lester, *Journey through Despair*, 105.

65. For Surrealism and spiritualism, Daniel Cottom, *Abyss of Reason: Cultural Movements, Revelations, and Betrayals* (Oxford University Press, 1991).

66. V. Kolocotroni, J. A. Goldman and O. Taxidou, *Modernism: An Anthology of Sources and Documents* (Edinburgh University Press, 1998), 31.

67. Excerpted from the 1977 Penguin edition, 12–14.

68. Henderson, *Fourth Dimension*, 207–8.

69. Marina Yaguello, *Lunatic Lovers of Language: Imaginary Languages and Their Inventors* (New Jersey: Fairleigh Dickinson University Press, 1991), 100.

70. Susan Sontag, *Artaud: Selected Writings* (Berkeley and Los Angeles: University of California Press, 1988), 220.

71. Elderfield, *Flight Out of Time*, 104.

72. Ronald Vroon in Vroon and Paul Schmidt, *Velimir Khlebnikov: Collected Works, Vol. III* (Boston: Harvard University Press, 1997), 1.

73. Douglas in Tuchman, *The Spiritual in Art*, 187.

74. Ibid. In touch with Khlebnikov, Roman Jacobsen was also interested Khlysty sect glossolalia: Yaguello, *Lunatic Lovers*, 103.

75. John Moffitt, *Occultism in Avant-Garde Art: The Case of Joseph Beuys* (Ann Arbor: UMI Research Press, 1988), 163.

76. H. E. Salisbury, preface to Bely's *The Silver Dove* (New York: Random House, 1974), xxxv.

77. Wassily Kandinsky, *Concerning the Spiritual in Art* (New York: Dover, 1977), 15.

78. J. Hahl-Koch, *Letters, Pictures and Documents by Arnold Schoenberg, Wassily Kandinsky* (London: Faber and Faber, 1984), 121.

79. For Kruchenykh, Marjorie Perloff, *The Futurist Moment* (University of Chicago Press, 1986), 123; for Ball, Michael Tucker, *Dreaming with Open Eyes: The Shamanic Spirit in Twentieth Century Art and Culture* (San Francisco: Harper, 1992), 189.

80. For Huidobro, Tucker, *Dreaming with Open Eyes*, 190; for Artaud, 192.

81. Joseph Straus, *The Music of Ruth Crawford Seeger* (Cambridge University Press, 1995), 207.

82. Fernand Ouellette, *Edgard Varese* (New York: Orion Press, 1973), 127.

83. Olivia Mattis in James Leggio, ed., *Music and Modern Art* (New York and London: Routledge, 2002), 139ff.

3 Destruction–Creation: From Decadence to Dada

1. Porter in Marijke Gijswijt-Hofstra, Brian Levack and Roy Porter, *The Athlone History of Witchcraft and Magic in Europe*, vol. 5 (London: Athlone, 1999), 255ff.

2. Gershom Scholem, *Sabbatai Sevi: The Mystical Messiah* (Bollingen Foundation, Princeton University Press, 1976), 8ff.

3. Alan Robinson, *Poetry, Painting and Ideas, 1885–1914* (London: MacMillan, 1985).

4. *Twilight in Italy*, 'The Lemon Gardens', 53–4, discussed by Peter Fjagesund, *The Apocalyptic World of D. H. Lawrence* (New York: Scandinavian University Press, 1992), 44.

5. I. F. Clarke, *The Pattern of Expectation, 1644–2001* (London: Jonathan Cape, 1979); idem, *Voices Prophesying War, 1793–3749* (Oxford University Press, 1992).

6. Richard Ellmann, *Yeats: The Man and His Masks* (London: Allen Lane, 1989), 100; Peter Kuch, *Yeats and AE* (Gerrards Cross: Colin Smythe, 1986), 106.

7. R. Pynsent, *Decadence and Innovation* (London: Weidenfeld and Nicolson, 1989), 148.

8. Quoted from Marc, *100 Aphorisms* (1915), by Donald Gordon, *Expressionism: Art and Idea* (New Haven: Yale University Press, 1991), 24.

9. Urs App, *Richard Wagner and Buddhism* (Rorschach and Kyoto: UniversityMedia, 2011); Stephen Cross, *Schopenhauer's Encounter with Indian Thought* (Honolulu: University of Hawaii Press, 2013).

10. Ronald Taylor, *Richard Wagner: His Life, Art and Thought* (London: Elek, 1979), 228, 231.

11. Raymond Schwab, *The Oriental Renaissance: Europe's Rediscovery of India and the East, 1680–1880* (New York: Columbia University Press, 1984), 418ff.

12. Frantisek Deak, *Symbolist Theater: The Formation of an Avant-Garde* (Baltimore: Johns Hopkins University Press, 1993), 82.

13. Eugen Weber, *France, Fin de Siecle* (Cambridge, MA: Harvard University Press, 1986), ch. 1.

14. Max Nordau, *Degeneration* (Lincoln: Nebraska University Press, 1993), 20.

15. Robert Orledge, *Debussy and The Theatre* (Cambridge University Press, 1982), 269.

16. For Belgian *Schopenhauerisme*, Louis Roberts-Jones, *Brussels Fin de Siecle* (Koln: Taschen, 1999), 92; for Kubin, Patrick Werkner, *Austrian Expressionism* (Oxford: Premier Book Marketing, 1994), 205.

17. Munch apparently owned a book of selections from Schopenhauer. The implications of this for his art need spelling out.

18. For Rodenbach, Khnopff and Schopenhauer, Judi Freeman in Maurice Tuchman, ed., *The Spiritual in Art: Abstract Painting 1890–1985* (New York: Abbeville Press, 1986), 405; for Klimt's Schopenhauerian Vienna University murals, Carl Schorske, *Fin de Siecle Vienna: Politics and Culture* (Cambridge University Press, 1981), 205ff; for Klinger and Schopenhauer, Manfred Boetzkes, *Max Klinger, Wege zum Gesamtkunstwerk* (Mainz am Rhein: von Zabern, 1984).

19. Bryan Magee, *The Philosophy of Schopenhauer* (Oxford University Press, 1983), appendix 7.

20. James Robinson, *Eugene O'Neill and Oriental Thought* (Carbondale and Edwardsville: Southern Illinois University Press, 1982), 64. Strindberg's friends, Munch (note his *Madonna*) and Przybyszweski ('in the beginning was sex') were similarly obsessed by will's original sin.

21. Joseph Horowitz, *Wagner Nights: An American History* (Berkeley and Los Angeles: University of California Press, 1994), 114.

22. Dale Riepe, *Philosophy of India and Its Impact on American Thought* (Springfield, IL: Charles C. Thomas, 1970), 120–1.

23. Christian Kloeckner, 'Re-Orienting Impersonality: T. S. Eliot and the Far East', in Zaoming Qian, ed., *Modernism and the Orient* (Ezra Pound Center: University of New Orleans Press, 2012), 163ff.; Devin Zuber, '"Poking around in the Dust of Asia": Wallace Stevens, Modernism, and the Aesthetics of the East', in Sabine Sielke and Christian Kloeckner, eds, *Orient and Orientalisms in US-American Poetry and Poetics* (Frankfurt am Main: Lang, 2009), 189ff.

24. Robert Pincus-Witten, *Les Salons de la Rose + Croix, 1892–1897* (London: Piccadilly Gallery, 1968).

25. For Symbolism's decline, Jean Pierrot, *The Decadent Imagination, 1880–1900* (Chicago and London: University of Chicago Press, 1981), 238ff.

26. Mary Greer, *Women of the Golden Dawn: Rebels and Priestesses* (Rochester, VT: Park Street Press, 1995).

27. John Bowlt in Tuchman, *The Spiritual in Art*, 170, quoting Berdyaev: 'painting is passing from physical bodies to ether and astral ones … the terrifying pulverization of … material bodies began with Vrubel. The transition to the other plane can be sensed in Ciurlionis.'

28. Alain Mercier, *Les Sources Esoteriques et Occultes de la Poesie Symboliste 1870–1914* (Paris: Nizet, 1969), two volumes.

29. Nordau, *Degeneration*, 539, 544.

30. 'Chaos, disintegrated music, proto-plasma' was one critic's verdict on Busoni's occultist *Nocturne symphonique*: Antony Beaumont, *Busoni the Composer* (London: Faber and Faber, 1985), 180.

31. For the *mundus imaginalis*, Tom Cheetham, *The World Turned Inside Out: Henry Corbin and Islamic Mysticism* (Woodstock: Spring Journal Books, 2003).

32. Stanley Rabinowitz, *The Noise of Change; Russian Literature and the Critics, 1891–1917* (Ann Arbor: Ardis, 1986), 198ff.

33. Maria Carlson, *'No Religion Higher Than Truth': A History of the Theosophical Movement in Russia, 1875–1922* (Princeton University Press, 1993), 201–2.

34. For Blok and Briusov, Daniel Gerould, *Doubles, Demons and Dreamers: An International Collection of Symbolist Drama* (New York: Performing Arts Journal Publications, 1985), 16, 22.

35. Solov'ev's influence explains why Bely's 'thought-form' technique is more nihilistic than Kandinsky's. Like Scriabin, Kandinsky foresaw an imminent Theosophical millennium; Bely adopted Solov'ev's vision of a 'pan-mongolist' reign of Antichrist before the Second Coming.

36. Adam Crabtree, *From Mesmer to Freud: Magnetic Sleep and the Roots of Psychological Healing* (New Haven: Yale University Press, 1993), 197.

37. Carlson, *'No Religion Higher Than Truth'*, 201.

38. Linda Henderson, *The Fourth Dimension and Non-Euclidean Geometry in Modern Art* (Princeton University Press, 1983), 203.

39. Stephen Stepanchev in Gay Allen and E. Folsom, *Walt Whitman and the World* (Iowa City: Iowa University Press, 1995), 303. For 'world-making' and 'life-creation', Irena Paperno and Joan Grossman, *Creating Life: The Aesthetic Utopia of Russian Modernism* (Stanford University Press, 1994). For Bal'mont and Theosophy, Carlson, *'No Religion Higher Than Truth'*, 159.

40. Beongcheon Yu, *The Great Circle: American Writers and the Orient* (Detroit: Wayne State University Press, 1983), 61.

41. For Whitman and India, Chari in Allen and Folsom, *Whitman*, 399, 402; for Lawrence, Brown, in Allen and Folsom, *Whitman*, 149; for Whitman's 'Superior Soul', Asselineau, in Allen and Folsom, *Whitman*, 270.

42. Christoph Asendorf, *Batteries of Life: On the History of Things and Their Perception in Modernity* (Berkeley and Los Angeles: University of California Press, 1993), 153, 163–4.

43. Asselineau in Allen and Folsom, *Whitman*, 242, 237.

44. Constant Lambert, *Music Ho!* (London, Faber and Faber, 1934).

45. For 'unselving of objects', Chari in Allen and Folsom, *Whitman*, 491.

46. R. C. Washton Long, *German Expressionism: Documents from the End of the Wilhelmine Empire to the Rise of National Socialism* (Berkeley and Los Angeles: University of California Press, 1995), 93, 264.

47. For Ouspensky, Patricia Railing, ed., *From Science to Systems of Art: On Russian Abstract Art and Language 1910/1920* (Forest Row: Artists Bookworks, 1989), 41–2; for Yeats, Shiro Naito, *Yeats and Zen: A Study of the Transformation of His Mask* (Kyoto: Yamaguchi, 1984), 122.

48. Charlotte Douglas in Tuchman, *The Spiritual in Art*, 186–7.

49. For Vivekananda and Malevich, Bernard Smith, *Modernism's History: A Study in Twentieth Century Art and Ideas* (New Haven: Yale University Press, 1998), 161.

50. Pynsent, *Decadence and Innovation*, 224.

51. Gerould, *Doubles, Demons and Dreamers*, 7.

52. For apocalyptic time versus historical time, Susan Buck-Morss, *Dreamworld and Catastrophe: The Passing of Mass Utopia in East and West* (Cambridge, MA: MIT Press, 2002), ch. 2.

53. John Elderfield, ed., *Flight Out Of Time: A Dada Diary by Hugo Ball* (Berkeley and Los Angeles: University of California Press, 1996), 224–5.

54. Long, *German Expressionism*, 264. Strindberg had described Gauguin as 'a sort of Titan, who jealous of the creator, creates his own microcosm'.

55. For Kandinsky and Theosophy, Sixtus Ringbom, *The Sounding Cosmos* (Helsingfors: Acta Academiae Aboensis, 1970); for Theosophy and the abstract pioneers generally, Ringbom in Tuchman, *The Spiritual in Art*, 131ff.

56. Long, *German Expressionism*, 83 for Hartlaub, 87 for Daubler.

57. For the Lowells, Sanehide Kodama, *American Poetry and Japanese Culture* (Hamden, CT: Archon Books, 1984).

58. Elderfield, *Flight out of Time*, 53.

59. Jelena Hahl-Koch, *Arnold Schoenberg, Wassily Kandinsky: Letters, Pictures and Documents* (London: Faber and Faber, 1984), 142.

60. Glenn Watkins, *Pyramids at the Louvre: Music, Culture and Collage from Stravinsky to the Postmodernists* (Cambridge, MA: Harvard University Press, 1994), 58.

61. Richard Sheppard, *Modernism – Dada – Postmodernism* (Evanston, IL: Northwestern University Press, 2000), 174–5, 228.

62. Jonathan Herman, *I and Tao: Martin Buber's Encounter with Chuang Tzu* (Albany: SUNY Press, 1996).

63. Sheppard, *Modernism – Dada*, 75–6, adding that the Bakhtin circle in 1920s Leningrad 'was … interested in Eastern … religion and … Bergson'.

64. Robinson, *Eugene O'Neill and Oriental Thought*; Yu, *Great Circle*, 141ff.

65. For Dadaist precursors, M. L. Grossman, *Dada: Paradox, Mystification, and Ambiguity in European Literature* (New York: Pegasus, 1971).

66. For Hausmann on abstraction, Timothy Benson, *Raoul Hausmann and Berlin Dada* (Ann Arbor: UMI Research Press, 1987), 50; for Herzfelde and Hartlaub, Long, *German Expressionism*, 274, 290.

67. Sheppard, *Modernism – Dada*, 256, 283.

68. Benson, *Haussmann*, 46, 49.

69. Ibid., 48; for Hausmann's reading, Sheppard, *Modernism – Dada*, 276.

70. For Flake, Arp and Ball, Sheppard, ibid., 268–9.

71. Elderfield, *Flight out of Time*, 221.

72. Sheppard, *Modernism – Dada*, 269ff.

73. For what follows, see Sheppard in Stephen Foster and Rudolph Kuenzli, eds, *Dada Spectrum: The Dialectics of Revolt* (Madison, WI: Coda Press, 1979), esp. 96–7, and Sheppard, *Modernism – Dada*, 269ff.

74. For Hausmann, Benson, *Haussmann*, 49; for Evola, Sheppard, *Modernism – Dada*, 277.

75. Sheppard, *Dada Spectrum*, 98.

76. Benson, *Haussmann*, 51. A novelist and satirist of Expressionism, Friedlander wrote as 'Mynona'. His *Creative Indifference* appeared in 1918.

77. Quoted by Ko Won, *Buddhist Elements in Dada: A Comparison of Tristan Tzara, Takahashi Shinkichi and Their Fellow Poets* (New York University Press, 1977), 85.

78. Sheppard, *Dada Spectrum*, 99.

79. For the urinal, Wanda Corn, *The Great American Thing: Modern Art and National Identity, 1915–1935* (Berkeley and Los Angeles: University of California Press, 1999), 49 n. 10, 76, 89.

80. Sheppard, *Modernism – Dada*, 176.

81. Quoted by Peter Conrad, *Modern Times, Modern Places: Life and Art in the Twentieth Century* (London: Thames and Hudson, 1998), 696.

4 Call to Order, Occultist Geopolitics, Spirit Wars

1. John Milner, *Symbolists and Decadents* (London: Studio Vista, 1971), 115.

2. Jacques Le Rider, *Modernity and Crises of Identity: Culture and Society in Fin de Siècle Vienna* (Cambridge: Polity, 1993), 57.

3. James Webb, *The Occult Establishment* (Glasgow: Drew 1981), 48. Generally, Sophie Treitel, *A Science for the Soul: Occultism and the Genesis of the German Modern* (Baltimore and London: Johns Hopkins University Press, 2004).

4. Nicholas Goodrick-Clarke, *The Occult Roots of Nazism* (London: Tauris Parke, 1992).

5. Andrei Znamenski, *Red Shambhala: Magic, Prophecy and Geopolitics in the Heart of Asia* (Wheaton IL: Quest Books, 2011).

6. Warwick Gould and Marjorie Reeves, *Joachim of Fiore and the Myth of the Eternal Evangel in the Nineteenth and Twentieth Centuries* (Oxford University Press, 2001).

7. 'A Letter from Germany' (1928), *Phoenix: The Posthumous Papers of D. H. Lawrence* (New York: Penguin USA, 1972), 107ff.

8. Edward Timms and Peter Collier, eds, *Visions and Blueprints: Avant-Garde Culture and Radical Politics in Early Twentieth Century Europe* (Manchester University Press, 1988).

9. Daniel Pick, *Svengali's Web: The Alien Encounter in Modern Culture* (New Haven: Yale University Press, 2000).

10. R. C. Grogin, *The Bergsonian Controversy in France, 1900–1914* (Alberta: Calgary University Press, 1988).

11. Susan Manning, *Ecstasy and the Demon: Feminism and Nationalism in the Dance of Mary Wigman* (Berkeley and Los Angeles: University of California Press, 1993).

12. Quoted from Wyndham Lewis, *Paleface: The Philosophy of the Melting Pot* (London: Chatto and Windus, 1929), 29ff.

13. John Fisher, *Gentleman Spies* (Stroud: Sutton Publishing, 2002), 112; Sean McMeekin, *The Berlin–Baghdad Express: The Ottoman Empire and Germany's Bid for World Power, 1896–1918* (London: Allen Lane, 2010).

14. Tom Reiss, *The Orientalist: In Search of a Man Caught between East and West* (London: Vintage, 2006).

15. Ibid., 208–9.

16. Ibid., 228ff.

17. Ibid., 236–7. For Masterman, Robert MacDonald, *Sons of Empire: The Frontier and the Boy Scout Movement, 1890–1918* (University of Toronto Press, 1993), 15.

18. For old imperial religious tolerance, Mark Mazower, *Salonika, City of Ghosts: Christians, Muslims and Jews, 1430–1950* (London: Harper Perennial, 2005).

19. Reiss, *The Orientalist*, 309.

20. Ibid., 244–5.

21. Dominic Green, *Armies of God: Islam and Empire on the Nile, 1869–1899* (London: Century, 2007), 196.

22. For this poorly covered controversy, Barry Cadwallader, *Crisis of the European Mind: A Study of André Malraux and Drieu La Rochelle* (Cardiff: University of Wales Press, 1981), ch. 2.

23. Peter Wollen, *Raiding the Icebox: Reflections of Twentieth Century Culture* (London: Verso, 1993), 24–5 (my italics).

24. Peter Heehs, *The Bomb in Bengal: The Rise of Revolutionary Terrorism in India* (New Delhi: Oxford University Press, 1993), 30ff.

25. Dale Riepe, *Philosophy of India and Its Impact on American Thought* (Springfield, IL: Charles C. Thomas, 1970), 127.

26. Mark Sedgwick, *Against the Modern World: Traditionalism and the Secret Intellectual History of the Twentieth Century* (New York: Oxford University Press, 2004).

27. Eugen Weber, *Satan Franc Macon: la Mystification de Leo Taxil* (Paris: Juillard, 1964).

28. For *The Protocols*, Webb, *Occult Establishment*, ch. 4.

29. Lewis, *Paleface*, 255.

30. Martin Green, *The Von Richthofen Sisters: The Triumphant and the Tragic Modes of Love* (Albuquerque: University of New Mexico Press, 1988); Gerald Doherty, *Oriental Lawrence: the Quest for the Secrets of Sex* (New York: Lang, 2001).

31. Hermann Rauschning, *Hitler Speaks* (London: Thornton Butterworth, 1939), 49.

32. Roger Griffin, *Fascism* (Oxford University Press, 1995), 357, for Ernst Niekisch's hope for a German–Russian alliance against the West; G. D. Stark, *Entrepreneurs of Ideology: Neoconservative Publishers in Germany, 1890–1933* (Chapel Hill: University of North Carolina Press, 1981), for Eugen Diederichs's Orientalism, Russian publications and liking for Eastern Europe.

33. *Phoenix*, 109.

34. Joscelyn Godwin, *Arktos: The Polar Myth in Science, Symbolism and Nazi Survival* (Kempton, IL: Adventures Unlimited Press, 1996), 82–8.

35. Webb, *Occult Establishment*, 198–204.

36. James Moore, *Gurdjieff and Mansfield* (London: Routledge and Kegan Paul, 1980); P. B. Taylor, *Gurdjieff and Orage: Brothers in Elysium* (York Beach: Weiser, 2001); Jon Woodson, *To Make a New Race: Gurdjieff, Toomer and the Harlem Renaissance* (Jackson: University Press of Mississippi, 1999).

37. Grogin, *Bergsonian Controversy*, 142; Richard Griffiths, *The Reactionary Revolution: The Catholic Revival in French Literature, 1870–1914* (London: Constable, 1966). Claudel Orientalized, as did Messiaen, another Catholic.

38. Thomas Tweed, *The American Encounter with Buddhism, 1844–1912* (Bloomington: Indiana University Press, 1992), 158: 'processive, nonsubstantialist views of the universe and the self were advanced by natural scientists and philosophers and given expression in ... Modernist fiction and painting.'

39. Cadwallader, *Crisis*, 36.

40. Mulk Raj Anand, *Conversations in Bloomsbury* (New Delhi: Oxford University Press, 1981).

41. Ibid., 162.

42. Ibid., 38–9.

43. Ibid., 108ff.

44. Ibid., 125ff.

45. Ibid., 174–5.

46. Ibid., 106 for Virginia's venom.

47. Ibid., 173, 176.

48. Ibid., 172.

49. Rachel Shteir, *Striptease: The Untold History of the Girlie Show* (New York: Oxford University Press, 2006).

50. Sherrill Tippins, *February House* (New York: Houghton Mifflin Harcourt, 2005).

51. Comparing Kiralfy's '*Gesamtkunstwerk* for the masses' with de Mille's epics, L. Senelick, 'Spectacle and the Kiralfys', *Dance Chronicle*, 12/1 (1989), 151.

52. Suzanne Shelton, *Divine Dancer: A Biography of Ruth St. Denis* (Garden City, NY: Doubleday, 1981); Joseph H. Mazo, *Prime Movers: The Makers of Dance in America* (Pennington: Princeton Book Company, 1986), 61ff.

53. Mazo, *Prime Movers*, 75. For dance criticism, Marshall Cohen and Roger Copeland, eds, *What is Dance? Readings in Theory and Criticism* (New York: Oxford University Press, 1983); for New Thought and St Denis, Nancy Ruyter, *The*

Cultivation of Body and Mind in Nineteenth-Century American Delsartism (Westport: Praeger, 1999).

54. Ruyter, *Cultivation*, 63.

55. Jonathan Massey, *Crystal and Arabesque: Claude Bradgon, Ornament and Modern Architecture* (University of Pittsburgh Press, 2009).

56. Elisabeth de Jong-Keesing, *Inayat Khan: A Biography* (The Hague and London: East West Publications, 1974), 94–5. Mata Hari's debut was at the Parisian Musee Guimet in 1905: Lynn Garafola, *Diaghilev's Ballets Russes* (New York: Oxford University Press, 1989), 282.

57. The photograph is reproduced in an essay on *Ballets Russes* Orientalism in Nancy Baer, ed., *The Art of Enchantment: Diaghilev's Ballets Russes, 1909–1929* (San Francisco: Fine Arts Museums/Universe Books, 1988).

58. For 'music-hall modernism', avant-garde alliances with popular culture and Futurist use of advertising techniques, Jeffrey Weiss, *The Popular Culture of Modern Art* (New Haven: Yale University Press, 1994); also Kirk Varnedoe and Adam Gopnik, eds, *Modern Art and Popular Culture: Readings in High and Low* (New York: Abrams, 1990).

59. For the elephant, Arthur Saxon, *P. T. Barnum: The Legend and the Man* (New York: Columbia University Press, 1989), 306. Paul Greenhalgh, *Ephemeral Vistas: History of the Expositions Universelles, Great Exhibitions and World's Fairs* (Manchester University Press, 1990), 43, notes how Kiralfy made a gigantic circus out of the imperial theme; see also John Mackenzie, *Orientalism: History, Theory and the Arts* (Manchester University Press, 1995), 86ff. and 196.

60. For Prampolini on Bakst, Garafola, *Ballets Russes*, 82.

61. Jane Sherman, *Soaring: The Diary and Letters of a Denishawn Dancer in the Far East, 1925–1926* (Middletown: Wesleyan University Press, 1977).

62. 'Grand Hotel Metaphysics' is the title of a chapter in Ball's (1914–20) Dada novel *Tenderenda the Fantast*.

5 'Zen' in the Second Abstraction

1. In the forties, Breton forecast a return of the 'accursed sciences' through 'accursed poetry'; Etienne-Martin and Remedio Varo followed Gurdjieff; Victor Brauner, a Spiritualist, pursued alchemy, magic, Tarot and Cabala; Kurt Seligman wrote on alchemy and the gnostics in *View* 1945, publishing a survey, *Magic*, in 1948. See also M. E. Warlick, *Max Ernst and Alchemy: A Magician in Search of Myth* (Austin: University of Texas Press, 2001).

2. Stephen Polcari, *Abstract Expressionism and the Modern Experience* (Cambridge University Press, 1993), ch. 2.

3. For *Pacific Era*, Klaus Berger, *Japonisme in Western Painting from Whistler to Matisse* (Cambridge University Press, 1992), 265. A June 1954 *Cimaise* article claimed Graves, Tobey, Pollock, Rothko and Clyfford Still for an *École du Pacifique*. In 1955 the Getty Museum director added Wolfgang Paalen, Onslow-Ford and Lee Mullican.

4. Helen Westgeest, *Zen in the Fifties: Interaction in Art between East and West* (Amstelveen: Wanders, 1996), 44–5.

5. Bert Winther in Alexandra Munroe, ed., *Japanese Art after 1945: Scream against the Sky* (New York: Abrams, 1994), 61.

6. Ibid., 59.

7. For Zen's 'collapsed *trikaya*', Bernard Faure, *The Rhetoric of Immediacy: A Cultural Critique of Chan/Zen Buddhism* (Princeton University Press, 1991).

8. Winther in Munroe, *Japanese Art*, 57.

9. Ibid., 59–60.

10. Ellen Pearlman, *Nothing and Everything: The Influence of Buddhism on the American Avant-Garde, 1942–1962* (Berkeley: Evolver, 2012).

11. Zhaoming Qian, *Orientalism and Modernism: The Legacy of China in Pound and Williams* (Durham: Duke University Press, 1995).

12. Beongcheon Yu, *The Great Circle: American Writers and the Orient* (Detroit: Wayne University Press, 1983), ch. 4; Jonathan Spence, *The Chan's Great Continent: China in Western Minds* (New York and London: Norton, 1998); William Schwartz, *The Imaginative Interpretation of the Far East in Modern French Literature, 1800–1925* (Paris: Champion, 1927).

13. D. J. Clarke, *The Influence of Oriental Thought on Postwar American Painting and Sculpture* (New York and London: Garland, 1988), ch. 2.

14. Reinhard May, *Heidegger's Hidden Sources: East Asian Influences on His Work* (London and New York: Routledge, 1996), noting 'thefts' from Taoism, Zen and Kyoto School philosophy.

15. Doris in Ken Friedman, ed., *A Fluxus Reader* (Chichester: Academy Editions, 1998), 91ff.

16. Jacqueline Decter, *Nicholas Roerich: The Life and Art of a Russian Master* (London: Thames and Hudson, 1989), 136.

17. William McGuire, *Bollingen: An Adventure in Collecting the Past* (Princeton University Press, 1982), 208ff.

18. Pearlman, *Nothing and Everything*, 95–6.

19. Stefan Tanaka, *Japan's Orient: Rendering Pasts into History* (Berkeley and Los Angeles: University of California Press, 1995), chs 3–6.

20. Harold Bloom, *The American Religion: The Emergence of a Post-Christian Nation* (New York: Simon and Schuster, 1992).

21. R. H. Scharf, 'The Zen of Japanese Nationalism', in Donald Lopez, ed., *Curators of the Buddha: The Study of Buddhism under Colonialism* (University of Chicago Press, 1995), 140.

22. Gustavo Benavides, 'Giuseppe Tucci, or Buddhology in the Age of Fascism', in Lopez, ed., *Curators of the Buddha*, ch. 4.

23. For context, Frances Stonor Saunders, *The Cultural Cold-War: The CIA and the World of Arts and Letters* (New York: The New Press, 2013).

24. Serge Guibault, *How America Stole the Idea of Modern Art: Abstract Expressionism, Freedom, and the Cold War* (University of Chicago Press, 1985).

25. Kay Larson, *Where the Heart Beats: John Cage, Zen Buddhism, and the Inner life of Artists* (New York: Penguin, 2013), 165–7.

26. Sulagna Sengupta, *Jung in India* (New Orleans: Spring Journal Books, 2013), 82ff.

27. J. W. de Gruchy, *Orienting Arthur Waley: Japonism, Orientalism and the Creation of Japanese Literature in English* (Honolulu: University of Hawaii Press, 2003), 164.

28. Winther in Munroe, *Japanese Art*, 57. For a good bibliography, Alexandra Munroe, ed., *The Third Mind: American Artists Contemplate Asia, 1860–1989* (New York: Guggenheim Museum, 2009).

29. Pearlman, *Nothing and Everything*, xii.
30. Gail Levin and Marianne Lorenz, *Theme and Improvisation: Kandinsky and the American Avant-Garde, 1912–50* (Ohio: Dayton Art Institute, 1992).
31. James Monte and Anne Glusker, *The Transcendental Painting Group: New Mexico 1938–1941* (New Mexico: Albuquerque Museum, 1982).
32. For music, John Mackenzie, *Orientalism: History, Theory and the Arts* (Manchester University Press, 1995), 138ff.
33. For pioneers of the second *Japonisme*, Francoise Will-Levaillant, 'La Chine d'Andre Masson', *Revue de l'Art* (1971) 12, 64–74. For Western knowledge of calligraphy, Westgeest, *Zen in the Fifties*, 100–1.
34. Westgeest, *Zen in the Fifties*, 9.
35. Isaac Luria was a renowned sixteenth-century Cabalist. See Chapter 6 on Bob Dylan.
36. Dore Ashton, *Noguchi: East and West* (Berkeley and Los Angeles: University of California Press, 1993).
37. Robert Weinberg, *Spinning the Clay into Stars: Bernard Leach and the Baha'i Faith* (Oxford: George Ronald, 1999), 14–15.
38. Domiciled in Ireland from the late fifties, Graves met Paul Tillich, Campbell and Rothko in 1960. He revisited the East in 1971 and 1977: Freeman in Maurice Tuchman, ed., *The Spiritual in Art: Abstract Painting, 1890–1985* (New York: Abbeville, 1987), 400.
39. Wulf Herzogenrath and Andreas Kreul, eds, *Sounds of the Inner Eye: John Cage, Mark Tobey, Morris Graves* (Seattle: University of Washington Press, 2002).
40. Between spells in Seattle, Tobey was associated with Dartington from 1930–38.
41. Linda Henderson, *The Fourth Dimension and Non-Euclidean Geometry in Modern Art* (Princeton University Press, 1983), 345 n. 9.
42. Weinberg, *Spinning the Clay*, 117.
43. Freeman in Tuchman, *The Spiritual in Art*, 414; Steven Naifeh and Gregory Smith, *Jackson Pollock: An American Saga* (New York: Clarkson N. Potter, 1990).
44. Moritz in Tuchman, *The Spiritual in Art*, 309–10.
45. For Fischinger's 'animistic Buddhism', Moritz in Tuchman, *The Spiritual in Art*, 301; for his Kandinskyism, Levin and Lorenz, *Theme and Improvisation*, 159ff.
46. Moritz in Tuchman, *The Spiritual in Art*, 309–10.
47. For the Indians, who taught Hindu dance and philosophy at Black Mountain College in 1949, Clarke, *Influence of Oriental Thought*, ch. 3 n. 106.
48. Henderson, *Fourth Dimension*, 227.
49. Freeman in Tuchman, *The Spiritual in Art*, 415.
50. Carole Tonkinson, ed., *Big Sky Mind: Buddhism and the Beat Generation* (London: Thorsons, 1996), 326–7.
51. Stephen Schwartz, *From West to East: California and the Making of the American Mind* (New York: Free Press, 1998).
52. Perle Epstein, *The Private Labyrinth of Malcolm Lowry: Under the Volcano and Cabbala* (New York: Holt, Rinehart and Winston, 1969); for Duncan, Timothy Materer, *Modernist Alchemy: Poetry and the Occult* (Ithaca: Cornell University Press, 1995), 107ff.
53. David Nicholls, ed., *The Whole World of Music: A Henry Cowell Symposium* (Amsterdam: Harwood Academic Press, 1997), 76ff.
54. Henderson, *Fourth Dimension*, 224ff.
55. For Rauschenberg, Andreas Papadakis, *New Art International* (New York: St Martin's Press, 1990), 23; for Cage on Fischinger, Richard Kostelanetz, *Conversing with Cage* (New York: Limelight Editions, 1988), 8.

56. James Pritchett, *The Music of John Cage* (Cambridge University Press, 1993), 36ff.

57. For the '*objet-poème*', Westgeest, *Zen in the Fifties*, 102ff.

58. Werner Schmalenbach, *Bissier* (New York: Abrams, 1963), gives conflicting dates (1919 and 1927). I choose the latter.

59. Roger Lipsey, *An Art of Our Own: The Spiritual in Twentieth Century Art* (Boston and Shaftesbury: Shambhala, 1988), 367ff.

60. Wols worked with closed eyes, the better to follow his 'unconscious'. For Degottex, Westgeest, *Zen in the Fifties*, 117–18.

61. K. F. Rosenblatt, *Rene Daumal: The Life and Work of a Mystic Guide* (Albany: SUNY Press, 1999).

62. Westgeest, *Zen in the Fifties*, 144–5.

63. Thomas McEvilley in Dominique de Menil, *Yves Klein 1918–62: A Retrospective* (Houston: Rice University Institute for the Arts, 1982).

64. Rustom Bharucha, *Theatre and the World: Performance and the Politics of Culture* (India: Manohar, 1990), 14: 'Artaud was drawn to a vast ... range of cultural stimuli, including Yoga, oriental religions, drugs, magic, the Tibetan Book of the Dead, mysticism, acupuncture, astrology.'

65. Rupert Arrowsmith, *Modernism and the Museum: Asian, African and Pacific Art and the London Avant-Garde* (Oxford University Press, 2010), 117.

66. Michael Tucker, *Alan Davie: The Quest for the Miraculous* (London: Lund Humphries, 1993.)

67. For the monochrome, Thomas McEvilley, *The Exile's Return: Toward a Redefinition of Painting for the Post-Modern Era* (Cambridge University Press, 1994), ch. 2.

68. Barbara Rose, *Art as Art: Selected Writings of Ad Reinhardt* (Berkeley and Los Angeles: University of California Press, 1991), xvi. Renouncing colour in 1953, Reinhardt painted residually Mondrianesque black monochromes until his death in 1967. Asian art contained nothing 'romantic, spontaneous, unconscious, primitive, expressionistic, accidental, or informal' (Rose, 217): none of the qualities prized by Abstract Expressionists! He disparaged 'cafe-and-club primitives and neo-Zen bohemians' (Rose, 202).

69. Rose, *Art as Art*, 87, 98, 157.

70. A painter with a cellular/cosmogonic angle on Zen, Francis knew Mallarme's *blancs*: compare Reinhardt (Rose, *Art as Art*, 106), who called Mallarme, Melville and Flaubert 'masters of voidness'.

71. For Martin and Taoism, McEvilley, *Exile's Return*, ch. 4, noting her interest in Buddhism's 'intermediate' *Sambhogakaya* realm. This distinguishes her from would-be *Dharmakaya*-level abstractionists like Reinhardt and Marden.

72. For Tapies on Eastern influences, Barbara Catoir, *Conversations with Antoni Tapies* (Munich: Prestel, 1991).

73. Clarke, *Influence of Oriental Thought*, 307 n. 85; Will-Levaillant, 'La Chine d' Andre Masson', 68 n. 43.

6 Owning, Disowning and Trivializing the Occult

1. R. C. Grogin, *The Bergsonian Controversy in France, 1900–14* (Alberta: University of Calgary Press, 1988), 37.

2. James Robinson, *Eugene O'Neill and Oriental Thought* (Carbondale and Edwardsville: Southern Illinois University Press, 1982), 63.

3. For example, E. R. Dodds, *The Greeks and the Irrational* (Berkeley and Los Angeles: University of California Press, 1951); Frances Yates, *Giordano Bruno and the Hermetic Tradition* (University of Chicago Press, 1964).

4. J. Godwin, *The Theosophical Enlightenment* (Albany: SUNY Press, 1994).

5. For this meta-world ('the middle zone of experience'), Richard Sheppard, *Modernism–Dada–Postmodernism* (Evanston, IL: Northwestern University Press, 2000), 42ff.

6. Gary Lachman, *Turn Off Your Mind: The Mystic Sixties and the Dark Side of the Age of Aquarius* (London: Sidgwick and Jackson, 2001).

7. P. Caraciollo, 'Buddhist Typologies in "Heart of Darkness" and "Victory" and Their Contribution to the Modernism of Jacob Epstein, Wyndham Lewis and T. S. Eliot', *The Conradian*, 14/1/2 (1989), 67–91.

8. R. C. Zaehner, *Mysticism, Sacred and Profane* (Oxford University Press, 1957) and *Our Savage God* (New York: Sheed and Ward, 1974). Sadie Plant, *Writing On Drugs* (London: Faber and Faber, 1999), 96 n. 27, mentions Junger's mescalin use. William James, Havelock Ellis and Yeats were among the first to experiment with peyote.

9. For 'the vulgarization of elitism' during the sixties, Robert Pynsent, *Decadence and Innovation* (London: Weidenfeld and Nicolson, 1989), 226.

10. Max Nordau, *Degeneration* (Lincoln: University of Nebraska Press, 1993), 544.

11. Pynsent, *Decadence and Innovation*, 156. After Joachimite doctrine, Bahr notes elsewhere that *die Moderne* 'paint a new philosophy, a new religion, the dawn of the third realm'.

12. Stanley Rabinowitz, *The Noise of Change: Russian Literature and the Critics, 1891–1917* (Ann Arbor: Ardis, 1986), 194.

13. Daniel Gerould, *Doubles, Demons and Dreamers: An International Collection of Symbolist Drama* (New York: Performing Arts Journal Publications, 1985), 10.

14. For Surrealism's darker side, Petrine Archer-Straw, *Negrophilia: Avant-Garde Paris and Black Culture in the 1920s* (New York: Thames and Hudson, 2000), 134ff. For *Ankoku Butoh* (the 'Dance of Utter Darkness'), Alexandra Munroe in Munroe, ed., *Japanese Art after 1945: Scream against the Sky* (New York: Abrams, 1994), 189ff.

15. J. C. Bramble in G. Samuel and J. Johnston, eds, *Religion and the Subtle Body in Asia and the West* (London and New York: Routledge, 2013), 206ff. That argument is rewritten and extended here.

16. Christoph Asendorf, *Batteries of Life: On the History of Things and Their Perception in Modernity* (Berkeley and Los Angeles: University of California Press, 1993), 167; idem, *Strome und Strahlen: Das langsame Verschwinden der Materie um 1900* (Giessen: Anabas-Verlag, 1989).

17. Asendorf, *Batteries*, 174–5.

18. Ibid., 173.

19. *The Man Who Was Thursday*, ch. 8: the Professor 'insisted on a furious and incessant energy, rending all things in pieces. Energy he said was the All.'

20. For the king-making or -undoing Tantrika as 'occult cosmocrat', David Gordon White, *The Kiss of the Yogini: 'Tantric Sex' in Its South Asian Contexts* (University of Chicago Press, 2003), 32.

21. Asendorf, *Batteries*, 36ff.

22. Daniel Pick, *Svengali's Web: The Alien Enchanter in Modern Culture* (New Haven and London: Yale University Press, 2000).

23. M. H. Abrams, *Natural Supernaturalism: Tradition and Revolution in Romantic Literature* (New York: Norton, 1973).

24. Jay Winter, *Sites of Memory, Sites of Mourning: The Great War in European Cultural History* (Cambridge University Press, 1995), 64, 65 n. 54.

25. Weston La Barre, *The Ghost Dance: The Origins of Religion* (New York: Doubleday, 1970), 239ff.

26. Pascal Boyer, *Religion Explained: The Human Instincts That Fashion Gods, Spirits and Ancestors* (London: Heinemann, 2001).

SELECT BIBLIOGRAPHY

Allen, Gay, and Ed Folsom, eds. *Walt Whitman and the World*. Iowa City: Iowa University Press, 1995.

Anand, Mulk Raj. *Conversations in Bloomsbury*. New Delhi: Oxford University Press, 1981.

App, Urs. *Richard Wagner and Buddhism*. Rorschach and Kyoto: UniversityMedia, 2011.

Arrowsmith, Rupert. *Modernism and the Museum: Asian, African and Pacific Art and the London Avant-Garde*. Oxford University Press, 2011.

Asendorf, Christoph. *Batteries of Life: On the History of Things and Their Perception in Modernity*. Berkeley and Los Angeles: University of California Press, 1993.

Asendorf, Christoph. *Strome und Strahlen: das langsame Verschwinden der Materie um 1900*. Giessen: Anabas-Verlag, 1989.

Benson, Timothy. *Raoul Hausmann and Berlin Dada*. Ann Arbor: UMI Research Press, 1987.

Born, Georgina, and David Hesmondhalgh, eds. *Western Music and Its Others*. Berkeley and Los Angeles: University of California Press, 2000.

Bramble, J. C. 'Sinister Modernists', in Geoffrey Samuel and Jay Johnston, eds. *Religion and the Subtle Body in Asia and the West*. London and New York: Routledge, 2013, 192–210.

Brantlinger, Patrick. *Rule of Darkness: British Literature and Imperialism, 1830–1914*. Ithaca: Cornell University Press, 1988.

Cadwallader, Barry. *Crisis of the European Mind: A Study of Andre Malraux and Drieu La Rochelle*. Cardiff: University of Wales Press, 1981.

Cannadine, David. *Ornamentalism: How the British Saw Their Empire*. London: Allen Lane, 2001.

Carlson, Maria. 'No Religion Higher Than Truth': A History of the Theosophical Movement in Russia, 1875–1922*. Princeton University Press, 1993.

Catoir, Barbara. *Conversations with Antoni Tapies*. Munich: Prestel, 1991.

Clarke, D. J. *The Influence of Oriental Thought on Postwar American Painting and Sculpture*. New York: Garland, 1988.

Cousineau, Phil, ed. *The Hero's Journey: Joseph Campbell on His Life and Work*. New York: Harper and Row, 1990.

Crabtree, Adam. *From Mesmer to Freud: Magnetic Sleep and the Roots of Psychological Healing*. New Haven: Yale University Press, 1993.

Crary, Jonathan. *Suspensions of Perception: Attention, Spectacle and Modern Culture*. Cambridge and London: MIT Press, 1999.

Dixon, Joy. *Divine Feminine: Theosophy and Feminism*. Baltimore and London: Johns Hopkins University Press, 2001.

Doherty, Gerald. *Oriental Lawrence: The Quest for the Secrets of Sex*. New York: Lang, 2001.

Elderfield, John, ed. *Flight out of Time: A Dada Diary by Hugo Ball*. Berkeley and Los Angeles: University of California Press, 1996.

163

Eliade, Mircea. *Occultism, Witchcraft and Cultural Patterns*. University of Chicago Press, 1976.

Ellenberger, Henri. *The Discovery of the Unconscious*. New York: Basic Books, 1981.

Ellwood, Robert, ed. *Eastern Spirituality in America, Selected Writings*. New York: Paulist Press, 1987.

Epstein, Perle. *The Private Labyrinth of Malcolm Lowry: Under the Volcano and Cabbala*. New York: Holt, Rinehart and Winston, 1969.

Figal, Gerald. *Civilization and Monsters: Spirits of Modernity in Meiji Japan*. Durham, NC: Duke University Press, 1999.

Foster, Stephen, and Rudolph Kuenzli, eds. *Dada Spectrum: The Dialectics of Revolt*. Madison, WI: Coda Press, 1979.

Friedman, Ken, ed. *A Fluxus Reader*. Chichester: Academy Editions, 1998.

Garafola, Lynn. *Diaghilev's Ballets Russes*. New York: Oxford University Press, 1989.

Gauld, Alan. *A History of Hypnotism*. Cambridge University Press, 1992.

Gijswijt-Hofstra, Marijke, Brian Levack and Roy Porter. *The Athlone History of Witchcraft and Magic in Europe*, vol 5. London: Athlone, 1999.

Godwin, Joscelyn. *The Theosophical Enlightenment*. Albany: SUNY Press, 1994.

Gordon, Donald. *Expressionism: Art and Idea*. New Haven: Yale University Press, 1991.

Gould, Warwick, and Marjorie Reeves. *Joachim of Fiore and the Myth of the Eternal Evangel in the Nineteenth and Twentieth Centuries*. Oxford University Press, 2001.

Green, Martin. *Mountain of Truth: The Counterculture Begins, Ascona, 1900–1920*. Hanover and London: University Press of New England, 1986.

Greenhalgh, Paul. *Ephemeral Vistas: History of the Expositions Universelles, Great Exhibitions and World's Fairs*. Manchester University Press, 1990.

Greenhalgh, Paul. *The Modern Ideal: The Rise and Collapse of Idealism in the Visual Arts*. London: V&A Publications, 2005.

Greer, Mary. *Women of the Golden Dawn: Rebels and Priestesses*. Rochester, VT: Park Street Press, 1995.

Griffin, Roger. *Modernism and Fascism: The Sense of a Beginning under Mussolini and Hitler*. Basingstoke: Palgrave Macmillan, 2007.

Griffiths, Richard. *The Reactionary Revolution: The Catholic Revival in French Literature. 1870–1914*. London: Constable, 1966.

Grogin, R. C. *The Bergsonian Controversy in France, 1900–1914*. Alberta: University of Calgary Press, 1988.

Grossman, Manuel. *Dada: Paradox, Mystification, and Ambiguity in European Literature*. New York: Pegasus, 1971.

Hahl-Koch, Jelena. *Arnold Schoenberg, Wassily Kandinsky: Letters, Pictures and Documents*. London: Faber and Faber, 1984.

Hay, Stephen. *Asian Ideas of East and West: Tagore and His Critics*. Cambridge, MA: Harvard University Press, 1970.

Heehs, Peter. *The Bomb in Bengal: The Rise of Revolutionary Terrorism in India*. New Delhi: Oxford University Press, 1993.

Henderson, Linda. *The Fourth Dimension and Non-Euclidean Geometry in Modern Art*. Princeton University Press, 1983.

Herman, Jonathan. *I and Tao: Martin Buber's Encounter with Chuang Tzu*. Albany: SUNY Press, 1996.

Hopkins, A. G., ed. *Globalization in World History*. London: Pimlico, 2002.

Jacob, Margaret. *Living the Enlightenment: Freemasonry and Politics in Eighteenth-Century Europe*. New York: Oxford University Press, 1992.

Kearns, C. McNelly. *T. S. Eliot and Indic Traditions*. Cambridge University Press, 2008.

Kodama, Sanehide. *American Poetry and Japanese Culture*. Hamden, CT: Archon Books, 1984.

Kuryluk, Eva. *Judas and Salome in the Cave of Sex: The Grotesque, Origins, Iconography, Techniques*. Evanston, IL: Northwestern University Press, 1987.

Lachman, Gary. *Turn Off Your Mind: The Mystic Sixties and the Dark Side of the Age of Aquarius*. London: Sidgwick and Jackson, 2001.

Lears, T. J. Jackson. *No Place of Grace: Antimodernism and the Transformation of American Culture*. University of Chicago Press, 1994.

Lester, John A. *Journey through Despair, 1880–1914: Transformations in British Literary Culture*. Princeton University Press, 1969.

Liebersohn, Harry. *Aristocratic Encounters: European Travellers and North American Indians*. Cambridge University Press, 1998.

Lipsey, Roger. *An Art of Our Own: The Spiritual in Twentieth Century Art*. Boston and Shaftesbury: Shambhala, 1988.

Lloyd, Jill. *German Expressionism: Primitivism and Modernity*. Newhaven: Yale University Press, 1991.

Lopez, Donald, ed. *Curators of the Buddha: The Study of Buddhism under Colonialism*. University of Chicago Press, 1995.

Mackenzie, John. *Orientalism: History, Theory and the Arts*. Manchester University Press, 1995.

Marchand, Suzanne. *German Orientalism in the Age of Empire: Religion, Race, and Scholarship*. New York: Cambridge University Press, 2010.

Martin, Stoddard. *Orthodox Heresy, The Rise of 'Magic' as Religion and Its Relation to Literature*. London: MacMillan, 1989.

May, Reinhard. *Heidegger's Hidden Sources: East Asian Influences on His Work*. London: Routledge, 1996.

Mazo, Joseph H. *Prime Movers: The Makers of Dance in America*. Pennington: Princeton Book Company, 1986.

McEvilley, Thomas. *The Exile's Return: Toward a Redefinition of Painting for the Post-Modern Era*. Cambridge University Press, 1994.

McGuire, William. *Bollingen: An Adventure in Collecting the Past*. Princeton University Press, 1989.

Melman, Billie. *Women's Orients: English Women in the Middle East, 1718–1918*. London: Macmillan, 1995.

Mercier, Alain. *Les Sources Esoteriques et Occultes de la Poesie Symboliste 1870–1914*. Paris: Nizet, 1969, two volumes.

Moffitt, John. *Occultism in Avant-Garde Art: The Case of Joseph Beuys*. Ann Arbor: UMI Research Press, 1988.

Moore, James. *Gurdjieff and Mansfield*. London: Routledge and Kegan Paul, 1980.

Munroe, Alexandra, ed. *Japanese Art after 1945: Scream against the Sky*. New York: Abrams, 1994.

Munroe, Alexandra, ed. *The Third Mind: American Artists Contemplate Asia, 1860–1989*. New York: Guggenheim Museum, 2009.

Naito, Shiro. *Yeats and Zen: A Study of the Transformation of His Mask*. Kyoto: Yamaguchi, 1984.

Noll, Richard. *The Jung Cult: Origins of a Charismatic Movement*. Princeton University Press, 1994.

Nordau, Max. *Degeneration*. Lincoln: Nebraska University Press, 1993.

Paperno, Irena, and Joan Grossman. *Creating Life: The Aesthetic Utopia of Russian Modernism*. Stanford University Press, 1994.

Pearlman, Ellen. *Nothing and Everything: The Influence of Buddhism on the American Avant-Garde, 1942–1962.* Berkeley: Evolver, 2012.

Pick, Daniel. *Svengali's Web: The Alien Encounter in Modern Culture.* New Haven: Yale University Press, 2000.

Polcari, Stephen. *Abstract Expressionism and the Modern Experience.* Cambridge University Press, 1993.

Prothero, Stephen. *The White Buddhist: The Asian Odyssey of Henry Steel Olcott.* Bloomington: Indiana University Press, 2012.

Qian, Zhaoming, ed. *Modernism and the Orient.* Ezra Pound Center: University of New Orleans Press, 2012.

Qian, Zhaoming, ed. *Orientalism and Modernism: The Legacy of China in Pound and Williams.* Durham: Duke University Press, 1995.

Rabinowitz, Stanley. *The Noise of Change: Russian Literature and the Critics, 1891–1917.* Ann Arbor: Ardis, 1986.

Reiss, Tom. *The Orientalist: In Search of a Man Caught between East and West.* London: Vintage, 2006.

Rider, Jacques Le. *Modernity and Crises of Identity: Culture and Society in Fin de Siècle Vienna 1993.* Cambridge: Polity, 1993.

Ridley, Hugh. *Images of Imperial Rule.* London: Croom Helm, 1983.

Riepe, Dale. *Philosophy of India and Its Impact on American Thought.* Springfield, IL: Charles C. Thomas, 1970.

Ringbom, Sixtus. *The Sounding Cosmos.* Helsingfors: Acta Academiae Aboensis, 1970.

Robinson, James. *Eugene O'Neill and Oriental Thought.* Carbondale and Edwardsville: Southern Illinois University Press, 1982.

Rose, Barbara. *Art as Art: Selected Writings of Ad Reinhardt.* Berkeley and Los Angeles: University of California Press, 1991.

Rosenblatt, Kathleen. *Rene Daumal: The Life and Work of a Mystic Guide.* Albany: SUNY Press, 1999.

Rosenthal, Beatrice Glatzer, ed. *The Occult in Russian and Soviet Culture.* Ithaca and London: Cornell University Press, 1997.

Rudnick, Lois. *Utopian Vistas: The Mabel Dodge Luhan House and the American Counterculture.* Albuquerque: University of New Mexico Press, 1998.

Schwab, Raymond. *The Oriental Renaissance: Europe's Rediscovery of India and the East, 1680–1880.* New York: Columbia University Press, 1984.

Schwartz, William. *The Imaginative Interpretation of the Far East in Modern French Literature, 1800–1925.* Paris: Champion, 1927.

Seager, Richard. *The World's Parliament of Religions: The East–West Encounter, Chicago, 1883.* Bloomington: Indiana University Press, 2009.

Sedgwick, Mark. *Against the Modern World: Traditionalism and the Secret Intellectual History of the Twentieth Century.* New York: Oxford University Press, 2004.

Sengupta, Sulagna. *Jung in India.* New Orleans: Spring Journal Books, 2013.

Shelton, Suzanne. *Divine Dancer: A Biography of Ruth St. Denis.* Garden City, NY: Doubleday, 1981.

Sheppard, Richard. *Modernism–Dada–Postmodernism.* Evanston, IL: Northwestern University Press, 2000.

Smith, Bernard. *Modernism and Post-Modernism, a neo-Colonial Viewpoint.* Working Papers in Australian Studies, Sir Robert Menzies Centre for Australian Studies, Institute of Commonwealth Studies, University of London, 1992.

Smith, Bernard. *Modernism's History: A Study in Twentieth Century Art and Ideas.* New Haven: Yale University Press, 1998.

Steele, Tom. *Alfred Orage and the Leeds Art Club 1893–1923.* Aldershot: Scolar Press, 1990.

Tanaka, Stefan. *Japan's Orient: Rendering Pasts into History.* Berkeley and Los Angeles: University of California Press, 1995.

Taylor, Kathleen. *Sir John Woodroffe, Tantra and Bengal.* Richmond: Curzon, 2001.

Taylor, P. B. *Gurdjieff and Orage: Brothers in Elysium.* York Beach: Weiser, 2001.

Tonkinson, Carole, ed. *Big Sky Mind: Buddhism and the Beat Generation.* London: Thorsons, 1996.

Treitel, Sophie. *A Science for the Soul: Occultism and the Genesis of the German Modern.* Baltimore and London: Johns Hopkins University Press, 2004.

Tuchman, Maurice, ed. *The Spiritual in Art: Abstract Painting 1890–1985.* New York: Abbeville Press, 1987.

Tucker, Michael. *Dreaming with Open Eyes: The Shamanic Spirit in Twentieth Century Art and Culture.* San Francisco: Harper, 1992.

Tweed, Thomas. *The American Encounter with Buddhism, 1844–1912.* Bloomington: Indiana University Press, 1992.

Tweed, Thomas, and Stephen Prothero. *Asian Religions in America: A Documentary History.* New York: Oxford University Press, 1999.

Van Gogh, Vincent. 2003. *The Letters of Vincent Van Gogh.* London: Penguin.

Warlick, M. E. *Max Ernst and Alchemy: A Magician in Search of Myth.* Austin: University of Texas Press, 2001.

Watkins, Glenn. *Pyramids at the Louvre: Music, Culture and Collage from Stravinsky to the Postmodernists.* Cambridge, MA: Harvard University Press, 1994.

Webb, James. *The Occult Establishment.* Glasgow: Drew, 1981.

Weber, Eugen. *France, Fin de Siècle.* Cambridge, MA: Harvard University Press, 1986.

Weinberg, Robert. *Spinning the Clay into Stars: Bernard Leach and the Baha'i Faith.* Oxford: George Ronald, 1999.

Werkner, Patrick. *Austrian Expressionism: The Formative Years.* Oxford: Premier Book Marketing, 1994.

Wessinger, Catherine. *Annie Besant and Progressive Messianism, 1874–1933.* Lewiston, NY: Edwin Mellen Press, 1989.

West, James, *Russian Symbolism: A Study of Vyacheslav Ivanov and the Russian Symbolist Aesthetic.* London: Methuen, 1970.

Westgeest, Helen. *Zen in the Fifties: Interaction in Art between East and West.* Amstelveen: Wanders, 1996.

Will-Levaillant, Francoise.'La Chine d'Andre Masson'. *Revue de l'Art*, 12 (1971), 64–74.

Willson, A. L. *Mythical Image: The Ideal of India in German Romanticism.* Durham: Duke University Press, 1964.

Woodson, Jon. *To Make a New Race: Gurdjieff, Toomer and the Harlem Renaissance.* Jackson: University Press of Mississippi, 1999.

Yaguello, Marina. *Lunatic Lovers of Language: Imaginary Languages and Their Inventors.* New Jersey: Fairleigh Dickinson University Press, 1991.

Yu, Beongcheon. *The Great Circle: American Writers and the Orient.* Detroit: Wayne State University Press, 1983.

Znamenski, Andrei. *Red Shambhala: Magic, Prophecy and Geopolitics in the Heart of Asia.* Wheaton, IL: Quest Books, 2011.

INDEX

73535788R00113

Made in the USA
Middletown, DE
15 May 2018